THE PERSISTENT ADVOCATE AND THE USE OF FORCE

The Ashgate International Law Series

Series Editor: Alex Conte, Consultant on Security and Human Rights

The Ashgate International Law Series brings together top-quality titles, principally in the area of public international law but also in private international law, under the label of a single international series. Each title represents work which is the result of high-level research, aimed at both the professorial and postgraduate academic market as well as the expert practitioner.

Also in the series

Public Interest Rules of International Law
Towards Effective Implementation
Edited by Teruo Komori and Karel Wellens
ISBN 978 0 7546 7823 6

Terrorism, War and International Law
The Legality of the Use of Force Against Afghanistan in 2001
Myra Williamson
ISBN 978 0 7546 7403 0

A Dual Approach to Ocean Governance
The Cases of Zonal and Integrated Management
in International Law of the Sea
Yoshifumi Tanaka
ISBN 978 0 7546 7170 1

The Persistent Advocate and the Use of Force

The Impact of the United States upon the *Jus ad Bellum* in the Post-Cold War Era

CHRISTIAN HENDERSON
Oxford Brookes University, UK

Routledge
Taylor & Francis Group
LONDON AND NEW YORK

First published 2010 by Ashgate Publishing

2 Park Square, Milton Park, Abingdon, Oxon OX14 4RN
711 Third Avenue, New York, NY 10017, USA

Routledge is an imprint of the Taylor & Francis Group, an informa business

First issued in paperback 2016

British Library Cataloguing in Publication Data
Henderson, Christian.
The persistent advocate and the use of force : the impact
of the United States upon the jus ad bellum in the
post-Cold War era. -- (The Ashgate international law series)
1. Just war doctrine. 2. United States--Military policy.
3. War (International law) 4. Unilateral acts
(International law) 5. United States--Foreign relations--
1945-1989. 6. United States--Foreign relations--1989-
7. United Nations. Security Council.
I. Title II. Series
341.6-dc22

Library of Congress Cataloging-in-Publication Data
Henderson, Christian.
The persistent advocate and the use of force : the impact of the United States upon the jus ad bellum in the post-cold war era / by Christian Henderson.
p. cm. -- (Ashgate international law series)
Includes index.
ISBN 978-1-4094-0173-5 (hbk)
1. Just war doctrine. 2. Preemptive attack (Military science) 3. Self-defense (International law) 4. War on Terrorism, 2001-2009. 5. United States--Foreign relations--1945-
6. United Nations. Security Council. 7. United Nations--Military policy. I. Title.
KZ6396.H46 2010
341.6'2--dc22

2010010569

ISBN 978-1-4094-0173-5 (hbk)
ISBN 978-1-138-27217-0 (pbk)

Contents

For Sanna and Minttu

Foreword

This impressive book considers the impact of the attitude and practice of the United States on the development of the laws governing the use of force and collective security in the post-Cold War and post-9/11 eras. By applying the theory of interpretive communities in a systematic way to key areas of the *jus ad bellum* where American influence is very strong, both in collective security and self-defence, the book makes a genuine contribution to knowledge.

After outlining his theoretical stance, the author considers the impact of the United States on Chapter VII of the UN Charter by analyzing the method of authorization of Coalitions of the Willing, the development of auto-interpretation of Security Council resolutions, and the arguments concerning enforcement of such resolutions. The conclusions drawn are sound in this regard, and the search for inter-subjective agreement on these matters is illuminating. The argument then turns to issues of self-defence by considering the attempt to expand the test of attribution that applies to the actions/presence of terrorists; and then the most controversial attempted extension of the right to allow for pre-emptive self-defence on the basis of a perceived threat.

The book represents a clear-sighted counter-weight to the rush to reconsider well-established and legitimate principles of international law on the basis that either the fall of the Berlin Wall or the events of 9/11 were turning points in international relations, replacing or rather necessitating the replacement of the old rules drawn up principally in the UN Charter of 1945. The basic rules governing violence agreed upon by representatives of states in 1945 took many centuries to achieve, but even so they are a product of a dated consensus and their enforcement depends on an alliance of powers in the Security Council that only enjoyed brief unity of purpose. This book develops a method which allows that consensus to be challenged, not by unilateral actions and re-interpretations of the rules, but by the development of a new and meaningful multilateral consensus. The argument of the author is not that of a formalist insisting upon the letter of rules drawn up in 1945, but is one based on the need to achieve real consensus if new and lasting rules are to be formulated.

Nigel D. White
Professor of Public International Law
University of Nottingham

Preface

The period of research from which the monograph emerged was embarked upon just over a year after the United States of America had used force against Iraq and toppled its Government in an enforcement action that was justified upon compelling this state to comply with its disarmament obligations. The central argument advanced by the United States was that it had the authority to do this under a United Nations Security Council resolution that had been adopted over a decade previously. This claim was made and persisted with despite the objections of the majority of other members of the United Nations Security Council, including several permanent members, and indeed large swathes of other states and actors within the international community at large. The apparent conviction with which this argument was made, along with the stated belief that its actions were lawful despite the objections of many, initiated an interest in whether, despite the undoubted power of this state, it could determine what the law was and as such have an impact upon the actions which the law permits or denies.

Whilst this was one example of the United States advocating a view that was perceived by others to lie outside of the contemporary interpretation of the law, thoughts turned to the question of whether it had made other such attempts and whether these had had an impact upon the law. Indeed, in connection with the *jus ad bellum*, was the United States a 'persistent advocate' and, more importantly, was it a successful one?

I wish to express my gratitude to the School of Law at the University of Nottingham for providing me with a place and the necessary funding to write this work. The School and the University more widely was an inspiring place in which to carry out research of this nature. During my time at Nottingham I also had the opportunity to spend time at The Hague Academy of International Law and the University of Virginia. These experiences widened my knowledge of international law and provided me with different resources to facilitate the writing of this work.

There are also many people whom I have to acknowledge for their help, support and inspiration during the course of this research and its subsequent transformation into this book. Firstly, I would like to express my thanks to Professor Robert Cryer (University of Birmingham) for his assistance and guidance over the years. I also wish to express my deepest appreciation to Professor Nigel White (University of Nottingham) and Dr Olympia Bekou (University of Nottingham) who made me think more deeply about the issues raised in my research and have thus made a substantial contribution to its transposition into this monograph. Others whom I would like to thank in regards to this process are Professor Ian Johnstone (The

Fletcher School of Law and Diplomacy, Tufts University) and Dr James Green (University of Reading) who kindly took the time to read and comment upon parts of various chapters. Discussions with Professor John Norton Moore (University of Virginia) were valuable and insightful and I appreciate the time that he gave me.

I am also indebted to friends and colleagues at all stages of my academic career so far and to my colleagues within the Department of Law at Oxford Brookes University for their patience and understanding during my first weeks of work there which happened to coincide with the final weeks of finishing this research.

The publishing process was made as smooth as possible by Alison Kirk, Jude Chillman, Sarah Horsley and Adam Guppy at Ashgate Publishing, so my thanks to them.

Lastly, my mother and father have been a constant source of support and encouragement and my wife, Sanna, has been an avenue of strength and inspiration throughout the years of writing this work. I would not have been able to complete it without her and so it is to her that it is dedicated.

It has been the intention to state the material found in this book to be current as of December 2009. Any errors are my sole responsibility.

Christian Henderson
Oxford
January 2010

List of Abbreviations

9/11	The terrorist attacks of 11 September 2001
AMIS	African Union Mission in Sudan
ANZUS	Australia, New Zealand, United States Security Treaty
AU	African Union
BFSP	British and Foreign State Papers
CIA	Central Intelligence Agency
DASR	Draft Articles on State Responsibility
DPRK	Democratic People's Republic of Korea
DRC	Democratic Republic of Congo
ECOWAS	Economic Community of West African States
EU	European Union
FRY	Federal Republic of Yugoslavia
IAEA	International Atomic Energy Agency
ICJ	International Court of Justice
ICJ Rep.	International Court of Justice Reports
ICTY	International Criminal Tribunal for the Former Yugoslavia
ILA	International Law Association
ILC	International Law Commission
ILM	International Legal Materials
KLA	Kosovo Liberation Army
NAM	Non-Aligned Movement
NATO	North Atlantic Treaty Organization
NGO	Non-Governmental Organization
NILR	Netherlands International Law Review
NSS	National Security Strategy
OAS	Organization of American States
OSCE	Organization for Security and Cooperation in Europe

PCIJ	Permanent Court of International Justice
PKK	Kurdistan Workers' Party
PLO	Palestine Liberation Organization
UK	United Kingdom
UN	United Nations
UNGA	United Nations General Assembly
UNIFIL	United Nations Interim Force in Lebanon
UNIKOM	United Nations Iraq-Kuwait Observation Mission
UNMOVIC	United Nations Monitoring, Verification and Inspection Commission
UNSC	United Nations Security Council
UNSCOM	United Nations Special Commission
UNSG	United Nations Secretary-General
UNYB	United Nations Yearbook
US	United States of America
VCLT	The Vienna Convention on the Law of Treaties
WMD	Weapons of Mass Destruction

Journals and Publications

AJICL African Journal of International and Comparative Law
AJIL American Journal of International Law
Aust YBIL Australian Yearbook of International Law
BYBIL British Yearbook of International Law
Cal.W.Int'l L.J. California Western International Law Journal
Cal.W.L.Rev. California Western Law Review
Cardozo J.Int'l & Comp.L. Cardozo Journal of International and Comparative Law
Chicago J.Int'l L. Chicago Journal of International Law
Chinese J.Int'l L. Chinese Journal of International Law
Colum.J.Transnat'l L. Columbia Journal of Transnational Law
Cornell Int'l L.J. Cornell International Law Journal
Duke J.Comp.& Int'l L. Duke Journal of Comparative and International Law
EJIL European Journal of International Law
Fletcher F. World Aff. Fletcher Forum of World Affairs
Ga.J.Int'l.& Comp.L. Georgia Journal of International and Comparative Law
Geo.Int'l Envtl.L.Rev. Georgetown International Environmental Law Review
Geo.L.J. Georgetown Law Journal
German Y.B.Int'l L. German Yearbook of International Law
Hague Yrbk Int'l L. Hague Yearbook of International Law
Harv.Int'l L.J. Harvard International Law Journal
Harv.J.L.& Pub.Pol'y Harvard Journal of Law and Public Policy

ICLQ International and Comparative Law Quarterly
Indian J.Int'l L. Indian Journal of International Law
Iowa L.Rev. Iowa Law Review
Israel Y.B.Hum.Rts. Israel Yearbook on Human Rights
JCSL Journal of Conflict and Security Law
Keesing's Keesing's Record of World Events
LJIL Leiden Journal of International Law
Max Planck Yrbk UN L. Max Planck Yearbook of United Nations Law
Mich.J.Int'l L. Michigan Journal of International Law
Mich.L.Rev. Michigan Law Review
MLR Modern Law Review
Stan.J.Int'l L. Stanford Journal of International Law
Syracuse L.Rev. Syracuse Law Review
Tex.Int'l L.J. Texas International Law Journal
Transnat'l L.& Contemp.Probs. Transnational Law and Contemporary Problems
Tul.J.Int'l & Comp.L. Tulane Journal of International and Comparative Law
Tul.L.Rev. Tulane Law Review
Tulsa J.Comp.& Int'l L. Tulsa Journal of Comparative and International Law
U.Chi.L.Rev. University of Chicago Law Review
U.Pitt.L.Rev. University of Pittsburgh Law Review
UNYBILC United Nations Yearbook of the International Law Commission
W.Va.L.Rev. West Virginia Law Review
Yale J.Int'l L. Yale Journal of International Law
Y.B.N.Z.Juris. Yearbook of New Zealand Jurisprudence

Chapter 1
Introduction

The formal notion of sovereign equality provides that all states are equal before the law.[1] However, whilst this notion is deeply ingrained at the theoretical level within the international system it might not appear so clearly visible in practice. Indeed, states are of differing wealth, size, and power which could be viewed as creating varying possibilities to make and shape international law as well as varying possibilities to evade its enforcement.[2] In this respect the United States of America, which since the end of the Cold War in 1989 and the collapse of the Soviet Union has been recognized as the world's 'sole remaining superpower',[3] may be viewed as being in the possession of greater powers than any other state. Whilst this status is subject to change, or to be challenged by other states such as China or India, since the end of the Cold War we have arguably been living in a 'unipolar moment'.[4]

During this period of superior power, the US has been a 'persistent objector' to the development of international law on many contemporary issues.[5] In particular, under the administration of former President George W. Bush international efforts to combat climate change through international law and the establishment of an International Criminal Court have been persistently objected to and, whilst the US has not ultimately been able to prevent them from being realized, it has remained outside of these regimes thus inhibiting their effectiveness.[6] However, during this period, which has witnessed the US moving from a war fought using the principles

1 I. Brownlie, *Principles of Public International Law*, 7th edn (Oxford: Oxford University Press, 2008), 289; M. Shaw, *International Law*, 6th edn (Cambridge: Cambridge University Press, 2008), 214–15.

2 M. Byers, *Custom, Power, and the Power of Rules* (Cambridge: Cambridge University Press, 1999), 5.

3 See, for example, J. Murphy, *The United States and the Rule of Law in International Affairs* (Cambridge: Cambridge University Press, 2004), 7.

4 C. Krauthammer, 'The Unipolar Moment' (1991) 70 *Foreign Affairs* 23, 24.

5 Whilst this notion is found in the rules governing the formation of customary international law, it is used here in a general sense to depict the way in which the US has approached many international legal issues. See, generally, J. Charney, 'The Persistent Objector Rule and the Development of Customary International Law' (1985) 56 *BYBIL* 1.

6 See, generally, R. Wedgwood, 'The International Criminal Court: An American View' (1999) 10 *EJIL* 93; C. Kormos, B. Groskos, and R.A. Mittermeier, 'US Participation in International Environmental Law and Policy' (2001) 13 *Geo.Int'l Envtl.L.Rev.* 661.

of containment and deterrence[7] to the adoption of a pre-emptive strategy,[8] it has used force both unilaterally and collectively in a number of situations.[9] In contrast to its objections to any changes to the legal regime in other areas, in its justifications for these uses of force, or occasionally in the abstract, it has interpreted, applied and, in many cases, attempted to modify the law governing when force is permitted under international law (the *jus ad bellum*).[10] Indeed, in connection with many aspects of this particular branch of international law the US may be termed a 'persistent advocate'.[11]

Given the US's power, one may be led into thinking that it has thus been able to modify and develop the law to suit its present and future interests. Indeed, some have claimed dramatic changes to the *jus ad bellum*, or even the death of the prohibition of the use of force completely,[12] as a result of the actions and discourse of the US, especially since the terrorist attacks of 9/11 and the subsequent declaration of a 'war on terror'.[13] The aim of this book is to provide a sober and dispassionate analysis and assessment of the impact of not only the key actions taken, justifications provided and policies adopted since 9/11 now

7 See, generally, J.L. Gaddis, *Strategies of Containment: A Critical Appraisal of Post-War American National Security Policy* (New York: Oxford University Press, 1982).

8 The doctrine of pre-emptive self-defence will be the focus of Chapter 7.

9 The US's military, diplomatic, political, and economic assets have provided it with the capabilities 'to be a decisive player in any conflict in whatever part of the world it chooses to involve itself'. Krauthammer, supra n. 4, 24. Michael Byers has commented that '[i]n terms of its military strength relative to other countries, the United States is more powerful than any state since the Roman Empire. With a diversified air, sea and land-based nuclear arsenal, twelve aircraft carriers, thousands of advanced warplanes and substantial stocks of precision-guided missiles and bombs, it has little reason to fear any other country'. See M. Byers, 'Preemptive Self-defense: Hegemony, Equality and Strategies of Legal Change' (2003) 11 *Journal of Political Philosophy* 171, 171.

10 The *jus ad bellum* is the body of rules of international law which govern *when* force can be used in international affairs and is the focus of this book. The *jus in bello*, that is the rules of international law which govern *how* military force should be used during times of armed conflict, is not covered here.

11 This term is used in this work to depict the relative persistence by which the US has either implicitly or explicitly advocated changes to the *jus ad bellum*.

12 See, for example, T.M. Franck, 'What happens Now? The UN After Iraq' (2003) 97 *AJIL* 607; M.J. Glennon, 'Why the Security Council Failed?' (2003) 82 *Foreign Affairs* 16; M.J. Glennon, 'How International Rules Die' (2005) 83 *Geo.L.J.* 939.

13 In the President's Address to a Joint Session of Congress and the American People on 20 September 2001, President Bush stated that '[o]n September 11th, enemies of freedom committed an act of war against our country … Americans are asking: how will we fight and win this war? … this war will not be like the war against Iraq a decade ago … it will not look like the air war above Kosovo …' President George W. Bush, 'Address to a Joint Session of Congress and the American People' (20 September 2001). Available at: http://www.washingtonpost.com/wp-srv/nation/specials/attacked/transcripts/bushaddress_092001.html [Accessed: 15 December 2009].

that the dust has had a chance to settle, but also in the time since it became endowed with the title of 'sole remaining superpower'. A comprehensive and up to date analysis and assessment of the impact of the US upon the *jus ad bellum* in this time period has not as yet been produced. Furthermore, the book does not fail to address the recent changing of the guard at the White House and the taking up of residence by President Barack Obama. Given that this was hailed by many at the time as being a momentous event, it is thus perhaps a good time to take stock of the impact of the US's persistent advocacy up to the end of the second Bush administration, but at the same time consciously looking forward to the future. Consequently, the Postscript to this book has sought to discern the approach to the *jus ad bellum* that appears to have been initially adopted by the Obama administration and address whether, and if so how, this is proving to be any different from previous US administrations, particularly that of his predecessor.

In attempting to gauge any impact upon this fundamental area of international law, the book has drawn upon insights from the theory of interpretive communities in constructing a framework of analysis. This has as one of its key tenets the importance of discerning 'intersubjective agreement' amongst those with authority for interpretation within the international community. Under this framework it becomes clear that whilst in certain areas of the *jus ad bellum* a widening of the terms of the debate is recognizable, modifications to the *lex lata* are generally not. This is due essentially to a lack of intersubjective agreement between the US and other relevant actors as to the proposed interpretations either at the time or as exhibited through subsequent practice. Given that the position of the US as 'sole' superpower could be viewed as being under threat from other competitors,[14] this book provides a comprehensive reaffirmation of the robustness of international law governing the use of force to superpower manipulation, regardless of which state happens to be given this label. Whilst it is not possible to predict the future, it is hoped that the conclusions formed in this book will provide at least some reassurance.

It should be made clear at the outset that this book does *not* attempt to provide a complete account of the US's relationship with the *jus ad bellum* in the post-Cold War era. It does not, for example, examine the influence of the law upon decisions of the US to use, or to refrain from using, force, which is a study perhaps best left to be dealt with by international relations theorists.[15] Furthermore, this book is not a comprehensive assessment of changes to the *jus ad bellum* over this time period, which would of course involve an assessment of the practice of all states. There are

14 See, for example, J. Kynge, *China Shakes the World: A Titan's Rise and Troubled Future – and the Challenge for America* (Boston, MA: Mariner Books, 2007).

15 Although this is not to say that international lawyers have not approached such questions. See, for example, A. Chayes, *The Cuban Missile Crisis: International Crises and the Role of Law* (New York: Oxford University Press, 1974).

already works which provide a more general assessment of this nature.[16] Rather, it focuses on the substantive areas of the *jus ad bellum* with which the US has most often and significantly engaged with through either its actions, justifications for actions, or adopted policies.

The book is divided into two main Parts. After having addressed in more detail the framework of how it will assess impact in Chapter 2, the first Part goes on to examine the US's engagement with, and impact upon, the collective use of force. In particular, it focuses upon the uses of force by the US which, at least appear to, come under the authority of the UNSC. Chapter 3 addresses the US's role in the contemporary functioning of the collective security system. Whilst this has not functioned as envisaged in the UN Charter, the US has played a pivotal role in its development which began with the response to Iraq's invasion of Kuwait in 1990. More specifically, the chapter addresses the development of what has been termed in this work the 'authorization technique'.

Building on this, Chapter 4 is the first of two connected branches of the authorization technique. In particular, given the legitimacy with which this technique came to be viewed, the US took to arguing that the authorization provided could be unilaterally 'revived' on subsequent occasions. Chapter 5 then addresses a related, yet more controversial, argument that states are able to unilaterally enforce what can be viewed as the collective will, either that which is contained in resolutions of the UNSC, or connected with a major concern of the international community; the violation of human rights.

The second Part of the book focuses on the US's practice in connection with self-defence, the sole unilateral exception to the prohibition of the use of force found in the UN Charter. Since 11 September 2001 global terrorism has been a concern not just for the US but for the international community as a whole, as witnessed, for example, by the adoption of the 'legislative' UNSC Resolution 1373 (2001).[17] However, the US has attempted to push the boundaries of the traditional law governing responses to attacks by non-state actors, in particularly by adopting a 'harbouring' standard in the attribution of these attacks to states for the purposes of self-defence. The impact of this is addressed in Chapter 6, the penultimate chapter.

As part of its anti-terror strategies after 9/11, the Bush administration also attempted to expand the permissible norms of behaviour so as to incorporate the

---

16 See, for example, C. Antonopoulos, *The Unilateral Use of Force by States in International Law* (Athens: A.N. Sakkoulas, 1997); A.C. Arend and R.J. Beck, *International Law and the Use of Force: Beyond the UN Charter Paradigm* (New York: Routledge, 1993); J. Gardam, *Necessity, Proportionality and the Use of Force by States* (Cambridge: Cambridge University Press, 2004); C. Gray, *International Law and the Use of Force*, 3rd edn (Oxford: Oxford University Press, 2008); T. Gazzini, *The Changing Rules on the Use of Force in International Law* (Manchester: Manchester University Press, 2005).

17 See, generally, P. Szasz, 'The Security Council Starts Legislating' (2002) 96 *AJIL* 90.

possibility of taking pre-emptive forcible defensive measures. Chapter 7, the final chapter, focuses on the doctrine of expanded self-defence that has been championed by the Bush administration during this time. Finally, the book will attempt to draw some conclusions as to the impact of the US upon international law governing the use of force since the end of the Cold War and what the implications are for the future.

Chapter 2
Assessing Impact upon the *Jus ad Bellum*

Introduction

There is no distinct prescribed method of measuring the impact that a state has had upon international law. Therefore it is important to set out in this chapter how this will be undertaken prior to commencing the main substantive analysis in Part I of the book. Before this is done, however, it is necessary to say a few words about the nature and content of the object of assessment for impact; the *jus ad bellum*. The purpose of this chapter is not to be exhaustive in its treatment of these issues, but aims instead to establish a suitable basis from which to carry out the substantive analysis in the book.

The Sources of International Law with Special Reference to the *Jus ad Bellum*

The *jus ad bellum* is the *lex specialis* of international law governing the use of force. Thus, to gain a picture of the sources of the *jus ad bellum*, it first needs to be determined what the sources of international law *lex generalis* are.[1] A common starting point for an examination of the general sources is Article 38(1) of the Statute of the International Court of Justice which states that:

> The Court, whose function is to decide in accordance with international law such disputes as are submitted to it, shall apply:
>
> a. international conventions, whether general or particular, establishing rules expressly recognised by the contesting states;
> b. international custom, as evidence of a general practice accepted as law;
> c. the general principles of law recognized by civilized nations;

---

1 On the sources of international law see, generally, C. Parry, *The Sources and Evidences of International Law* (Manchester: Manchester University Press, 1965); G.J.H. van Hoof, *Rethinking the Sources of International Law* (Hague: Kluwer, 1983); M.E. Villiger, *Customary International Law and Treaties: A Manual on the Theory and Practice of the Interrelation of Sources*, 2nd edn (Hague: Kluwer, 1997); V.D. Degan, *Sources of International Law* (Hague: Martinus Nijhoff, 1997).

d. subject to the provisions of Article 59, judicial decisions and the teachings of the most qualified publicists of the nations, as subsidiary means for the determination of rules of law.[2]

Although this provision does not purport to be an exhaustive list of the sources of international law, but rather an authorization for the ICJ to consider certain materials when determining cases, it has been generally accepted by states as an authoritative list of the sources[3] and is also commonly cited by writers as such,[4] and by the ICJ itself.[5]

Whilst 'Article 38 is generally regarded as a complete statement of the sources of international law',[6] for the purposes of this work mention should be made of a sub-category of the international convention source: resolutions containing decisions of the UNSC.[7] The obligatory nature of these resolutions flows from Article 25 of the UN Charter,[8] that is, an international convention, and are consequently perhaps only general sources of law to the extent that membership of the UN is nearly universal.[9] However, they are nonetheless particularly relevant in this work due to the UNSC's primary responsibility for the maintenance of international

2 Whereas paragraphs (a)–(c) contain the 'law-creating processes', paragraph (d) contains the 'law-determining agencies', that is, the means of verifying the law. See G. Schwarzenberger, *International Law*, 3rd edn, vol. 1 (London: Stevens, 1957), 27. For more on the 'law-determining' sources see infra *The secondary interpretive community*.

3 It has also been commented that Article 38(1) of the Statute of the International Court of Justice is 'authoritative generally because it reflects state practice'. R. Jennings, *Oppenheim's International Law*, 9th edn, vol. 1 (Harlow: Longman, 1997), 24.

4 See, for example, I. Brownlie, *Principles of Public International Law*, 7th edn (Oxford: Oxford University Press, 2008), 4–5; A. Cassese, *International Law*, 2nd edn (Oxford: Oxford University Press, 2005), 156; R. Higgins, *Problems and Process: International Law and How We Use It* (Oxford: Clarendon Press, 1994), 17–18; J. Murphy, *The United States and the Rule of Law in International Affairs* (Cambridge: Cambridge University Press, 2004), 13.

5 See, for example, *North Sea Continental Shelf Cases (Federal Republic of Germany v Denmark; Federal Republic of Germany v The Netherlands)* [1969] ICJ Rep. 3, para. 88.

6 Brownlie, supra n. 4, 5.

7 Byers talks of 'the "sources" of international law, including treaties, customary international law and, since 1945, UN Security Council resolutions adopted under Chapter VII of the UN Charter'. See M. Byers, *War Law: International Law and Armed Conflict* (London: Atlantic Books, 2005), 45.

8 This provision states that '[t]he Members of the United Nations agree to accept and carry out the decisions of the Security Council in accordance with the present Charter'.

9 For example, during the Gulf War in 1990–91, Switzerland was not bound to apply the sanctions imposed against Iraq in UNSC Resolution 661 (1990) as it was not a member of the UN. However, Article 2(6) of the UN Charter (1945) states that '[t]he Organization shall ensure that states which are not Members of the United Nations act in accordance with [the Principles and Purposes] so far as may be necessary for the maintenance of international peace and security'.

peace and security[10] and to the fact that in the institutional context if debates regarding the use of force are to take place they do so almost exclusively within the chamber of the Council.[11]

In this section the main sources for the purposes of this work will be discussed, that is, international conventions, customary international law, and resolutions of the UNSC. This is not intended to be an exhaustive study of these sources but merely as a point of departure from which to begin the analysis in subsequent chapters.[12]

International Conventions: The Charter of the United Nations

The UN Charter is the most important treaty in force today and has been since its adoption in 1945. Its importance, along with its virtually unanimous ratification, has led some commentators to refer to it as the 'constitution of the international community'.[13] However, the Charter is also the main textual source of the *jus ad bellum*. It not only contains the prohibition of the threat or use of force in Article 2(4), arguably the Charter's most important provision,[14] but also the exceptions to this prohibition; individual and collective self-defence under Article 51 and collective forcible measures under the auspices of the UNSC in Chapter VII. Given that it is the cornerstone provision in connection with the use of force and thus has relevance for all of the chapters of this book, some of Article 2(4)'s salient features and the scholarly debate that has surrounded this provision will be addressed here. The other relevant provisions of the Charter, including the exceptions to the prohibition, will be addressed as and when they arise in the subsequent chapters.

Article 2(4): The prohibition of the threat or use of force Although regulation of the use of force in some form in international relations dates back to long before the UN Charter was adopted in 1945,[15] Article 2(4) of the Charter is the basis for

10 UN Charter (1945), Article 24(1).

11 See infra *Resolutions of the United Nations Security Council.*

12 They will be addressed in more detail where relevant in subsequent chapters. More specifically, what is set out here, along with where indicated in connection with the other aspects of the *jus ad bellum* set out in these subsequent chapters, is intended to be, as far as possible, a summary of how the law stood at the end of the Cold War in 1989.

13 See, generally, B. Fassbender, 'The United Nations Charter as Constitution of the International Community' (1998) 36 *Colum.J.Transnat'l L.* 529.

14 This is due to the UN 's stated primary purpose 'to save succeeding generations from the scourge of war'. UN Charter (1945), preamble. Brierly describes it as 'the corner-stone of the Charter system'. See J.L. Brierly, *The Law of Nations*, 6th edn (revised by H. Waldock) (Oxford: Oxford University Press, 1963), 414.

15 For a classic account of the history of the regulation of war and the use of force see, generally, I. Brownlie, *International Law and the Use of Force by States* (Oxford: Clarendon Press, 1963).

the prohibition of the threat or use of force in contemporary public international law. It provides that:

> All Members shall refrain in their international relations from the threat or use of force against the territorial integrity or political independence of any state, or in any other manner inconsistent with the Purposes of the United Nations.

Addressing itself to 'all Members', the prohibition was intended to be binding on member states, whether individually or as members of other international or regional organizations. Although the provision does not elucidate the type of 'force' that was the intended target of the prohibition, it is generally accepted that this was military force, as opposed to that of a political, economic, or technological nature.[16] Significantly, the provision does not simply prohibit the resort to 'war', but also covers those acts involving the use of force that stop short of war.[17] However, regardless of whether the use of force stops short of war or not, threats of such force are prohibited if it would be unlawful to employ actual force in the same circumstances.[18] It is also notable that, in addition to being addressed solely to member states, by using the phrases 'international relations' and 'any state' the prohibition contained in Article 2(4) only covers inter-state and not intra-state conflicts. This is generally the case with the provisions of the Charter as it was adopted at a time when the primacy of the state as the subject of, and actor within, international law was clearer than it is today.[19]

---

16 Cassese, supra n. 4, 56. Although for some doubt expressed regarding the exclusion of technological force from the reach of this provision see M.N. Schmitt, 'Computer Network Attack and the Use of Force in International Law: Thoughts on a Normative Framework' (1999) 37 *Colum.J.Transnat'l L.* 885.

17 This is in contrast to the predecessors of the UN Charter – the League of Nations Covenant of 1919 and the Kellogg-Briand Pact of Paris of 1928 – where the term 'war' was used instead of 'force'. See E. Gordon, 'Article 2(4) in Historical Context' (1985) 10 *Yale J.Int'l L.* 271, 273–74.

18 This has most recently been pronounced by the ICJ to be the correct interpretation of the threat of force in *Legality of the Treat or Use of Nuclear Weapons* (Advisory Opinion) [1996] ICJ Rep. 226, paras. 47–8. See, generally, N. Stürchler, *The Threat of Force in International Law* (Cambridge: Cambridge University Press, 2007). Whilst the prohibition of the *threat* of force constitutes a part of the *jus ad bellum* and threats to use force will be referenced at different places in the succeeding chapters of this book, this work restricts its analysis to assessing the US's impact upon the law governing the *use* of force. Whilst caution must be taken in making any direct inferences, it could be argued that, on the basis of the jurisprudence of the ICJ, if it is shown that the an impact has been made upon the law governing the actual *use* of force, it can be inferred that one has also been made upon the law governing the *threat* to use force in the same circumstances.

19 If the Charter was to be re-written today, it is possible that, due to the rise in frequency of internal conflicts and the reality of global terrorism, the use of force between states and non-state entities would be addressed in some form in the provisions regulating

The provision has historically proved to be the focal point of much debate between commentators regarding the breadth and scope of the prohibition contained within. For example, some have relied on a textual analysis to argue for limited constraints, asserting that use of the phrase 'against the territorial integrity or political independence of any state' suggests that force is permitted so long as it does not target these two fundamental elements of statehood.[20] However, many scholars have been critical of this particular reading of Article 2(4). Oscar Schachter, for example, has rejected this interpretation by commenting that it demands an Orwellian construction of the terms of this provision.[21] Others have also argued for a more watertight prohibition.[22] There was also an implicit rejection of this argument by the ICJ after it had been advanced by the UK in the *Corfu Channel* case.[23] Additionally, Article 2(4) states that force that is used in a 'manner inconsistent with the purposes of the United Nations' is prohibited. Given that the fundamental purpose of the UN is 'to maintain international peace and security',[24] it has been argued that the inclusion of the phrase 'against the territorial integrity or political independence of any state' should not be seen as limiting the prohibition of the use of force but instead to give 'particular emphasis' to it in these circumstances.[25]

---

the use of force. However, by contrast to Article 2(4), the sole unilateral exception of self-defence to this prohibition contained in Article 51 does not expressly restrict itself only to responses to 'armed attacks' by state actors. See Part II for more on self-defence.

20 See, for example, D. Bowett, *Self-Defence in International Law* (Manchester: Manchester University Press, 1958), 152. This kind of narrow interpretation was used by Anthony D'Amato when, in an article regarding the Israeli missile strike against the Iraqi nuclear reactor in Osiraq in 1981, it was argued that:

> … it is open to serious question whether Israel's strike was a use of force against either Iraq's territorial integrity or its political independence. No portion of Iraq's territory was taken away from Iraq by the bombardment. A *use* of the territory – namely, to construct a nuclear reactor – was interfered with, but the territory itself remained integral. Nor was Iraq's political independence compromised. Iraq's *power* was undoubtedly lessened, but in what sense was its governmental authority *vis-à-vis* other sovereign governments diminished?

See 'Israel's Air Strike Upon the Iraqi Nuclear Reactor' (1983) 77 *AJIL* 584, 585.

21 See O. Schachter, 'The Legality of Pro-Democratic Invasion' (1984) 78 *AJIL* 645, 649.

22 See, for example, Brownlie, supra n. 15, 267–68; Y. Dinstein, *War Aggression and Self-Defense*, 4th edn (Cambridge: Cambridge University Press, 2005), 87.

23 *Corfu Channel Case (United Kingdom v Albania)* [1949] ICJ Rep. 4, p. 35.

24 This is found, in particular, in the preamble and Article 1(1) of the UN Charter. For the other purposes and principles of the UN see Chapter I of the Charter.

25 This is revealed in the *travaux préparatoires*. See A. Randelzhofer, 'Article 2(4)' in B. Simma (ed.), *The Charter of the United Nations: A Commentary*, 2nd edn (Oxford: Oxford University Press, 2002), 112, paras. 37–9. Michael Akehurst has stated

Lastly, it has been argued by a few scholars that due to numerous violations of the prohibition since 1945 it can be pronounced 'dead'.[26] However, others have taken the view that an assault upon this key provision of the Charter, based upon the record of violations, does not lead to it becoming a dead letter.[27] Indeed, what is important to these commentators is the fact that no state itself has ever pronounced the death of the prohibition[28] and that governments do not freely violate this provision but instead 'tend to hold to the sweeping Article 2(4) prohibition against the threat or use of force, except where self-defence or Security Council enforcement action is involved'.[29] Indeed, the prohibition has been reaffirmed by states themselves in various resolutions of the UNGA.[30] These facts, along with the undisputed importance of the norm within the UN Charter, have led many to regard the prohibition of the threat or use of force as a norm of *jus cogens*[31] and, as such, one that would consequently require a considerable

that 'the *travaux préparatoires* indicate that the reference to territorial integrity, political independence, and the purposes of the United Nations was added to Article 2(4), not in order to limit the prohibition on the use of force, but in a clumsy attempt to strengthen it'. See M. Akehurst, 'Humanitarian Intervention' in H. Bull (ed.), *Intervention in World Politics* (Oxford: Clarendon Press, 1986), 95. See also I. Brownlie, *The Rule of Law in International Affairs* (Hague: Martinus Nijhoff, 1998), 198.

26 For the original claim see, generally, T.M. Franck, 'Who Killed Article 2(4)?' (1970) 64 *AJIL* 809. This has been pronounced again more recently, as noted in Chapter 1 (n. 12).

27 See, generally, L. Henkin, 'The Reports of the Death of Article 2(4) Are Greatly Exaggerated' (1971) 65 *AJIL* 544.

28 L. Henkin, *How Nations Behave: Law and Foreign Policy*, 2nd edn (New York: Columbia University Press, 1979), 138. Schachter notes that 'no state has ever suggested that violations of Article 2(4) have opened the door to free use of force'. O. Schachter, 'In Defense of International Rules on the Use of Force' (1986) 53 *U.Chi.L.Rev.* 113, 131. For the importance of the views of states in the interpretive process see infra *The primary interpretive communities*.

29 O. Schachter, 'The Right of States to Use Armed Force' (1984) 82 *Mich.L.Rev.* 1620, 1632.

30 See, for example, Declaration on Principles of International Law Concerning Friendly Relations and Cooperation Among States in Accordance with the Charter of the United Nations, UNGA Res. 2625 (XXV) (24 October 1970) UN Doc. A/RES/25/2625 (XXV). This is not to say, however, that the exact parameters of the prohibition or the exceptions to it have been set out in these.

31 See, for example, Brownlie, supra n. 4, 511. The International Law Commission expressed the view that 'the law of the Charter concerning the prohibition of the use of force in itself constitutes a conspicuous example of a rule in international law having the character of *jus cogens*'. See (1996-II) UNYBILC, 247. Furthermore, the ICJ in the *Nicaragua* case noted that the prohibition of the use of force 'is frequently referred to in statements by *state representatives* as being not only a principle of customary international law but also a fundamental or cardinal principle of such law'. *Case Concerning Military and Paramilitary Activities in and Against Nicaragua (Nicaragua v United States of America)* (Merits) [1986] ICJ Rep. 14, para. 190 (emphasis added).

amount of intent on behalf of the international community to modify it, let alone render it completely invalid.[32]

International Customary Law

The *jus ad bellum* is not simply located in the UN Charter. Indeed, most of its important rules are found in, and often derive from, customary international law.[33] This source of international law can be described as being formed from the practice of states which is followed out of a sense of legal obligation, as opposed to habit, politeness, or comity.[34] However, as the ICJ in the *Nicaragua* case of 1986 clearly stated, the two sources of the law retain their separate existence and identity so that '[o]n a number of points, the areas governed by the two sources of law do not exactly overlap, and the substantive rules in which they are framed are not identical in content'.[35]

Nevertheless, although it is possible for conventional and customary norms to develop autonomously and in divergent ways, because there has now been over 60 years of state practice subsequent to the introduction of the UN Charter and because the addressees of the Charter and those of customary international law almost completely coincide, there has been a 'certain degree of uniformity and coherence in their respective development'[36] so that the two sources of the *jus ad*

32 Article 53 of the Vienna Convention on the Law of Treaties (1969) states that 'a peremptory norm of general international law is a norm accepted and recognized by the international community of states as a whole as a norm from which no derogation is permitted and which can be *modified* by a subsequent norm of general international law having the same character' (emphasis added). This will be expanded upon infra in *The limitations of the theory of interpretive communities in assessing impact.*

33 This was stated most famously by the ICJ in the *Nicaragua* case in 1986: 'There can be no doubt that the issues of the use of force ... are issues which are regulated both by customary international law and by treaties, in particular by the United Nations Charter'. See *Nicaragua Case*, supra n. 31, para. 34.

34 In forming and modifying customary international law the two necessary elements are the practice of states (*usus*) accompanied by a belief that this practice is permitted or required by law (*opinio juris sive necessitatis*). Article 38(1)(b) of the Statute of the International Court of Justice (1945) includes 'international custom, as evidence of a general practice accepted as law' as a source of international law. See also, for example, *North Sea Continental Shelf Cases*, supra n. 5, para. 73; 'Final Report of the Committee on Formation of Customary (General) International Law', ILA London Conference (2000), 7.

35 *Nicaragua Case*, supra n. 31, para. 175. For example, the requirement of an 'armed attack' before an action in self-defence can commence is found in Article 51 of the UN Charter, whereas the requirements that actions taken in self-defence be 'necessary' and 'proportional' emanate from customary international law. For more on necessity and proportionality see Chapter 6.

36 T. Gazzini, 'The Rules on the Use of Force at the Beginning of the XXI Century' (2007) 11 *JCSL* 319, 320.

bellum 'are substantially identical'.[37] Arguments to the contrary have not been made by states and when discussing forcible actions a distinction is not generally made between the two sources. For example, the ICJ noted in the *Nicaragua* case of 1986 that 'both Parties [in their pleadings] take the view that the principles as to the use of force incorporated in the United Nations Charter correspond, in essentials, to those found in customary international law'.[38]

Resolutions of the United Nations Security Council

Resolutions containing decisions of the UNSC are legally binding upon member states of the UN.[39] As Chapter 3 will demonstrate, this organ has a fundamental role to play in the *jus ad bellum* through being endowed with primary responsibility for the maintenance of international peace and security.[40] As such, it has a particular role in connection with incidences involving the use of force, whether unilaterally[41] or due to it having the sole power to use force outside of the context of self-defence.[42] Today this latter power operates by the UNSC 'authorizing' states to use force on its behalf.[43] This authorization is expressed in the form of a UNSC resolution and the existence, extent, or breadth of this authorization has on occasion proved a source of controversy.[44] Furthermore, the UNSC may condemn, or express concern over, a situation or take control of one after a prior use of force by declaring a ceasefire and in building the peace.[45] Again, the will of this organ of the UN is normally expressed in the form of a resolution.[46]

However, due to its responsibility for maintaining international peace and security, it has been argued that the UNSC's significance and importance in the context of the *jus ad bellum* goes further than simply being sole interpreter of its resolutions and general competence.[47] Indeed, some have given special weight to

---

37 Ibid. As will be demonstrated at certain points in this book there has been a certain amount of reciprocal conditioning between the two sources.

38 *Nicaragua Case*, supra n. 31, para. 188.

39 UN Charter (1945), Article 25.

40 Ibid., Article 24(1).

41 UN member states are required to report measures taken in self-defence, which may only last until the UNSC has 'taken measures necessary to maintain international peace and security'. Ibid., Article 51.

42 Ibid., Articles 39–50.

43 The development of this technique under the influence of the US will be discussed in Chapter 3.

44 See Chapter 4 on the 'revival' doctrine.

45 See UNSC Resolution 46 (1948) as an example of one of many such instances in the Israeli-Palestinian context.

46 See Chapter 5 for the argument of the US that unilateral decisions to employ force may be taken to enforce this 'will'.

47 As Zweifel notes, '[a]t the San Francisco conference that launched the UN, the founders preferred to let each organ interpret its own competence'. T.D. Zweifel,

UNSC evaluations of state practice in the realms of the use of force beyond this immediate sphere.[48] However, whilst debates within the chamber of the UNSC and communications made to it are of particular relevance as a focal point in gathering the views of states on issues connected with international peace and security and, more specifically, the use of force,[49] legally speaking this does not provide it as a body with any more authority in terms of interpreting the general *jus ad bellum* outside of the context of its own competence.[50]

Assessing Impact Upon the Sources of the *Jus ad Bellum*

The exercise of assessing the impact that the US has had upon the *jus ad bellum* is essentially one of gauging whether this particular branch of international law has undergone a process of change as a result of the actions and discourse of this particular state.[51] The extent of any impact that a state can be said to have had upon any branch of international law is affected by two intrinsic structural realities of the international legal system. First, the international legal system, unlike domestic systems, is decentralized. Rather than operating in a vertical, hierarchical way, with a sovereign at the apex handing down laws to its subjects, it operates horizontally with the makers of the law also its subjects. Second, as

---

International Organizations and Democracy: Accountability, Politics, and Power (Boulder, CO: Lynne Rienner, 2005), 72. Although this has been questioned. See, generally, T.M. Franck, 'The "Powers of Appreciation" Who is the Ultimate Guardian of UN Legality?' (1992) 86 *AJIL* 519.

48 See, for example, T.M. Franck, *Recourse to Force: State Action Against Threats and Armed Attacks* (Cambridge: Cambridge University Press, 2002).

49 As Johnstone notes, 'discourse about the meaning and implementation of legal norms ... takes place in the Council' on a regular basis. I. Johnstone, 'Security Council Deliberations: The Power of the Better Argument' (2003) 14 *EJIL* 437, 453.

50 It should be borne in mind that the UNSC is a political, as opposed to a legal, organ of the UN.

51 The discourse engaged in will often form part of a justification for action. There is not now, nor has there ever been, an obligation upon states under international law to offer a justification, legal or otherwise, for their actions. Nevertheless, as Kritsiotis has remarked, whilst '[n]o formal obligation is placed on states outside the arena of litigation or official reporting commitments to justify their actions in international law ... we find that even the most powerful states invoke international law principles and argument to defend their conduct'. See D. Kritsiotis, 'The Power of International Law as Language' (1997–98) 34 *Cal.W.L.Rev.* 397, 402. The amorphous nature of the practice of state justification for action means that its form and procedure, either preceding, during, or after an action is taken, or in the abstract, is not formally established. However, in judging impact upon the law, what one is aiming to discern from any justification advanced by the acting state, especially where multiple justifications are proffered, is the justification with the greatest 'characterization of legality'. See A. D'Amato, *The Concept of Custom in International Law* (New York: Cornell University Press, 1971), 76–7.

well as not possessing an efficient distinct centralized lawmaker, like Congress in the US or Parliament in the UK, the international system also lacks a compulsory centralized legal adjudicator. Consequently, whilst in a domestic legal system courts are usually the primary interpreters, the international legal system is what can be described as auto-interpretative so that in the majority of cases states are the actors involved in interpreting and applying the law.

Whilst there is no distinct prescribed method to measure impact under these conditions there are certain rules that have emerged regarding the formation, interpretation, modification and termination of the sources of international law that are of assistance. Indeed, if it can be demonstrated that new law has been formed or existing law reinterpreted, modified or terminated following the actions and discourse of the US then this would suggest that it has had an impact. Although it is not within the scope of this work to offer a comprehensive description and analysis of these rules,[52] given that the interpretation and modification of the sources described in the above section of this chapter is under focus in this work, some brief treatment is necessary in connection with these types of changes to these particular sources.

Interpreting and Modifying the Sources of the Jus ad Bellum

The rules governing the formation of treaties and their interpretation, modification, and termination are set out in the Vienna Convention on the Law of Treaties (1969) (VCLT (1969)).[53] Given that this is a multilateral treaty these rules have been expressly agreed to by those states that are a party to it.[54] Furthermore, whilst there has been no explicit guidance from the UN, or the UNSC more specifically, on the rules governing the interpretation of resolutions of the UNSC, some scholars have employed many of the principles from the VCLT as guidance in this enterprise.[55]

On the other hand, the rules governing customary international law formation and modification have not arisen through the adoption of a treaty or through the direct discourse and expression of states. They have, instead, emerged through the jurisprudence and observations of state practice by the ICJ,[56] and

52 For more on these rules see the sources cited supra in n. 1.

53 Although strictly speaking these rules only apply to treaties concluded after the coming into force of the VCLT they still apply to the UN Charter as the rules are a codification of those found in customary international law. See A. Aust, *Modern Treaty Law and Practice*, 2nd edn (Cambridge: Cambridge University Press, 2007), 12–13.

54 This treaty only has 108 parties, although, as noted Ibid., these rules are found in customary international law.

55 See M. Wood, 'The Interpretation of Security Council Resolutions' (1998) 2 *Max Planck Yrbk UN L.* 73; E. Papastavridis, 'Interpretation of Security Council Resolutions Under Chapter VII in the Aftermath of the Iraqi Crisis' (2007) 56 *ICLQ* 83.

56 See, for example, *North Sea Continental Shelf Cases*, supra n. 5; *Nicaragua Case*, supra n. 31.

its predecessor the PCIJ,[57] and by scholars of international law, although (to the knowledge of the present author) no real disagreement with them has been discernible amongst states.[58]

Consequently, upon first appearance the two sets of rules seem to be very different, both in origin and form. However, if we are to use these established 'rules about rules'[59] as an aid in assessing change to the sources under focus in this work, that is, whether the UN Charter or UNSC resolutions have been reinterpreted or the customary regulation of the use of force modified,[60] there are similarities on the essential points.[61]

The VCLT is primarily aimed at how one should interpret a treaty at any given point, rather than assessing if and how the interpretation has changed over a given period. Consequently, it takes as its primary indicator the text of the treaty and the 'ordinary meaning' of its terms.[62] However, as noted in the above section of this chapter, and as will be seen in the succeeding chapters of this book, the textual provisions of the UN Charter dealing with the use of force have not brought all to agreement over their permissible limits.[63]

---

57 See, for example, *Lotus Case (France v Turkey)* (1927) PCIJ Rep. Series A no. 10.

58 If one peruses the key works of international law, it is noticeable that the majority of the discussion in the relevant chapters on customary international law focuses on the debate amongst scholars and the jurisprudence of the ICJ as opposed to the practice of states directly. See, for example, Brownlie, supra n. 4, 6–12; M. Shaw, *International Law*, 6th edn (Cambridge: Cambridge University Press, 2008), 72–93.

59 M. Byers and S. Chesterman, 'Changing the Rules About Rules? Unilateral Humanitarian Intervention and the Future of International Law' in J.L. Holzgrefe and R. Keohane, *Humanitarian Intervention: Ethical, Legal and Political Dilemmas* (Cambridge: Cambridge University Press, 2003), 177.

60 As noted in the above section of this chapter, the two sources of the *jus ad bellum* are virtually identical. See supra *International Customary Law*.

61 As Byers has noted, whilst a strict analogy between the two processes is inappropriate, it remains nonetheless true that one of the ways in which the UN Charter may be modified is 'informally, through a process of reinterpretation that is not unrelated to the way in which customary international law evolves'. M. Byers, 'Review of T.M. Franck, Recourse to Force: State Action against Threats and Armed Attacks' (2003) 97 *AJIL* 721, 721.

62 This 'general rule of interpretation' is found in Article 31(1) of the VCLT (1969). However, as Ian Johnstone has commented, '[w]hatever its merits as a theory of interpretation in domestic settings, the "textualist" approach is particularly implausible in the international context … In the heterogeneous international system, treaties are typically concluded by states with different cultures and, often, different languages. Thus, the notion that the interpreter's task is merely to construe the words of the instrument, with little recourse to context or extrinsic evidence, has been largely discredited'. See I. Johnstone, 'Treaty Interpretation: The Authority of Interpretive Communities' (1990–91) 12 *Mich. J.Int'l L.* 371, 372.

63 As Gray notes, '[e]ven in inter-state conflicts the apparently simple words of the Charter have given rise to fundamental differences between states'. C. Gray, *International Law and the Use of Force*, 3rd edn (Oxford: Oxford University Press, 2008), 7.

If the text of a treaty does not provide a clear interpretation the VCLT provides for further information to be taken into account. This primarily includes 'any subsequent *agreement* between the parties regarding the interpretation of the treaty or the application of its provisions'[64] or 'any subsequent practice in the application of the treaty which establishes the *agreement* of the parties regarding its interpretation'.[65] The essential element here is 'agreement' amongst the community of party members to the treaty,[66] whether exhibited expressly through verbal means or implicitly through practice. Indeed, the element of agreement is of such importance that it can provide a 'special meaning' to a term outside of its ordinary textual bounds 'if it is established that the parties so intended'.[67]

However, the element of agreement is also central to the rules on determining whether a new customary international legal norm has formed or an existing one been modified. Whilst this element is not expressly mentioned in the definition provided in Article 38(1)(b) of the Statute of the International Court of Justice of 'a general practice accepted as law' or in the pronouncements on the formation and modification of customary international law of the ICJ during its enquiries into the existence of a customary norm, this is clearly an implicit requirement. For example, the ICJ has required a 'settled practice'[68] involving 'widespread and representative participation'[69] in which 'the states concerned ... *feel* that they are conforming to what amounts to a legal obligation' before it could be said that such a norm was in existence.[70] The notion that a particular practice has become 'settled'

64 VCLT (1969), Article 31(3)(a) (emphasis added).

65 Ibid., Article 31(3)(b) (emphasis added). Aust asserts that subsequent practice 'is the most important element in the interpretation of any treaty, and reference to practice is well established in the jurisprudence of international tribunals'. See A. Aust, *Modern Treaty Law and Practice*, 2nd edn (Cambridge: Cambridge University Press, 2007), 241. The importance of this notion in interpreting UNSC resolutions has also been stressed. See Wood, supra n. 55, 92.

66 In the case of the UN Charter, this is virtually all states. The problems with finding agreement in this context are discussed below. See infra *The limitations of the theory of interpretive communities in assessing impact.*

67 VCLT (1969), Article 31(4).

68 *North Sea Continental Shelf Cases*, supra n. 5, para. 77.

69 Ibid., para. 73.

70 Ibid., para. 77 (emphasis added). This is the *opinio juris sive necessitatis* element of customary international law. See supra n. 34. Whilst it is beyond the scope of this work to offer a critical analysis of this subjective element, a key problem worth drawing attention to is that it is not possible to know what states actually believe or feel. Because it is simply not possible to get into the minds of states to determine this, what they claim as to the law must be taken as indicative of what they actually believe. Furthermore, at the outset states do not necessarily always believe, or indeed claim, that a particular practice falls within the *lex lata*. Instead, as Cassese eloquently describes:

> a practice evolves among certain states under the impulse of economic, political, or military demands. At this stage the practice may thus be regarded as being imposed

and with the states involved believing that they are complying with international law implies that states are in agreement as to the legality of the practice concerned, whether they are aware of this agreement or not.

Furthermore, as with the interpretation of treaties, this settled agreement does not need to be demonstrated through actual physical practice. Whilst some scholars have advocated the view that physical acts are an essential ingredient in forming the agreement over the formation and modification of customary international law,[71] this view has not found wide support and many scholars have discounted it.[72] Although it is undoubtedly true that acts may carry more weight on occasion, if it were a general rule it would lead to the conclusion that the only way that customary international law could change was through violations of it. As Michael Akehurst notes, this approach is 'hardly one to be recommended by anyone who wishes to strengthen the rule of law in international relations'.[73] Others argue that it would provide more powerful states with increased opportunities to modify customary international law thus impinging upon sovereign equality.[74] Furthermore, this approach has not found acceptance by the ICJ.[75] Indeed, the general approach appears to be that the legality of the practice in question should be 'shared *in principle* by other states'[76] so that their general 'conduct' is not inconsistent with it.[77]

Challenges to the Requirement of 'Agreement'

Whilst it could be argued that the structural realities of decentralization and auto-interpretation mentioned above simply highlight the necessity of agreement in

---

> by social or economic or political needs (*opinio necessitatis*). If it does not encounter strong and consistent opposition from other states but is increasingly accepted, or acquiesced in, a customary rule gradually crystallizes. At this later stage it may be held that the practice is dictated by international law (*opinio juris*).

Cassese, supra n. 4, 157–58. Given the 'chronological paradox' associated with *opinio juris*, that is, states should believe that a practice is either legally obligatory or permitted before it can actually take its place as law, the notion of *opinio necessitatis* is an accurate descriptor of the initial phase of the customary process on many occasions.

71 See, for example, D'Amato, supra n. 51; M. Weisburd, *Use of Force: The Practice of States since World War II* (Pennsylvania: Pennsylvania State University Press, 1997).

72 See, for example, M. Akehurst, 'Custom as a Source of International Law' (1974–75) 47 *BYBIL* 1, 41; N. Onuf, 'Review of Karol Wolfke, Custom in Present International Law (2nd edn)' (1994) 88 *AJIL* 556.

73 Akehurst, Ibid., 8.

74 Byers and Chesterman, supra n. 59, 188.

75 In the *Nicaragua case* in 1986 the court specifically acknowledged that UNGA resolutions were important in forming the customary prohibition of aggression and intervention. *Nicaragua Case*, supra n. 31, paras 183–90.

76 Ibid., para. 207 (emphasis added).

77 Ibid., para. 186.

the process of treaty interpretation and customary international law modification, they have, nonetheless, led to several challenges to it. For example, it has been recognized that there is often a tendency in literature emanating from the US to make references to 'leading' and 'major' states in discussions concerning customary international law, indicating that these states are somehow more significant in its formation.[78] Furthermore, Oscar Schachter has commented that 'custom gives weight to effective power and responsibility'.[79] However, this is a misconception; it is not custom itself which gives weight to power, but rather some scholars in assessing the current status of customary international law. Similarly, in the context of treaty interpretation, Ian Johnstone has observed that '[s]kepticism about the determinacy of meaning combined with the absence of an impartial interpreter can lead to the discomforting conclusion that treaty auto-interpretation is an unconstrained activity determined entirely by short-term national interests and power politics'.[80]

In responding to accusations of this type, Ian Brownlie has commented that 'those who hold that inequalities of power between states should be reflected in the way in which the law is made and applied' are engaging in 'what may be called the hegemonial approach to law-making'.[81] Simply because a state is in the possession of greater power permitting it to engage in more practice due to a broader range of interests and activities and perhaps persuasive capabilities, these are political factors in the law making process which, strictly speaking, lie outside of jurisprudential considerations. As Byers and Chesterman note, 'paying less attention to some states is one thing: having a legal justification for doing so is another'.[82] Even though the view that power provides more rights in the legal interpretive process is one that is persistently asserted by some commentators, there has never been an acceptance of this as a legal principle by states themselves. Indeed, for it to become a rule of customary international law and displace the legal principle of sovereign equality it would have to be generally accepted by other states.[83] This, for obvious reasons, is not a proposition that would get past the first hurdle.

However, whilst *de facto* power does not have any more weight, *de jure*, in the development of international law, in some cases it is expressly accepted that equal agreement is displaced by the notion that certain 'specially affected' states may

---

78 As observed by Byers and Chesterman, supra n. 59, 193.

79 See O. Schachter, 'Entangled Treaty and Custom' in Y. Dinstein (ed.), *International Law at a Time of Perplexity: Essays in Honour of Shabtai Rosenne* (Hague: Martinus Nijhoff, 1989), 717, 720–21.

80 I. Johnstone, 'Treaty Interpretation: The Authority of Interpretive Communities' (1990–91) 12 *Mich.J.Int'l L.* 371, 372.

81 I. Brownlie, 'International Law at the Fiftieth Anniversary of the United Nations' 255 *Recueil des Cours* (1996-I), 49.

82 Byers and Chesterman, supra n. 59, 193.

83 Byers and Chesterman have described sovereign equality as 'a principle which operates, in a multitude of contexts, to constrain the law-making influence of the powerful'. Ibid., 194.

be of more importance in the process of customary international law formation and modification.[84] Nevertheless, this is a limited doctrine which does not extend to the granting of more rights to powerful states, but instead to those which are, for example, coastal states in determining issues regarding the law of the sea[85] or states which possess nuclear weapons in determining the legality of their use.[86] In other words, this provides certain states in certain positions, geographical or otherwise, a greater impact on the question of whether a new norm has formed rather than granting the powerful more rights in law formation and modification more generally. Whilst the argument can be made that due to the fact that powerful states often engage more frequently in a broader range of activities they are more likely to be 'specially affected' there has been 'no indication that their special status in customary law-making is recognized as a matter of law'.[87]

Furthermore, whilst it is possible for treaties to provide otherwise, this notion of 'specially affected' states does not extend to the interpretation of the UN Charter. On the contrary, in this context and in searching for agreement as to the interpretation of this treaty, the VCLT provides for the taking into account of 'any relevant rules of international law applicable in the relations between the parties'.[88] This would, presumably, include sovereign equality so as not permitting one party to have a greater authority in its interpretation than others.

The only source under analysis in this work which provides a *de jure* weighting in favour of more powerful states are resolutions of the UNSC. In this respect there is a form of 'legalized hegemony'[89] due to the fact that when the Charter was drafted the victors of the Second World War and the other most significant states at the time were granted a veto in the adoption of resolutions containing decisions on substantive issues. Indeed, if a resolution on such an issue is to be adopted, agreement has to be reached between nine of the 15 members sitting with no veto by any of the five permanent members.[90] This system

---

84 *North Sea Continental Shelf Cases*, supra n. 5, para. 74.

85 Ibid.

86 See *Nuclear Weapons Advisory Opinion*, supra n. 18. Although the Court did not comment directly on this point.

87 G. Danilenko, *Law-Making in the International Community* (Hague: Martinus Nijhoff, 1993), 96.

88 VCLT (1969), Article 31(3)(c).

89 G. Simpson, *Great Powers and Outlaw States: Unequal Sovereigns in the International Legal Order* (Cambridge: Cambridge University Press, 2004), 67.

90 UN Charter (1945), Article 27(3). This is the case, for example, if an 'authorization' resolution is to be adopted. See Chapter 3 for more on the 'authorization technique'. The permanent members of the UNSC, otherwise known as the 'P5' include China, France, Russia, the UK and the US. Very early on in the UN era Article 27(3) began to be interpreted so as to allow an absence or abstention by a permanent member on the vote not to count as a veto thereby permitting the adoption of a resolution. This has now become an accepted part of UNSC practice. See S. Bailey and S. Daws, *The Procedure of the UN Security Council*, 3rd edn (Oxford: Clarendon Press, 1998), 251. See also, generally, C.A. Stavropoulos, 'The

survived the Cold War so that even though the positions of these states within the international legal order today may not be as they were in 1945, decisions on when to use collective force are still ultimately subject to their agreement. However, in interpreting and applying the terms of resolutions of the UNSC, as well as in judging actions taken under them, the power of the veto is not directly relevant and all states within the UNSC have equal weighting unless, of course, they come to adopt a resolution presenting the collective view of the organ.[91]

Ultimately, notwithstanding these limited exceptions, the fact that the international legal system is decentralized and auto-interpretive does not mean that a state, regardless of how powerful it is, can unilaterally make new law and interpret existing law for itself, thus having an impact. Although certain attributes may provide a state with the possibilities to act *as* it wishes, *when* it wishes, perhaps with little repercussions,[92] the argument that more powerful states have greater *de jure* rights to interpret and change the law finds no place in the context of the sources of international law under discussion in this work.

The Theory of Interpretive Communities

The texts and state practice associated with the sources of the *jus ad bellum* do not exist in an objective vacuum and they must be interpreted and given legal significance in changing contexts. However, as argued above, this exercise is also not a purely subjective one undertaken by the individual interpreter in isolation. Whilst actions and justifications for actions, as with proposed changes in the abstract, are important in discerning whether a state is claiming to be acting within the existing boundaries of the *lex lata*, or whether any changes are being proposed, simply because a particular interpretation has been advanced by a state this does not mean that it acquires authoritative status.[93] Instead, when an interpretation has been advanced it triggers a process of evaluation and judgment by others to gauge whether it conforms to the conventions and purposes of the particular enterprise in which the practice sits.[94] Indeed, if the rule of law is to have any real substance in the international legal system, evaluations of proposals proffered by states for new interpretations or modifications of existing international law should be undertaken collectively in conjunction with other relevant actors within the interpretive process.

Practice of Voluntary Abstentions by Permanent Members of the Security Council Under Article 27, Paragraph 3, of the Charter of the United Nations' (1967) 61 AJIL 737.

91 See infra *Primary interpretive communities*.

92 This goes to the enforcement of international law which is not dealt with here.

93 As Johnstone has noted, '[i]n the decentralized international legal system, much law is interpreted not by an impartial arbiter but by domestic officials who are institutionally and politically predisposed to interpretations that favour their government or state'. Johnstone, supra n. 49, 443.

94 Ibid.

In this sense, the groupings of the actors relevant to the interpretation of each of the sources of the *jus ad bellum* can be seen in the framework of an 'interpretive community'.[95] This community represents the collective judgment from those concerned with accepting or rejecting proffered interpretations, assessing legal arguments, and weighing legal significance in regards to each of the sources of international law. In assessing the impact of a proposed modification to the law the objective is to discern the 'intersubjective' interpretation of it provided by the members of the relevant interpretive community.[96]

The theory of interpretive communities has been employed to demonstrate that intersubjectivity is more complicated than these actors simply striking a deal.[97] Instead, it is a process of shared understandings and interpretations emerging from a deliberative process within these communities.[98] However, whilst it is acknowledged that the underlying process is more complicated than the actors arriving at a simple agreement, in employing the theory in this work to assess impact it will be necessary to demonstrate that agreement has ultimately emerged amongst the members of the relevant community as to whether any proposed interpretations of the law by the US fit within these shared understandings and interpretations. In other words, and relating it to the rules regarding treaty interpretation and custom modification where agreement has been argued above to be the essential element,[99] in determining whether

95 This concept was first developed by Stanley Fish who, although a literary theorist, claimed that it had explanatory power in the field of domestic legal interpretation. See, generally, S. Fish, *Is There a Text in the Class? The Authority of Interpretive Communities* (Cambridge, MA: Harvard University Press, 1980). It has been subsequently applied in the international legal setting most prominently by Ian Johnston whose work will be drawn upon here in setting out its application in this work. See, generally, Johnstone, supra n. 80; Johnstone, supra n. 49; I. Johnstone, 'US-UN Relations after Iraq: The End of the World (Order) As We Know It?' (2004) 15 *EJIL* 813.

96 Johnston, 'Treaty Interpretation', Ibid., 381. Whilst Johnstone's application of the theory is essentially descriptive in explaining that this is what *does* happen in these communities, given what has been said above regarding the nature of the international legal system, the point is made here that interpretation within this system also *should* be an intersubjective activity.

97 The theory of interpretive communities has been used to explain the conditions conducive to giving rise to 'intersubjective' agreement (Johnstone, supra n. 49, 443–50). Furthermore, it has been employed in the international legal setting to explain why legal arguments are used in political forums such as the UNSC to justify and critique action (Ibid., generally), to make the argument that there are limits upon the enterprise of treaty interpretation (Johnstone, supra n. 80), and to explain the process of impact upon the sources of international law in wider terms than the traditional rules permit (Johnstone, 'US-UN Relations after Iraq', supra n. 95, 819).

98 It has been commented that '[i]ntersubjectivity … does not connote simple agreement, but rather is about engaging in a collectively meaningful activity, an activity collectively understood'. Johnstone, supra n. 49, 449.

99 It should be noted that Johnstone does not give these rules any real attention in his work on the theory.

an impact has occurred, one is attempting to discern the 'intersubjective *agreement*' of the particular interpretive community in regards to the proposed change.

Indeed, the theory is employed here not in disregard of, or as a substitute for, the traditional rules regarding treaty and UNSC resolution interpretation and customary international law modification. Instead, it is used to emphasize the fact that ultimately what matters in both processes is discerning intersubjective agreement as to the contemporary interpretation of the rules are.[100] In uncontroversial situations this process may be relatively unmarked. On other occasions a period of protracted negotiation may ensue.

However, the theory is also employed in the subsequent analysis of this work to highlight and give appropriate weight to the different actors involved in forming, influencing, and baring witness to this agreement and thus both the actors instrumental in facilitating an impact and in it becoming discernible. As opposed to simply claiming that there is agreement amongst 'states' in regard to the acceptability of a particular interpretation, the theory provides a clearer separation of, and focus to, those actors that possess authority in determining the acceptable boundaries of legal interpretation in each enterprise. Viewed in this way, the international legal interpretive process can be seen as comprised of two distinct constitutive parts. The key elements of each of these parts will be set out next.

Primary interpretive communities First, each of the sources has a 'primary' interpretive community associated with it. These communities consist of states, that is, the actors that ultimately bring rules into existence and then participate directly in their implementation and application.[101] However, more specifically they consist of the states associated with the particular enterprise in which the practice falls.

The most easily identifiable primary interpretive community that is of concern to this work is that charged with interpreting the competence of the UNSC,[102]

100 The notion of agreement is implicitly discernible in Ian Johnstone's exposition of the theory in connection with the sources of international law: 'Because the parties to a treaty or customary law regime constitute a collective law-making body, when disputes over interpretation arise, the interpretive task is to ascertain what the law means to the parties collectively rather than to each individually'. Johnstone, 'US-UN Relations after Iraq', supra n. 95, 819.

101 Johnstone, supra n. 49, 450. Corten has observed that '[i]nternational law does not exist in the abstract: it is rather what states make of it'. O. Corten, 'The Controversies over the Customary Prohibition of the Use of Force: A Methodological Debate' (2005) 16 *EJIL* 803, 811.

102 The competence of the UNSC can be found in the powers granted to it in the UN Charter. Although interpreting this competence requires interpreting a treaty – the UN Charter – so that one would assume that it is the primary interpretive community associated with this source which is relevant, the founders of the UN Charter decided to let each organ interpret its own competence so that this section of the UN Charter concerning the powers and competence of the UNSC has the primary interpretive community of the UNSC associated with it. See supra n. 47.

interpreting resolutions adopted by this body, and weighing actions taken under them. This comprises 15 members of the Council at any one time as they have a right to sit in the chamber during any discussion on such issues.[103] However, more indirectly, it also consists of '[a]ny Member of the United Nations which is not a member of the Security Council' whenever the Council 'considers that the interests of that Member are specially affected'.[104] In these circumstances, the particular state 'may participate, without vote, in the discussion of any question brought before the Security Council'.[105]

The relatively structured institutional community of the UNSC stands in contrast to the more diffuse primary interpretive community associated with the UN Charter and customary international law, that is, essentially, *all* states. Obviously this community contains a 'broader range of interests, concerns and understandings' than the relatively confined and structured UNSC.[106] Additionally, lacking the institutional environment within which the Council operates makes 'diverging interpretations more difficult to reconcile through consultation and negotiation'.[107] Instead, '[t]he interpretive process tends to be more evolutionary as shared meanings are worked out over time' with subsequent practice.[108] Nevertheless, the theory of interpretive communities is no less relevant, it is just that discerning intersubjective agreement regarding the interpretation of the UN Charter and the customary practice of states 'is, at root, a matter of uncovering shared expectations and understandings about international life' more generally and whether proposed modifications fit within these.[109]

The secondary interpretive community Although elaborate and detailed legal discussion and debate is not common between members of the primary interpretive communities, this takes place to a greater extent within the secondary interpretive community. This community is naturally wide ranging and includes all individuals, entities, groups, or organizations that possess an interest or expertise in connection with the particular enterprise. Furthermore, those within this community have either as their main purpose, or as a subsidiary function to their main purpose, the commenting upon, discussion, and debate of state practice and international law.[110]

---

103 For the composition of the UNSC see Chapter 3. As Article 28 of the UN Charter states, '[e]ach member of the Security Council shall ... be represented at all times at the seat of the Organization', although given the protracted nature of some issues and disputes the non-permanent members are not always on the Council for their full duration.

104 UN Charter (1945), Article 31.

105 Ibid.

106 Johnstone, supra n. 80, 407.

107 Ibid.

108 Ibid.

109 Ibid., 413.

110 The statements and pronouncements of the members of this community are frequently referenced in works of international law in support of the position of the particular author. However, the legal significance of these actors is rarely acknowledged.

For example, this group includes scholars, the UNSG, lawyers, judges, courts, international law bodies, NGOs, regional organizations, think-tanks, pressure groups or indeed anybody 'who participates in some way to the particular field of international law or practice in which the interpretive dispute arises'.[111] Whilst those within this community are not formally decisive as to normative change and do not have any direct authority for determining what the rules of the *jus ad bellum* are,[112] they may influence the direction of the law through the impact of their pronouncements and discourse upon the behaviour and discourse of the primary actors.[113] However, whilst the extent of the influence of such actors is an interesting question in itself, it is not the one under examination in this work. Here, the community, and the pronouncements and discussion emanating from it, is used as a subsidiary means for determining and assessing any impact.[114]

Due to the relative openness as to membership of this community and its diffuse nature, the community as a whole is common to the various primary interpretive communities which differ according to the individual interpretive enterprise. Together the two communities constitute an 'international jury'[115] which possess interpretive authority and passes judgment on legal claims.

The limitations of the theory of interpretive communities in assessing impact The theory of interpretive communities posits authority for interpretation firmly in the collective hands of the relevant community and gives an identity and relevance to those involved in the process. Furthermore, it provides a useful lens through which to view the interpretive process, as well as the terminology for describing and discussing it. However, it must be acknowledged that a limitation in the utility of the theory to this work, in the form that it has been developed by others, is

---

111 Johnstone, supra n. 80, 450–51.

112 Corten goes as far as to say that '[t]he political organs of the UN, NGOs, scholars or other actors certainly play an essential political role in the evolution of the rule, to the extent that they influence official state positions. It is, however, these positions themselves that must be analysed when seeking to determine whether or not a custom has evolved'. Corten, supra n. 101, 819; Gray, supra n. 63, 27.

113 As Lowe points out, actors of this nature 'have a peculiarly important role in international law. They cannot create law, but their analyses can ease or impede the passage of new doctrines into legal rules … lubricating the movement of the engine of state practice in cases where there is a consensus among [them] that a particular development is in line with the logic and underlying policy of international law and, like grains of sand in the gears, impeding such movement where a development is opposed'. V. Lowe, 'The Iraq Crisis: What Now?' (2003) 52 *ICLQ* 859, 860. It also 'represents the institutional mechanism closest to an impartial arbiter that the structure of … auto-interpretation provides' by monitoring and supervising the primary interpretive communities so as to provide indirect reassurance against subjective interpretation. Johnstone, supra n. 80, 390.

114 See infra *Significant actors within the secondary interpretive community* for more discussion on this.

115 Corten, supra n. 101, 812.

that it does not provide a precise method by which to certify or measure whether the US has had an impact upon the law governing the use of force. Nevertheless, given that, as noted above, there is neither a distinct prescribed method by which to do this or an alternative theory or methodological approach which provides a way, by employing the theory of interpretive communities in conjunction with the traditional rules on the interpretation and modification of international law assessing any impact becomes a more transparent exercise.

The existence of intersubjective agreement both in quantitative and qualitative terms may be clearly established in the debates of the UNSC.[116] This is essentially due to the fact that for the outside observer 'the relevant information is publicly available as UN documentation and manageable, in quantitative terms'.[117] However, the UNSC is not an organ that requires unanimity. To claim that this agreement has formed does not require evidence of express positive agreement by *all* members. Rather, the evidence should demonstrate that it is an interpretation that is generally shared amongst its members. Indeed, if from the transcripts of a particular meeting where an issue is discussed it transpires that from the statements made by the states present that at least 60 per cent of them are in agreement regarding the competence of the UNSC or the interpretation of a particular resolution, then this is arguably sufficient to claim that there is intersubjective agreement.[118] However, under the collective security system as it currently stands, any decisions as to when to use force must have the agreement of the permanent members.

On the other hand, in viewing the practice of the primary interpretive communities associated with the UN Charter and customary international law one is 'confronted by a truly massive amount of potentially relevant behaviour'.[119] Attempting to find a general consensus amongst these primary interpretive communities is not an easy task with the assessment of state practice and reaction, far from being an exact science, often seeming to be more of a rough sketch. Indeed, the finding of intersubjective agreement in these contexts is still subject to the same practical difficulties as discerning amongst the 192 states of the international community a 'general practice accepted as law' or 'subsequent' agreement or practice regarding the interpretation of the UN Charter.[120]

These difficulties are compounded by the fact that, as noted above, the prohibition of the use of force is considered by many to be *jus cogens*.[121] Under this view, for any direct modification of this particular norm, and the acceptance of

116 See, for example, Chapter 3.

117 Byers, supra n. 61, 724.

118 This is the same percentage as required for the adoption of a resolution by the UNSC, that is, nine of the 15 members present. See text accompanying supra n. 90.

119 Byers, supra n. 61, 724.

120 Finding this agreement is arguably possible in the meetings of the UNGA and in the adoption of resolutions or other documents by this organ that address aspects of the use of force. However, the adoption of such documents is a relatively rare occurrence.

121 See supra n. 31.

a norm which conflicts with it or the widening of the exceptions to it, it would have to be demonstrated that the proposed change had been 'accepted and recognized by the international community of states *as a whole*' as a peremptory norm.[122] Even if one does not take the view that the prohibition is *jus cogens*, there is no doubt that it is a norm that the international community 'holds dear'.[123] Either way, one should hesitate before concluding that a change to the law has taken place in the light of an incident involving the use of force, even if there are initial signs of acceptance and agreement.

Generally speaking, the duration of time sufficient to demonstrate that a proffered interpretation has had an impact upon the law does not necessarily have to be extensive. Indeed, a short period of time is not necessarily a bar to interpretations finding a place within the *lex lata*.[124] However, any reaction after the occurrence of an incident is inherently caught up with the emotions of the moment, especially in the context of incidents involving the use of force. In these moments, it cannot be assumed that attention has been given to the broader ramifications of a practice and whether legal significance should flow from it. As such, it is only with the passing of time that one is able to discern with any certainty whether and, if so, in what form or to what extent a norm has been modified.[125] Indeed, given the undoubted importance of the norm prohibiting force under consideration it is arguable that any reinterpretation or modification would have to be particularly well settled.[126]

The point here is that to gain enough evidence, both quantitatively and temporally, to identify sufficient positive intersubjective agreement in connection with a proposed modification affecting the prohibition of the use of force is a far from easy task.[127] To ease the burden of this undertaking, it is possible to view the process from the opposite end, so that rather than searching for 'whole' or 'general' positive intersubjective agreement with a proposed modification the search is instead inverted so as to make it one of identifying *negative* intersubjective

---

122 VCLT (1969), Article 53 (emphasis added).

123 R. Higgins, *Problems and Process: International Law and How We Use It* (Oxford: Clarendon Press, 1994), 22.

124 *North Sea Continental Shelf Cases*, supra n. 5, para. 74.

125 As noted above, *opinio necessitatis* may be present at the outset but whether this solidifies into *opinio juris* is perhaps only discernible with the passing of such time. See supra n. 70.

126 Whilst it is not argued here that 'instant' changes to international law are not possible, this notion has only been discussed in regards to norms *jus dispositivum* requiring a general practice, as opposed to the agreement of the international community as a whole, as required in connection with those that have been considered *jus cogens*. See, generally, B. Cheng, 'United Nations Resolutions on Outer Space: "Instant" Customary International Law?' (1965) 5 *Indian J.Int'l L.* 23.

127 This task is complicated further by the difficulties associated with whether states which do not appear to have offered any reaction are acquiescing in the proposed change or not. See Akehurst, supra n. 72, 38–42.

agreement, that is, agreement amongst the relevant interpretive community rejecting the proposed interpretation.[128]

On this basis, if the view that the prohibition of the use of force is *jus cogens* is taken, we start from the proposition that for any substantive change in this particular area of international law to occur we are looking for 'whole' agreement with it. In other words, the finding of intersubjective agreement amongst virtually all states is necessary to conclude that the US has had an impact upon the *jus ad bellum*. It is perhaps to be expected that when a proposed change is made to such a controversial area of the law as that governing when states can use force, it will not be universally accepted or acquiesced in, with at least some states rejecting it. In this case, if one adopts a strict interpretation of 'whole' agreement then this negative reaction may be sufficient to quash the proposed change. Indeed, if the focus is instead placed on negative responses to the proposed modification as an indicator of impact, it could be argued that any identifiable cracks of whatever magnitude in this 'whole' are sufficient to certify that the norm has not been modified and that the general prohibition remains intact.

However, given that it is not universally accepted that the prohibition of the use of force is *jus cogens*, this approach can also be applied to the lower threshold of requiring 'general' agreement for a modification of the law to take place. In this case, however, a claim that a proposed change has not been accepted does not require a demonstration of general or widespread *negative* intersubjective agreement; a task that would prove equally as difficult as finding general positive intersubjective agreement. Instead, if what could be described as *significant* indicators of negative intersubjective agreement with the proposed modification are discernible it is arguable that this is sufficient to quash any proposition that there is general agreement that the law has changed as a result of the actions and discourse of the US.

Significant indicators of negative intersubjective agreement within the primary interpretive communities To categorize some reaction or subsequent practice as 'significant' is not to discredit the notion of sovereign equality or to provide some states with more formal authority in the law making process than others.[129] It is, rather, to

128 The phrase 'negative intersubjective agreement' is preferred to 'intersubjective disagreement' due to the latter indicating disagreement amongst the members of the primary interpretive community. On the other hand, 'negative intersubjective agreement' indicates that the community is in agreement as to its rejection of the proposed changes. Of course, it is arguable that any negative intersubjective agreement with a proposal can never be truly intersubjective, as at least one state (that proposing the change) has adopted a different view. However, in these circumstances the disagreeing state is no longer a part of the community. As Johnstone has noted, 'if the interpreter proffers an interpretation that reaches beyond the range of responses dictated by the conventions of the enterprise, he or she ceases to act as a member of the relevant community'. Johnstone, supra n. 49, 445.

129 This form of interpretation has been discounted above. See supra *Challenges to the Requirement of 'Agreement'*.

highlight that in different circumstances a negative reaction by certain states or groups of states within the primary interpretive communities concerned with interpreting the UN Charter or customary international law are indicative of a more general negative intersubjective agreement within the wider international community.

Whilst it is rarely ever easy to draw firm conclusions when talking about issues regarding the *jus ad bellum*, if such an indicator is identified as being present then this is suggestive of the fact that support has not been, and in some cases will not be, sufficient for an impact of a legal nature to be certified. In the context of this work, reaction and subsequent practice by the primary interpretive communities which could be classed as ‘significant’ include the following:

- If after either expressly or implicitly proposing a change to the law, the US then, in similar subsequent circumstances, fails to act in a similar way thereby failing to support the proposed modification. If a state advances a proposal as to a modification of the law but then itself fails to subsequently support it this is indicative of a lack of confidence in its viability and/or acceptability.
- If traditional or contemporary allies of the US are unsupportive to the proposed modification. Whilst if these states are in favour of the proposed changes to the *jus ad bellum* we could not say upon this basis alone that the *jus ad bellum* has been impacted upon, if these states prove to be unfavourable to the proposed changes then this provides a weighty indicator that there will be insufficient support for a change to the *jus ad bellum* to be discernible at that time. Indeed, if these states are not supportive of the US’s proposed modification then this is a good indicator that many others within the international community will similarly not be.
- If states that engage in subsequent uses of force in situations in which the proposed modification could be relied upon fail to do so in justifying their actions. If the US has attempted to set a precedent for action which is not then subsequently relied upon by other states when acting then this is a direct repudiation of the proposed change especially if no other justification is advanced by the acting state.
- If organizations which represent significant numbers of states expressly reject a proposed modification. Statements and resolutions from organizations such as the UN and the G77 which comprise of a totality or majority of states are indicative of the consensus amongst these states.

It must be acknowledged that this approach, which is more concerned with discrediting a proposal than supporting one, is not completely foolproof or quantitatively accurate. However, whilst it must be duly emphasized that these are only indicators, their distinguishing feature is that their existence arguably provides for wider conclusions to be drawn as to the presence of negative intersubjective agreement to a proposed change to the law within the wider primary interpretive community connected with the UN Charter and customary international law regulating the use of force.

Significant actors within the secondary interpretive community Just as certain types of practice and reaction of the primary interpretive communities are particularly significant, so it can be observed that certain actors within the secondary interpretive community are particularly significant depending upon the enterprise under focus. Indeed, within this community there is no notion of equality so that some are of more significance in discussing possible changes to the *jus ad bellum*. Although there is no formal hierarchy between those within this community and all are welcome to contribute, those with a particular interest, knowledge, or expertise in the interpretive enterprise arguably have more authority and experience in determining the status of the law and whether any impact has occurred. In this respect, due to their involvement with the issues under discussion in this work over the time period under focus, of notable importance here are the ICJ, the UNSG, and international legal scholars:

- The ICJ: The ICJ is the UN's 'principal judicial organ'.[130] Although there is no *stare decisis* in international law and 'the decision of the Court has no binding force except between the parties and in respect of that particular case'[131] it is 'indisputably pre-eminent'.[132] In this sense, the fact that its decisions are a 'subsidiary means for the determination of rules of law'[133] makes them particularly important in an assessment of any change in the law. Indeed, it has handed down some notable decisions and opinions connected with the *jus ad bellum*, and in particular in the post-Cold War era, such as the *Nicaragua* case of 1986, the *Nuclear Weapons* advisory opinion of 1996, the *Oil Platforms* case of 2003, the *Wall* advisory opinion of 2005, and the *DRC v Uganda* case of 2005. Whilst not claiming that the ICJ is always correct in its assessment,[134] if any clear changes have occurred in the law, one could expect them to be noted in its judgments and opinions.
- The UNSG: The UNSG is the 'chief administrative officer' of the UN.[135] Although the UNSG and the UNSC hold very distinct positions within the UN, he may, however, 'bring to the attention of the Security Council any matter which in his opinion may threaten the maintenance of international peace and security'.[136] Whilst there is nothing preventing the UNSG from

---

130 Statute of the International Court of Justice (1945), Article 1.

131 Ibid., Article 59.

132 D.J. Harris, *Cases and Materials on International Law*, 6th edn (London: Sweet and Maxwell, 2004), 53.

133 Statute of the International Court of Justice (1945), Article 38(1)(d).

134 There has been, for example, much disagreement over its judgment in the *Nicaragua* and *Oil Platforms* cases. See, for example, J.N. Moore, 'The Nicaragua Case and the Deterioration of World Order' (1987) 81 *AJIL* 151; J.A. Green, 'The Oil Platforms Case: An Error in Judgment?' (2004) 9 *JCSL* 357.

135 UN Charter (1945), Article 97.

136 Ibid., Article 99.

making general comments as to the legality of actions and impact upon the law, and he has done so on many occasions, it should be borne in mind that the UNSG has no constitutional basis for making such judgments. Nevertheless, he has been a key observer of the workings of the collective security system since the end of the Cold War and has produced a number of reports with observations and ideas to improve it.[137] Furthermore, the UNSG has been the inspiration behind much of the activity and publication of reports within and outside of the UN since 2000.[138] These reports will be drawn upon in this work as secondary indicators of the impact of the US's actions and justifications upon the *jus ad bellum*.

- International legal scholars: Although not as great as the immediate post-Westphalia period in the Middle Ages when the 'fathers of international law' virtually wrote its early beginnings, the contemporary role of scholars in international law should not be underestimated.[139] Indeed, the Statute of the ICJ explicitly mentions 'the teachings of the most highly qualified publicists of the various nations, as subsidiary means for the determination of rules of law'.[140] Ultimately, 'there would seem to be no legal order wherein the publicist – a peculiar term – has played a greater part than international law'[141] and the role they play in assessing international law and state practice so as to shed light upon it and analyse and assess its import is vital in any discussion.

Differences of opinion will always be present amongst these significant actors and amongst scholars in particular. As such, it is difficult to say that one scholar's determination as to the current state of the law is more conclusive than another's.[142] Indeed, it is not easy to use these actors to 'measure' impact. In their writings, scholars

137 See Report of the Secretary-General, 'An Agenda for Peace' (1992) UN Doc. A/47/277; Report of the Secretary-General, 'Supplement to an Agenda for Peace' (1995) UN Doc. A/50/60; Report of the Secretary-General, 'In Larger Freedom: Towards Security, Development and Human Rights for All' (2005) UN Doc. A/59/205.

138 Report of the High-Level Panel on Threats, Challenges and Change, 'A More Secure World: Our Shared Responsibility' (2004) UN Doc. A/59/565; The Report of the International Commission on Intervention and State Sovereignty, 'The Responsibility to Protect' (December 2001). Available at http:www.iciss.ca/report-en.asp [Accessed: 20 November 2009].

139 K. Wolfke, *Custom in Present International Law*, 2nd edn (Hague: Martinus Nijhoff, 1993), 76.

140 Statute of the International Court of Justice (1945), Article 38(1)(d). However, as Parry notes, 'it is as difficult to decide who "the most highly qualified publicists" are as it is to say what is a peace-loving nation within the meaning of the Charter of the United Nations'. Parry, supra n. 1, 108.

141 Parry, Ibid., 103.

142 Whilst the work of certain authors is particularly notable in the context of this work, such as that of Ian Brownlie, Christine Gray, Nigel White, Michael Reisman, and Mary

often draw upon and use the writings and pronouncements of other scholars to support their own position. In a sense, that is what is being done in this work. However, in determining impact in this work the assessment of the primary interpretive community is turned to first with no fixed agenda. The research behind this book did not commence with the intention to prove a hypothesis. Instead, it set out to accumulate and assess the available reaction from the primary interpretive community and then turn to the secondary interpretive community to either feed the debate or, most importantly, to confirm whether the initial conclusions drawn from the reaction and assessment of the primary interpretive community regarding the impact of the US can be supported. Where appropriate, different interpretations by scholars as to the response from the primary interpretive community or arguments surrounding the impact of the proposed modification under discussion have been included.

Using the framework and premises established in this chapter, this book will assess the impact that the US has had upon the *jus ad bellum* in the post-Cold War era. This begins in Part I, which addresses the impact that the US has had upon the first of the two exceptions to the general prohibition of the use of force – collective action under the auspices of the UNSC.

Ellen O'Connell, it is the particular interpretation of the reaction of the primary interpretive community as opposed to the particular author which this work is interested in.

PART I
The Use of Force Under the Auspices of the United Nations Security Council

Chapter 3

The Functioning of the United Nations Collective Security System: The Authorization Technique

The major changes since the fall of the Berlin Wall concerning the use of force relate to Security Council practice.[1]

Introduction

The contribution of the US was integral to the design and establishment of the UN at the end of the Second World War.[2] The system of collective security, which was a central part of the UN, aimed to restrict the occasions when armed force was employed, other than when it was resorted to in self-defence,[3] to those taken collectively in the 'common interest'.[4] However, for its full operation this system required a certain amount of cooperation between states and, with the onset of the Cold War, it failed to function as envisaged in the Charter both in terms of the quantity and quality of its work. With the end of the Cold War in 1989, and the

1 M.G. Kohen, 'The Use of Force by the United States after the End of the Cold War and its Impact Upon International Law' in M. Byers and G. Nolte (eds), *United States Hegemony and the Foundations of International Law* (Cambridge: Cambridge University Press, 2003), 197, 213.

2 See R.B. Russell and J.E. Muther, *A History of the United Nations Charter: The Role of the United States 1940–1945* (Washington: Brookings Institution, 1958), 96; F. Rawski and N. Miller, 'The United States in the Security Council: A Faustian Bargain?' in D. Malone (ed.), *The UN Security Council: From the Cold War to the 21st Century* (Boulder, CO: Lynne Rienner, 2004) 357, 357.

3 This sole unilateral right to use force is found in Article 51 of the UN Charter. See Part II of this work for more on this right.

4 See the preamble and Chapter VII of the UN Charter. Nigel White explains that '[a] collective security system entails the centralization of a society's coercive mechanisms'. See N.D. White, *Keeping the Peace: The United Nations and the Maintenance of International Peace and Security*, 2nd edn (Manchester: Manchester University Press, 1997), 5. See, generally, K.P. Saksena, *The United Nations and Collective Security* (Delhi: D.K. Publishing House, 1974); H. Kelsen, *The Law of the United Nations* (London: Stevens, 1951); L. Goodrich and A. Simons, *The United Nations and the Maintenance of International Peace and Security* (Washington: Brookings Institution, 1955).

collapse of the Soviet Union, a 'New World Order' was proclaimed by the US[5] and hopes for the improved functioning of the collective security system were raised.[6]

This chapter will demonstrate, with reference to the primary and secondary interpretive communities,[7] that to an extent this hope has been realized. Although not perfect, the UNSC has certainly been more active in its attempts to maintain international peace and security and in the use of force for this purpose. Furthermore, the US has had a heavy influence in the instigation and functioning of this new activism. This chapter will therefore examine the impact that this practice has had upon the *jus ad bellum* and demonstrate the method by which these changes have been effected. First, however, in order to set the context in which to view these changes, the collective security system as envisaged in the UN Charter will be briefly set out together with how it was utilized during the Cold War.[8]

The United Nations Collective Security System and the Use of Force: 1945–1989

In Theory: The Charter of the United Nations

The preamble of the UN Charter states the inspiration behind the Organization's founding as being 'to save succeeding generations from the scourge of war', 'to unite … strength to maintain international peace and security', and 'to ensure … that armed force shall not be used, save in the common interest'. Essentially, the intentions of the drafters of the Charter were to take the deliberations of when to use force other than in self-defence away from states. Similarly, foremost amongst the 'Purposes and Principles' of the UN, as set out in Chapter I of the Charter, is that of:

> maintain[ing] international peace and security, and to that end: to take effective collective measures for the prevention and removal of threats to the peace, and for the suppression of acts of aggression or other beaches of the peace, and to bring about by peaceful means, and in conformity with the principles of justice

5 See President George H.W. Bush, 'Toward a New World Order' (1991) 1 *United States Department of State Despatch* 91. See also, generally, G. Abi-Saab, 'A "New World Order"? Some Preliminary Reflections' (1994) 7 *Hague Yrbk Int'l L.* 87.

6 President Bush announced in his address to the UNGA on 1 October 1990 that '[t]he changes in the Soviet Union have been critical to the emergence of a stronger United Nations. The US-Soviet relationship is finally beyond containment and confrontation, and now we seek to fulfil the promise of mutually shared understanding'. See President George H.W. Bush, 'The UN: World Parliament of Peace' (1990) 1 *United States Department of State Despatch* 151.

7 For more on these communities see Chapter 1.

8 This section is also of use in setting the subsequent two chapters of Part I of this book in context.

> and international law, adjustment or settlement of international disputes or situations which might lead to a breach of the peace.

Consequently, the UNSC, which was ordained with 'primary responsibility for the maintenance of international peace and security'[9] and the power to take decisions binding on the members of the UN,[10] was envisaged as playing a key role within the system of collective security.[11] Commensurate with this responsibility, one of the exceptions to the general prohibition of the use of force[12] is action undertaken by the UNSC through its enforcement powers contained in Chapter VII of the UN Charter.[13]

The gateway provision to the availability of measures in Chapter VII is Article 39. This provides that:

> The Security Council shall determine the existence of any threat to the peace, breach of the peace, or act of aggression and shall make recommendations, or decide what measures shall be taken in accordance with Articles 41 and 42, to maintain or restore international peace and security.

The provision is unequivocal that prior to opening up the enforcement measures available to it under Chapter VII it is the UNSC itself that is to determine whether there exists a threat to the peace, breach of the peace, or act of aggression.[14] Once such a determination has been made, this organ of the UN can then either make recommendations, which are not binding upon member states,[15] or adopt a binding

---

9 UN Charter (1945), Article 24(1).

10 Ibid., Article 25.

11 Dinstein notes that '[t]he main objective of the framers of the Charter of the United Nations was to introduce into international relations a genuine mechanism of collective security. The UN organ entrusted with the task of activating and supervising the mechanism is the Security Council'. See Y. Dinstein, *War, Aggression and Self-Defence*, 4th edn (Cambridge: Cambridge University Press, 2005), 279.

12 UN Charter (1945), Article 2(4). For a discussion of this prohibition see Chapter 1.

13 The UNSC is a political rather than a legal organ that does not act to enforce international law *per se*, although this might be a collateral result of its decisions and actions. As Kelsen has noted, '[t]he purpose of enforcement action under Art. 39 is not to maintain or restore law, but to maintain and restore peace, which is not necessarily identical with the law'. See Kelsen, supra n. 4, 736. Furthermore, its decisions and deliberations might have more general legal consequences. See, generally, R. Higgins, *The Development of International Law through the Political Organs of the United Nations* (Oxford: Oxford University Press, 1963).

14 See J.A. Frowein and N. Krisch, 'Article 39' in B. Simma (ed.), *The Charter of the United Nations*, 2nd edn (Oxford: Oxford University Press, 2002), 717.

15 Article 25 of the UN Charter only states that '[t]he Members of the United Nations agree to accept and carry out the *decisions* of the Security Council …' (emphasis added).

decision to take either non-forcible measures under Article 41[16] or, if it decides that the 'measures provided for in Article 41 would be inadequate or have proved to be inadequate',[17] measures of a forcible nature under Article 42.[18] Furthermore, the text of the Charter provides that in order for the UNSC to fulfil its primary responsibility for the maintenance of international peace and security under Article 42, '[a]ll Members of the United Nations' shall make available to it armed forces 'in accordance with a special agreement or agreements'.[19]

In Practice: The Paradox of the Cold War

It has been widely documented and commented that the way in which these measures were utilized during the Cold War was neither what the drafters of the Charter initially envisaged nor what was expressly provided for in it.[20] The unforeseen onset of superpower rivalry led ultimately to an extensive paralysis of the UNSC during the first 45 years of its life and the 'special agreements' noted above never came to fruition due to the failure of member states to conclude such agreements. As a result, the model collective forcible measures system was never fully realized.[21]

However, this did not mean that the organ was completely idle during the Cold War in relation to its primary responsibility.[22] Although during this period of East-West ideological conflict the UNSC was often blocked from carrying out many enforcement measures due to the use of the veto by the permanent members,[23] the organ did recognize a 'threat to international peace and security' seven times,[24]

---

16 Action under Article 41 involves 'measures not involving the use of force'. As the provision itself spells out, '[t]hese may include complete or partial interruption of economic relations and of rail, sea, air, postal, telegraphic, radio, and other means of communication, and the severance of diplomatic relations'.

17 UN Charter (1945), Article 42.

18 Article 42 provides for the UNSC to 'take such action by air, sea, or land forces as may be necessary to maintain or restore international peace and security'. Action taken under this provision 'may include demonstrations, blockade, and other operations by air, sea, or land forces of Members of the United Nations'.

19 UN Charter (1945), Article 43(1). As Gray points out, '[t]he initial plan was that the Security Council would have its own standing army to use in response to threats to the peace, breaches of the peace, or acts of aggression'. See C. Gray, *International Law and the Use of Force*, 3rd edn (Oxford: Oxford University Press, 2008), 254.

20 See, for example, White, supra n. 4, 7; Gray, Ibid., 254.

21 Gray, ibid; White, Ibid., 115; D.J. Harris, *Cases and Materials on International Law*, 6th edn (London: Sweet and Maxwell, 2004), 980–81.

22 See, generally, F. Kirgis, 'The Security Council's First Fifty Years' (1995) 89 *AJIL* 506.

23 Gray, supra n. 19, 254.

24 Israel (UNSC Res. 573 (4 October 1985) UN Doc. S/RES/573); South Africa (UNSC Res. 418 (4 November 1977) UN Doc. S/RES/418); Cyprus (UNSC Res. 353 (20

label state action as 'aggression' twice,[25] determine that there had been a 'breach of the peace' three times,[26] employ non-military sanctions twice[27] and use military force three times.[28] Although these figures go some way to counter accusations of complete paralysis, as Koskenniemi notes, '[i]n light of the perhaps seventy-three interstate wars that broke out during the same period, the data clearly shows the dramatic extent of the Council's paralysis'.[29]

In the three instances where the UNSC employed military force during the Cold War, instead of this body using force itself by means of the model system described above, it permitted member states to do so. The collective use of force against the aggression of North Korea in 1950 came after a 'recommendation' from the UNSC under Chapter VII for 'members of the United Nations [to] furnish such assistance as may be necessary'.[30] Similarly, in the Congo in 1960 the UNSC, acting under Chapter VII, 'authorized' the UNSG to establish the UN Operation in Congo and 'to take the necessary steps ... to provide such military assistance as may be necessary'.[31] The organ also 'called upon' Great Britain in 1966 'to prevent, by the use of force if necessary', oil from reaching Southern Rhodesia.[32] As these incidences demonstrate, the UNSC was involved in the collective use of force and clothed certain actions with its unique legitimacy, but the full extent of its powers was never exhibited.

The end of the Cold War in 1989 and the emergence of the so-called 'New World Order' brought the possibility of consensus between member states,[33] thus

---

July 1974) UN Doc. S/RES/353); Pakistan (UNSC Res. 307 (21 December 1971) UN Doc. S/RES/307); Southern Rhodesia (UNSC Res. 232 (16 December 1966) UN Doc. S/RES/232); Congo (UNSC Res. 161 (21 February 1961) UN Doc. S/RES/161); Palestine (UNSC Res. 54 (15 July 1948) UN Doc. S/RES/54).

25 Israel (UNSC Res. 573 (4 October 1985) UN Doc. S/RES/573); South Africa (UNSC Res. 418 (4 November 1977) UN Doc. S/RES/418).

26 Iran-Iraq (UNSC Res. 598 (20 July 1987) UN Doc. S/RES/598); Falklands (UNSC Res. 502 (3 April 1982) UN Doc. S/RES/502); Korea (UNSC Res. 82 (25 June 1950) UN Doc. S/RES/82).

27 Economic blockade of Southern Rhodesia, 1966–79 (UNSC Res. 232 (16 December 1966) UN Doc. S/RES/232); Arms embargo of South Africa, 1977–94 (UNSC Res. 418 (4 November 1977) UN Doc. S/RES/418).

28 South Rhodesia (UNSC Res. 221 (9 April 1966) UN Doc. S/RES/221); The Congo (UNSC Res. 143 (17 July 1960) UN Doc. S/RES/143); Korea (UNSC Res. 83 (27 June 1950) UN Doc. S/RES/83).

29 M. Koskenniemi, 'The Place of Law in Collective Security' (1995–96) 17 *Mich. J.Int'l L.* 455, 458. Indeed, the collective security system 'did not stand up to the pressure of the Cold War'. Gray, supra n. 19, 255.

30 UNSC Res. 83, supra n. 28, preamble. This force was under US command. See Gray, supra n. 19, 258.

31 UNSC Res. 143, supra n. 28, para. 2.

32 UNSC Res. 221, supra n. 28, para. 5.

33 N. Blokker, 'Is the Authorization Authorized? Powers and Practice of the UN Security Council to Authorize the Use of Force by "Coalitions of the Able and Willing"'

fulfilling President Bush's hope for a 'mutually shared understanding'.[34] Indeed, this great shift in international relations established a basis upon which intersubjective agreement amongst members of the primary interpretive communities could be found in the future. At the time of writing, however, the UNSC has still not functioned as originally intended. Instead, it has firmly embedded within its practice, whilst drawing upon elements of the language of the Cold War permissions to use force, the method of 'authorizing' states to use 'all necessary means'. It is this practice, and the US's central role in instigating it, which is addressed next.

The Reinvigoration of the Collective Security System in the Post-Cold War Era

The Setting of a Precedent: Security Council Resolution 678 (1990)

The so-called 'New World Order' is said to have begun with the UNSC's response to Iraq's invasion and annexation of Kuwait on 2 August 1990.[35] The UNSC immediately determined that there existed 'a breach of international peace and security',[36] condemned the invasion,[37] and called for an immediate and unconditional withdrawal of Iraqi forces from Kuwait.[38] On 8 August 1990, Iraq formally annexed Kuwait.[39] In response, the UNSC rejected Iraq's annexation and declared it to be of 'no legal validity' and 'null and void'.[40]

However, the most significant action taken occurred on 29 November 1990 when Resolution 678 (1990) was adopted under Chapter VII of the UN Charter.[41] The key paragraph of this resolution:

> *Authorizes* Member States co-operating with the Government of Kuwait, unless Iraq on or before 15 January 1991, fully implements, as set forth in paragraph 1 above, the foregoing resolutions, to use *all necessary means* to uphold

(2000) 11 *EJIL* 541, 542. Gray also notes that '[t]he end of the Cold War brought with it a steep decline in the use of the veto and a massive increase in the activity of the Security Council'. See Gray, supra n. 19, 264.

34 See supra n. 6.

35 *Keesing's* (1990) 37632; Gray, supra n. 19, 264. This was the first time in the UN era when one member state sought to completely annex another. See C. Greenwood, 'New World Order or Old? The Invasion of Kuwait and the Rule of Law' (1992) 55 *MLR* 153, 153.

36 UNSC Res. 660 (2 August 1990) UN Doc. S/RES/660, preamble. It should be noted that the UNSC did not condemn the invasion as a violation of Article 2(4), as an act of aggression, or as an 'armed attack'.

37 Ibid., para. 1.

38 Ibid., para. 2.

39 *Keesing's* (1990) 37635.

40 UNSC Res. 662 (9 August 1990) UN Doc. S/RES/662, para. 1. The UNSC also imposed economic sanctions in UNSC Res. 661 (6 August 1990) UN Doc. S/RES/661.

41 UNSC Res. 678 (29 November 1990) UN Doc. S/RES/678.

> and implement resolution 660 and all subsequent resolutions and to restore international peace and security in the area.[42]

This paragraph, whilst not explicitly saying as such, was interpreted and accepted by those within the primary interpretive community of the UNSC at the time as an authorization to use *force*.[43] This state of affairs was, to an extent, engineered by the US. The phrase, 'all necessary means', which was devised by this particular state, was inserted into this paragraph with the intention that the primary interpretive community would accept it as alluding to forcible measures.[44] Whilst it is not clear whether there was any direct opposition to it at the outset by members of the primary interpretive community, or whether the US merely took precautions so as to ensure its smooth passage at the meeting where the resolution was to be adopted, the US nonetheless reportedly offered incentives and rewards to certain states in return for their support for the resolution and punished Cuba and Yemen for its lack of support.[45]

Although arguments critical of such a practice and in defence of the principle of sovereign equality can be made, the US, in flexing its *de facto* hegemonial muscles so as to ensure the smooth passage of a UNSC resolution, was not acting unlawfully.[46] In any event, during the course of the meeting when the resolution was adopted it became clear that there was positive intersubjective agreement amongst members of the community that the phrase 'all necessary means' alluded to military force.

---

42 Ibid., para. 2 (second emphasis added).

43 Gray notes that '[i]t is clear from the Security Council debates that this formula was understood to mean the use of force'. See Gray, supra n. 19, 265. See also Greenwood, supra n. 35, 166; N.D. White and R. Cryer, 'Unilateral Enforcement of Resolution 687: A Threat Too Far?' (1998–99) 29 *Cal.W.Int'l L.J.* 243, 261.

44 The phrase 'all necessary means' was devised by the US in a compromise with the Soviet Union. In response to concerns by the Soviet Union that the word 'force' should not be used, the US proposed five different euphemistic formulations before finally adopting the watered down version found in Resolution 678 (1990). D. Hoffman, 'Six Weeks of Intense Consultations Led to UN Resolution' *Washington Post* (2 December 1990), A1; B. Woodward, *The Commanders* (New York: Simon & Schuster, 1991), 334.

45 See B.H. Weston, 'Security Council Resolution 678 and Persian Gulf Decision Making: Precarious Legitimacy' (1991) 85 *AJIL* 516, 523–34. See also D.D. Caron, 'The Legitimacy of the Collective Authority of the Security Council' (1993) 87 *AJIL* 552, 563; S. Chesterman, *Just War or Just Peace? Humanitarian Intervention and International Law* (Oxford: Oxford University Press, 2001), 181; G. Simpson, *Great Powers and Outlaw States: Unequal Sovereigns in the International Legal Order* (Cambridge: Cambridge University Press, 2004), 57; T. Friedman, 'Mideast Tensions: How US Won Support to Use Mideast Forces. The Iraq Resolution: A US-Soviet Collaboration – A Special Report' *New York Times* (2 December 1990), A1.

46 Indeed, Reisman has correctly argued that all that the US was doing was engaging in a form of *realpolitik* by trading in 'the coin of exchange of the moment'. W.M. Reisman, 'Some Lessons from Iraq: International Law and Democratic Politics' (1991) 16 *Yale J.Int'l L.* 203, 206.

Whilst many stated this expressly,[47] those who did not do so also did not disagree or take issue with those that did.[48] Subsequently, on the night of 16 January 1991, a US-led international coalition of member states, acting under the authority granted to it in this resolution, launched an air offensive against Iraq, codenamed *Operation Desert Storm*,[49] and later, on 23 February 1991, a ground operation.[50]

The gravity of the occasion when Resolution 678 (1990) was adopted was reflected in the fact that the members of the UNSC met at the level of Foreign Minister and took to describing the occasion as an 'historic meeting',[51] an 'historic landmark'[52] and as 'a watershed in the history of the United Nations'.[53] US Secretary of State Baker, speaking as president of the UNSC, went as far as to say that 'the debate that we are about to begin will, I think, rank as one of the most important in the history of the United Nations'.[54] Furthermore, it was clear that many of those in the primary interpretive community on this occasion believed that the debate and the resolution would have precedential value.[55] Some

---

47 UNSC Verbatim Record (29 November 1990) UN Doc. S/PV. 2963, Yemen (32) and Cuba (58). China noted that 'in the draft resolution about to be voted on, the wording "use all necessary means" is used, which, in essence, permits the use of military action'. Ibid., China (62). See also Canada (71), Malaysia (76), UK (82) and US (103).

48 Kuwait, for example stated that 'the international community, represented by the Security Council, should now feel free, at this stage, to use all necessary means'. Ibid., Kuwait (17). See also Columbia (42) and Zaire (48). France noted that '[i]ts text constitutes one last invitation to implement our resolutions, coupled with a warning which itself opens the way to the use of direct means of action'. Ibid., France (67). See also USSR (91) and Romania (99–100). It appears that the authorization technique was only directly challenged by Iraq which, although referring to the cases 'in which the use of force may legally be *authorized* by the Security Council', went on to elaborate that this meant 'collective action under the command and control of the Security Council, in coordination with the Military Staff Committee' and that 'no individual Member state may by authorized to lynch a particular country for any reason'. Ibid., Iraq (21) (emphasis added). Blokker has termed this a 'case related' critique, seeing as Iraq was the state towards which the authorization was targeted. See Blokker, supra n. 33, 567. However, as discussed below, striking the correct balance between the unilateral and multilateral elements of the technique was something that was subsequently an issue amongst the primary interpretive community.

49 *Keesing's* (1991) 37936–39. On 12 January 1991, not long before the beginning of *Operation Desert Storm* and some time after the UNSC had authorized the operation, both houses of the US Congress authorized the use of force against Iraq. See *Keesing's* (1991) 37934; M.N. Leich, 'Contemporary Practice of the United States' (1991) 85 *AJIL* 340, 340–41.

50 See US letter to the UNSC of 5 March 1991, UN Doc. S/22341.

51 UN Doc. S/PV. 2963, supra n. 47, Yemen (31) and Romania (97).

52 Ibid., Kuwait (18).

53 Ibid., US (101).

54 Ibid., US (speaking as President of the UNSC) (6).

55 'It will surely do much to determine the future of the body'. Ibid., US (speaking as President of the UNSC) (6); the 'decision today will indeed lay down historic guidelines

scholars writing with hindsight within the secondary interpretive community made this point. For example, Christine Gray has noted that '*Operation Desert Storm* against Iraq may be seen as a revolutionary development, made possible by unprecedented agreement among states, and which proved to be the catalyst for fundamental change in the international regulation of the use of force'.[56]

Whilst the persuasiveness of the newly emerged 'sole' superpower assured the votes of some members of the primary interpretive community as described above,[57] the fact that the energy of the US appeared to be channelled through the multilateral context and towards a serious violator of international law no doubt assured the support of others.[58] At this point in time the confluence of these factors influenced the forming of a precedent and to this new paradigm of collective security becoming embedded within the practice of the UNSC.

The Subsequent Embedding of the Authorization Technique in the Practice of the Security Council

The example in Resolution 678 (1990) of the UNSC 'authorizing' states to use 'all necessary means' was subsequently consistently employed in the practice of the organ.[59] The difference is that whereas its use in the Gulf crisis of 1990–91 was in connection with an inter-state crisis of the kind envisaged in the UN Charter, its use since has been almost exclusively within the domain of intra-state

that will perhaps have an impact on the future of mankind'. Ibid., Kuwait (18); 'Today the Security Council has before it a draft resolution in effect authorizing states to use force in order to ensure compliance with those resolutions. In the annals of the United Nations this will long be remembered as the "war resolution"'. Ibid., Yemen (32). See also Yemen (37), Malaysia (76) and Cuba (59–60).

56 Gray, supra n. 19, 357.

57 As Weston articulates, 'the process by which Security Council Resolution 678 was won, while perhaps legally correct *stricto sensu*, confirms how complete the power of the United States over the UN policing mechanism had become in the absence of Cold War opposition'. Weston, supra n. 45, 525. Falk goes as far as to argue that this 'created the impression that the Security Council lacked autonomy and was appropriated by the United States to give a global community "cover" to what was in essence a traditional exercise of great power diplomacy'. See R. Falk, 'The United Nations and the Rule of Law' (1994) 4 *Transnat'l L.& Contemp.Probs.* 611, 617. This instance can be contrasted with the persuasiveness of the US 12 years later when the use of force was again being debated against the same state. See Chapter 4.

58 This incident led to the setting of what has been described in this work as the 'Iraq context'. See Chapter 4.

59 See F. Berman, 'The Authorization Model: Resolution 678 and its Effects' in D. Malone (ed.), supra n. 2, 153, 161. The fact that the technique has been used instead of the conclusion of Article 43 agreements perhaps suggests that the latter's absence during the Cold War was not simply down to divisions between member states during this time. See Blokker, supra n. 33, 567.

crises.[60] Furthermore, the technique has been employed to authorize states other than the US and even some organizations to use force. For example, whilst the US was authorized to use all necessary means 'to establish as soon as possible a secure environment for humanitarian relief operations' in Somalia,[61] authorizations with similar objectives have also been provided to France and Senegal in regards to operations in Rwanda,[62] Italy in regards to operations in Albania,[63] and Australia in regards to operations in East Timor.[64]

As the high-water mark of this new activism[65] and in what has come to be viewed by many within the secondary interpretive community as the UNSC employing the authorization technique to restore democracy,[66] the US was provided authorization to use all necessary means 'to facilitate the departure from Haiti of the military leadership, … the prompt return of the legitimately elected President and the restoration of the legitimate authorities of the Government of Haiti'.[67] Perhaps as an indication of the legitimacy with which the authorization technique had come to be viewed by its maker, 'this was the first time that the United States sought the imprimatur of the United Nations to use force within its own hemisphere'.[68]

The technique has also been employed to authorize organizations to use force.[69] For example, NATO has been authorized to use 'all necessary measures' to enforce a no-fly zone over Bosnian airspace[70] and ECOWAS has been authorized to 'take the necessary steps' to guarantee the security of their forces and the civilians at risk in the Ivory coast.[71]

---

60 As Gray has commented, '[i]t is in internal conflicts rather than inter-state conflicts that the experience of Iraq seems to have had a more significant impact'. See Gray, supra n. 19, 328.

61 UNSC Res. 794 (3 December 1992) UN Doc. S/RES/794, para. 10.

62 UNSC Res. 929 (22 June 1994) UN Doc. S/RES/929, paras 2 and 3.

63 UNSC Res. 1101 (28 March 1997) UN Doc. S/RES/1101, para. 4. See, generally, D. Kritsiotis, 'Security Council Resolution 1101 (1997) and the Multinational Protection Force or Operation Alba in Albania' (1999) 12 *LJIL* 511.

64 UNSC Res. 1264 (15 September 1999) UN Doc. S/RES/1264, para. 3.

65 M.E. O'Connell, 'Regulating the Use of Force in the 21st Century: The Continuing Importance of State Autonomy' (1997) *Colum.J.Transnat'l L.* 473, 474.

66 The action was 'unprecedented in authorizing force to remove one regime and install another (however democratically elected) within a Member state'. D. Malone, *Decision Making in the UN Security Council: The Case of Haiti, 1990–1997* (Oxford: Clarendon Press, 1998), 110. See also Gray, supra n. 19, 328–29; Chesterman, supra n. 45, 152.

67 UNSC Res. 940 (31 July 1994) UN Doc. S/RES/940, para. 4.

68 Chesterman, supra n. 45, 152.

69 However, this function was already provided for in the UN Charter. See Article 53 of the Charter.

70 UNSC Res. 816 (31 March 1993) UN Doc. S/RES/816, para. 4.

71 UNSC Res. 1464 (4 February 2003) UN Doc. S/RES/1464, para. 9.

On the face of it, what appears to be a clear shift in the context of application of the technique from that of Resolution 678 (1990) is in violation of the prohibition of intervention in the domestic affairs of states.[72] However, this prohibition is not applicable to actions taken under Chapter VII and the UNSC has generally stated that, despite the domestic contexts of the above examples, it was intervening in situations which constituted a threat to *international* peace and security in some way. Consequently, it has thereby confirmed that this prohibition still stands.[73] Although it is arguable that the international aspect of the threat has been invoked disingenuously by the UNSC so as to conceal a contextual refocus, this has, nonetheless, remained strictly speaking within the textual bounds of the UN Charter and its main purpose.[74]

From the above practice, it becomes apparent that the authorization technique has become generally accepted and employed beyond the inter-state context of Resolution 678 (1990) and the sole domain of the US. Indeed, whilst there were perhaps rumblings of discontent regarding the technique in general when it was first introduced by the US in 1990, no negative intersubjective agreement was discernible at the time amongst those within the primary interpretive community or has emerged since. On the contrary, positive intersubjective agreement has instead emerged that there were limited options for the UNSC itself to use force and the authorization technique was thus a necessary incremental shift regarding the competence of the organ.[75] This was reflected in the UNSG's *Supplement to an*

---

72 Article 2(7) of the UN Charter states that '[n]othing contained in the present Charter shall authorize the United Nations to intervene in matters which are essentially within the domestic jurisdiction of any state or shall require the Members to submit such matters to settlement under the present Charter; but this principle shall not prejudice the application of enforcement measures under Chapter VII'.

73 The ICTY stated in 1995 that 'there is a common understanding, manifested by the "subsequent practice" of the membership of the United Nations at large, that the "threat to the peace" of Article 39 may include, as one of its species, internal armed conflicts'. *Prosecutor v Tadic* (Appeals Chamber) IT-94-1-A (15 July 1995), para. 30.

74 Because of the Chapter VII context in which they occurred, and the inapplicability of the domestic jurisdiction clause in Article 2(7) in connection with measures undertaken in such a context, 'each of the instances in which the Council has used, or authorized coalitions of the willing to use collective measures in situations of civil war or against regimes engaged in egregious human rights violations can be fitted into the Charter text'. See T.M. Franck, *Recourse to Force: State Action Against Threats and Armed Attacks* (Cambridge: Cambridge University Press, 2002), 137.

75 For example, in the debate over Somalia, whilst Belgium voted in favour of Resolution 794 (1992) it made clear it 'would have preferred this to be a purely United Nations operation'. UNSC Verbatim Record (3 December 1992) UN Doc. S/PV. 3145, Belgium (24). However, Zimbabwe noted that 'in this new era – the post-cold-war era – it is not unreasonable to expect individual states or a group of states to provide the necessary resources, both human and material, to help resolve such a crisis as part of the international effort'. Ibid., Zimbabwe (7).

Agenda for Peace in 1995 where he noted that, although not without its faults, the authorization technique 'provides the Organization with an enforcement capacity it would not otherwise have and is greatly preferable to the unilateral use of force by Member states without reference to the United Nations'.[76]

However, the emergence of agreement with the technique generally paralleled the ironing out of some specific issues connected with it. Indeed, the technique, in response to the concerns of some of those within the primary interpretive community as to its unilateral elements and shared by some within the secondary interpretive community, has been refined and modified from that in Resolution 678 (1990) so as to keep the balance in favour of multilateralism.

Addressing the balance between unilateralism and multilateralism Whilst those within the interpretive communities on the whole found the technique generally acceptable, there was definite concern regarding UNSC involvement and control with several members of the primary interpretive community taking issue with the extent to which draft Resolution 678 (1990) had unilateralized the authority of the UNSC.[77] For example, although Malaysia stressed that 'this resolution does not provide a blank cheque for excessive and indiscriminate use of force',[78] Yemen claimed that the resolution was 'broad and vague' and unlimited. Consequently, 'the Security Council will have no control over those forces … the command of those forces will have nothing to do with the United Nations' which would constitute 'authority without accountability'.[79] Furthermore, Cuba claimed that this was 'equivalent to giving the United States and its allies *carte blanche* to use their enormous sophisticated military capability'.[80]

There was also some notable concern expressed from within the secondary interpretive community which criticized Resolution 678 (1990) as an *ultra vires* act by the UNSC.[81] For example, Burns Weston argued that the UNSC 'eschewed

76 Report of the Secretary-General, 'Supplement to an Agenda for Peace' (1995) UN Doc. A/50/60, para. 80. Furthermore, White notes that '[i]f the Council simply authorizes a state to use force to advance an objective within the ambit of the UN's security role, despite the fact that it is being performed by one state, it is still a collective authorization to use force, in that it is being performed to carry out the collective will of the Council on behalf of the UN'. See N.D. White, 'The Legality of Bombing in the Name of Humanity' (2000) 5 *JCSL* 27, 30. See also R. Higgins, *Problems and Process: International Law and How We Use It* (Oxford: Clarendon Press, 1994), 266.

77 Gray concurs that 'there was considerable controversy over lack of UN control over the operation conducted by the Coalition forces'. Gray, supra n. 19, 265.

78 UN Doc. S/PV. 2963, supra n. 47, Malaysia (76).

79 Ibid., Yemen (33).

80 Ibid., Cuba (58).

81 White is critical of earlier authorizations due to their vagueness and lack of UN control. See White, supra n. 4, 115–28; N.D. White, *The Law of International Organizations* (Manchester: Manchester University Press, 1996), 191–99. See also D. Sarooshi, *The United Nations and the Development of Collective Security: The Delegation by the Security*

direct UN responsibility and accountability for the military force that ultimately was deployed, favouring, instead, a delegated, essentially unilateralist determination and orchestration of world policy, coordinated and controlled almost exclusively by the United States'.[82] Consequently, the need for balancing the unilateral and multilateral elements of the technique in subsequent authorizations became a focal point in both the primary and secondary interpretive communities with the issue being refined into several categories:[83] control by the UNSC over the operation,[84] the involvement of the UNSG, the clarity and breadth of the mandates, the time limits, and the reporting requirements. The UNSC subsequently made attempts to respond to these concerns.

Although the US was in command of the military operation in Somalia and the mandate contained no time limit, the authorization for the use of force was, for the first time, subject to significant UNSC oversight.[85] For example, the authorizing resolution contained a provision requiring the participating states to report to the organ[86] and provided authority to this organ to decide when the member states' mission would end and control handed over to the UN.[87] Furthermore, the mission was to be undertaken in coordination with the UNSG.[88] In the meeting at the adoption of Resolution 794 (1992), Zimbabwe stressed that it:

> attaches a lot of importance to the idea that in any international enforcement action the United Nations must define the mandate, the United Nations must monitor and supervise its implementation, and the United Nations must determine when the mandate has been fulfilled. My delegation is happy that the draft resolution before us meets these very important requirements. This sets an important precedent for future operations under equally unique circumstances.[89]

Council of its Chapter VII Powers (Oxford: Clarendon Press, 1999), 179–80; D. Wembou, 'Reflexions sur la validité et la portee de la Resolution 678 du Conseil de Securité' (1993) 5 *AJICL* 34.

82 See Weston, supra n. 45, 517.

83 See, generally, G. Wilson, 'The Legal, Military and Political Consequences of the "Coalition of the Willing" Approach to UN Military Enforcement Action' (2007) 12 *JCSL* 295. See also Blokker, supra n. 33, 560–67.

84 Blokker has observed that if a close look is taken at the reports of the meetings of the Security Council during which post-Cold War authorization resolutions were adopted, 'it is striking how often these resolutions are criticized, precisely for the reason that the Council does not control the operation it authorizes'. Ibid., 555.

85 As Blokker notes, '[t]he actual involvement of the UN in the implementation of this operation was the *leitmotiv* of the meeting of the Security Council during which Resolution 794 was adopted'. Ibid., 557.

86 UNSC Res. 794, supra n. 61, para. 18.

87 Ibid. See also para. 19.

88 Ibid., para. 10.

89 UNSC Verbatim Record (3 December 1992) UN Doc. S/PV. 3145, Zimbabwe (7–8).

Other members in the meeting also commended the limited mandate,[90] the oversight and involvement of the UNSG,[91] the overall control by the UNSC,[92] and the reporting requirements,[93] whilst others commented directly on the improvement in the authorization technique since Resolution 678 (1990) due to the imposition of these controls.[94] The additional controls all proved to be important points when the resolution came to be adopted as less-developed members did not want the operation to be in the entire control of the US.[95] As Mark Hutchinson has noted: 'Recognizing less-developed country concerns surrounding a large American military action without political accountability to the world community, the Security Council agreed to trade authorization for the operation for provisions which gave the UN unprecedented oversight of the operation'.[96] Indeed, given the added legitimacy, the resolution was adopted unanimously, evidencing the positive intersubjective agreement which had emerged regarding the authorization technique in this context with the added controls.[97]

Outside of the context of operations led by the US, members of the primary interpretive community were similarly clearly aware of the need for greater UNSC control. In Resolution 929 (1994), for example, which provided authorization to France and Senegal to intervene in Rwanda, several members made reference to the clear mandate[98] and time limits.[99] Furthermore, an additional element of

---

90 For example, Ecuador noted that 'the operation that we are going to adopt will have a defined and limited objective'. Ibid., 13.

91 Ibid., Ecuador (13), China (16–17), France (29–30), Belgium (24) and Austria (32).

92 Ibid., Ecuador (14), China (17), France (29–30) and Belgium (24).

93 Ibid., France (29–30) and Japan (43).

94 Hungary noted that it was 'pleased that this new type of action has been planned and formulated in such a way as to establish an organic link with our world Organization. It also demonstrates how far the United Nations has come since adopting resolution 678 (1990) on the Gulf crisis. The distance we have covered eloquently demonstrates the more effective and dynamic role the United Nations can play in the creation of a new international environment'. Ibid., Hungary (48). See also Austria (32).

95 See J.M. Goshko, 'UN Orders US-Force Into Somalia' *Washington Post* (4 December 1992), A1.

96 M.R. Hutchinson, 'Restoring Hope: UN Security Council Resolution For Somalia and an Expanded Doctrine of Humanitarian Intervention' (1993) 34 *Harv.Int'l L.J.* 624, 637.

97 Although some states, for example India, Belgium and China, were more reluctant than others. See J. Quigley, 'The "Privatization" of Security Council Enforcement Action: A Threat to Multilateralsim' (1996) 17 *Mich.J.Int'l L.* 249, 267–68. See also H. Freudenschuβ, 'Between Unilateral and Collective Authorisations of the Use of Force by the UN Security Council' (1994) 5 *EJIL* 492, 514–15.

98 UNSC Verbatim Record (22 June 1994) UN Doc. S/PV. 3392, USSR (2) and Spain (8).

99 Ibid., USSR (2) and Oman (11).

importance to those within the primary interpretive community, and drawing upon elements of peacekeeping operations, was that this operation should be conducted in an impartial and neutral manner.[100]

More recently, there have been signs of a lessening concern regarding the maintaining of the multilateral element in resolutions authorizing the use of force. For example, in the debate preceding the adoption of Resolution 1511 (2003), which authorized a US-led multilateral force to provide 'security and stability' in Iraq,[101] very little was made of the specific controls. Instead, the focus was on the fact that the UNSC had overall control, especially the need for the reporting requirements,[102] and the temporary nature of the Coalition's authorization.[103]

Today, with the practice that has emerged in the UNSC and the general acceptance of the refined technique by both interpretive communities we have witnessed a modification to the practice and competence of the UNSC in regards to collective security. This is confirmed by the fact that the creases in the technique in its original form were ironed out over the years and thorough successive changes in the non-permanent membership of the organ. As Christine Gray points out:

> There now seems to be general agreement that the original scheme of Chapter VII of the UN Charter, even after the end of the Cold War, is not workable, and that it should not be for the UN itself to conduct enforcement operations. Instead there is consensus that it is for the Security Council to authorize member States to take enforcement action.[104]

Whilst this section has established that the authorization technique that was instigated by the US is today through its acceptance by the interpretive communities very much a settled part of the competence of the UNSC, given that it does not strictly fit within the original Charter scheme as outlined above, the question remains as to where the legal basis for this technique is to be found. That is, does it lie within the UN Charter and, if so, where, or is the legal basis to be found externally? The next section addresses this issue in more detail. Having discussed this change in practice of the UNSC and where its legal basis is to be found, it then becomes necessary to address the related issue of which of the sources of the *jus ad bellum* the new practice has had an impact upon.

---

100 Ibid., Spain (8), Oman (11), Czech Republic (9), Argentina (10) and USSR (2).

101 UNSC Res. 1511 (16 October 2003) UN Doc. S/RES/1551, para. 13.

102 UNSC Verbatim Record (16 October 2003) UN Doc. S/PV. 4844th meeting, USSR (3).

103 Ibid., UK (5), Pakistan (7) and US (10).

104 Gray, supra n. 19, 328.

The Legal Basis for the Authorization Technique

The constitutional legal basis of the authorization technique to this day has never been clearly expressed, with each of the various resolutions only ever making a general reference to acting under Chapter VII of the UN Charter. However, this has not been something that the primary interpretive community has been overly concerned with. Although there was some controversy over the legal basis for the authorization technique as it appeared in the draft of what became Resolution 678 (1990), with Yemen basing its criticism on the fact that 'the draft resolution … is not related to a specific article of Chapter VII of the Charter'[105] and Iraq claiming that 'the Council apparently thought that in this case the legal requirements were disposable niceties',[106] on other occasions this has not been an issue which has been raised in the meetings of those within the community with authority for interpreting the competence and resolutions of the UNSC.

Given the general acceptance of the technique by those within this community it is, as Gray suggests, perhaps of little 'practical significance' upon which basis the UNSC acts.[107] Indeed, the 'authorizing' of states to use 'all necessary means' has been subsequently adopted into the practice of the UNSC to such an extent that '[e]arly questions about the procedural legality of this adaptation of the Council's role now appear moot in light of state practice over the past decade'.[108] However, it is an area that has produced much debate amongst those within the secondary interpretive community, particularly scholars, where a number of possible bases have been proffered. Furthermore, and more importantly, identifying the legal basis may determine the breadth of permissible action available to states. As Christopher Greenwood correctly stated in connection with *Operation Desert Storm*, '[t]he question is by no means academic, since the answer has important implications for another difficult issue, namely the extent of authorization to use force and whether the resolution permitted the coalition to go beyond the objective of liberating Kuwait'.[109] As Chapter 4 will demonstrate, this issue become relevant as the US was to argue 12 years after the adoption of Resolution 678 (1990) that the authorization contained within that resolution could be 'revived' so as to provide legal authority for the use of force against Iraq for purposes other than that of liberating Kuwait.[110] Consequently, a brief discussion of this issue will be given here.

---

105 UN Doc. S/PV. 2963, supra n. 47, Yemen (33).

106 Ibid., Iraq (21).

107 Gray, supra n. 19, 259.

108 Chesterman, supra n. 45, 164; Kohen also notes that '[t]he practice of Security Council authorizations to member states to use force is today too well established to be contested'. See Kohen, supra n. 1, 215.

109 Greenwood, supra n. 35, 167.

110 Gray concedes that the question had 'great practical significance' in connection with the argument that the authorization in this resolution could be revived. See Gray, supra n. 19, 265 (n. 44).

Article 42

It is perhaps assumed that when the use of force is authorized it is done so under Article 42, this being the only article in Chapter VII, and indeed the whole of the UN Charter, which expressly permits an organ of the UN to use force.[111] However, it has been argued by some within the secondary interpretive community that the special agreements to provide forces under Article 43 are a condition precedent to the taking of collective military action by the UNSC under Article 42.[112] Indeed, Article 106 suggests this.[113] Although this argument has some merit, Oscar Schachter has observed that 'no explicit language in Article 42 or in Articles 43, 44, and 45 ... precludes states from voluntarily making armed forces available to carry out the resolutions of the Council adopted under Chapter VII'.[114] Furthermore, the subsequent practice in the implementation of these provisions demonstrates that forces and facilities have been provided by member states voluntarily as opposed to under legal compulsion.[115] However, in any case, Article 42 has never been expressly mentioned in any of the resolutions of the UNSC that have authorized the use of force.[116]

Collective Self-Defence 'Blessed' by the Security Council

In contrast to the absence of any mention of Article 42 in the authorizing resolutions, in the context of Iraq and *Operation Desert Storm* the right of self-defence was expressly affirmed in Resolution 661 (1990), which was 'subsequently recalled and reaffirmed' in Resolution 678 (1990).[117] As a result, an alternative possible

---

111 O. Schachter, 'United Nations Law in the Gulf Conflict' (1991) 85 *AJIL* 452, 461.

112 Goodrich and Simons, supra n. 4, 398–405; Kelsen, supra n. 4, 756; K.P. Saksena, supra n. 4, 93; Weston, supra n. 45, 519. The UNSG, in his 'Agenda for Peace', stated that action under Article 42 would 'require bringing into being, through negotiations, the special arrangements foreseen in Article 43 of the Charter'. Report of the Secretary-General, 'An Agenda for Peace' (1992) UN Doc. A/47/277, para. 43.

113 This provision states that '[p]ending the coming into force of such special agreements referred to in Article 43 as in the opinion of the Security Council enable it to begin the exercise of its responsibilities under Article 42...'.

114 Schachter, supra n. 111, 464. White notes that 'it would be incorrect to say that there is an inextricable link between Articles 42 and 43'. See White supra n. 4, 117. See also Greenwood, supra n. 35, 167.

115 As in Korea, the Congo and Southern Rhodesia. See supra *In Practice: The Paradox of the Cold War*.

116 Although specificity of articles upon which the UNSC is acting is not something that this particular organ is prone to.

117 UNSC Res. 661, supra n. 40, preamble; UNSC Res. 678, supra n. 41, preamble. This was the first time that the UNSC recognized and reaffirmed the right of self-defence. For a particularly interesting recognition of this right by the UNSC see the discussion on Resolution 1368 (2001) following the 11 September 2001 attacks in Chapter 6 of this work.

legal basis advanced by some within the secondary interpretive community for the authorization technique is that it is simply an action of collective self-defence under Article 51, but which has been provided with the 'blessing' of the UNSC.[118]

In the immediate aftermath of the annexation of Kuwait by Iraq in 1990, the US and its allies might have used collective self-defence under Article 51 of the Charter as the sole justification for the use of force to eject Iraq as the request had come from the legitimate government of the sovereign state of Kuwait which had declared itself the victim of an 'armed attack' by another state.[119] Indeed, after months of Iraqi occupation of Kuwait and the imposition of sanctions,[120] on 8 November 1990 the US began to deploy a large force of troops to the region[121] and was adamant that 'legally, [its] position and the position shared by others is that Article 51 provides a sufficient basis under international law for further action'.[122] Nevertheless, it also made clear that a mandate from the UNSC exhibiting support for the use of force to eject Iraq from Kuwait would 'provide a firmer political basis'.[123] Indeed, it could be argued that it is 'politically useful' to have action approved by the UNSC, regardless of the existence of the right of self-defence.[124]

However, in the debates within the UNSC chamber preceding the adoption of Resolution 678 (1990) a number of primary interpretive community members

---

118 A leading proponent of this view is Yoram Dinstein. See supra n. 11, 273–77.

119 Greenwood, supra n. 35, 161. These requirements for the invocation of the right of collective self-defence were noted in the *Nicaragua* case. See *Case Concerning Military and Paramilitary Activities in and Against Nicaragua (Nicaragua v United States of America)* (Merits) [1986] ICJ Rep. 14, para. 199.

120 See UNSC Res. 661, supra n. 40.

121 T. Gordon, 'Mideast Tensions: Bush Sends New Units to Gulf to Provide "Offensive Option": US Force Could Reach 380,000' *New York Times* (9 November 1990), A1.

122 T. Friedman, 'Allies Tell Baker Use of Force Needs UN Backing' *New York Times* (8 November 1990), A1.

123 Ibid. See also G.H.W. Bush and B. Scowcroft, *A World Transformed* (New York: Knopf, 1998), 491.

124 N. Rostow, 'The International Use of Force After the Cold War' (1991) 32 *Harv. Int'l L.J.* 412, 417. Oscar Schachter comments that Resolution 678 'served the political purpose of underlining the general support of the United Nations for the military measures if Iraq did not withdraw before January 16, 1991. In addition, the resolution, supported by all of the cooperating states committed to collective action, clarified the objectives of the collective defence action'. See Schachter, supra n. 111, 460. Eugene Rostow goes as far as to say that '[t]he UN defence of Kuwait was in fact an example of collective security in action – the exercise of the right of collective self-defence' and that '[t]he Gulf crisis showed that, when the Permanent Members agree, Article 51 rights can be exercized in the context of Security Council approval'. See E. Rostow, 'Until What? Enforcement Action or Collective Self-Defense' (1991) 85 *AJIL* 506, 509. Christopher Greenwood talks of the 'obvious advantages' in securing authorization, for example in holding the coalition together, helping to meet domestic criticism of a military campaign, and the fact that the right of self-defence would be limited to doing only what was necessary to defend Kuwait. See Greenwood, supra n. 35, 165.

expressly ruled out UNSC blessed collective self-defence of Kuwait. For example, Malaysia made clear that the organ had 'not agreed to any attempt unilaterally to apply Article 51 of the Charter once the Security Council is seized of the matter'.[125] Furthermore, Romania implicitly rejected this legal basis when it arrived 'at the logical conclusion that the Security Council should use all the means at its disposal, including those provided for in Chapter VII of the Charter with respect to threats to the peace, breaches of the peace and acts of aggression'.[126] Additionally, the lead state in the ejection of Iraq from Kuwait, the US, has not since depicted its actions on this occasion as self-defence.[127]

In any case, regardless of the debate that has arisen since within the secondary interpretive community around this possible basis for expelling Iraq from Kuwait, and there have been many arguments proposed both in favour[128] and against it being so,[129] it is ultimately limited to inter-state crises, which have not been the context of subsequent authorizations by the UNSC in the post-Cold War era.[130] Consequently, this legal basis is not applicable in the context of the authorization technique *per se*.

The Implied Powers Doctrine

Under the implied powers doctrine it is proposed that the UNSC may authorize the use of force under the implied powers it possesses based upon its primary responsibility for maintaining international peace and security under Chapter VII of the UN Charter.[131] Simply because Article 42 happens to expressly mention the

---

125 UN Doc. S/PV. 2963, supra n. 47, Malaysia (76). The fact that the UNSC 'remains seized of the matter' is generally mentioned in the last paragraph of each of its resolutions. See Chapter 4.

126 Ibid., Romania (99–100).

127 In particular, when setting out the revival argument in 2002–03, it did not claim that the operation to remove Iraq from Kuwait was one of self-defence. See Chapter 4.

128 Arguments in support of this basis include: the language of *cooperating with Kuwait* indicated collective self-defence; that there was no UN command or control of the operation; that it was President Bush who announced the initial ceasefire on 28 February 1991, not the UN; that unlike the operation in Korea in 1950, it did not take place under the flag of the UN; that the UNSG stated that it was not a UN war.

129 Arguments against this basis include: the fact that authorization for actions taken in self-defence is unnecessary; that this was a delayed response and the right of self-defence is reserved for situations in which force must be used quickly; that UNSC Res. 678 (1990) requested states to participate – not just giving its blessing to collective self-defence but rather attempting to organize the forces.

130 Gray, supra n. 19, 328. See supra *The Subsequent Embedding of the Authorization Technique in the Practice of the Security Council.*

131 On the powers it possesses under this responsibility see supra *In Theory: The Charter of the United Nations.*

use of forcible measures, this does not preclude the UNSC from authorizing the use of force under the general powers which it possesses.

This doctrine has received some support from those within the secondary interpretive community, in the form of both doctrinal analysis by scholars[132] and in the jurisprudence of the ICJ. In the *Certain Expenses* advisory opinion, the ICJ, in rejecting the idea that authorization for the use of armed force must be based on Article 42, stated that it could not assume such 'a limited ... view of the powers of the Security Council'.[133] Although the Court did not point to any other article in the Charter upon which the authorization for the use of force could be based, it was adamant that '[i]t cannot be said that the Charter has left the Security Council impotent in the face of an emergency situation when agreements under Article 43 have not been concluded'.[134] Furthermore, the Court, in the *Reparations* advisory opinion, stated that the Charter should be given an 'effective' interpretation so that 'the Organization must be deemed to have those powers which, though not expressly provided in the Charter, are conferred upon it by necessary implication as being essential to the performance of its duties'.[135]

It is not completely beyond the realms of possibility that the collective security system of the UN Charter may function in the future as originally intended, but at least for the present time this is an unrealistic prospect given the great symbolic step that would be required for the agreements under Article 43 to be concluded.[136] Nevertheless, the actions taken under the authorization technique are still generally viewed as examples of the contemporary paradigm of collective security, no matter how imperfect.[137] Given that the resolutions only specified that they were based

132 As Blokker poses: 'Is the Council, failing such agreement, barred from employing another, less far-reaching technique? Clearly not, as this would mean that not only the instrument, but also the power to take military action would become a dead letter and the UN collective security system would be without its *ultimum remedium*'. See Blokker, supra n. 33, 549. See also Greenwood, supra n. 35, 168; Kirgis, supra n. 22, 521; Freudenschuß, supra n. 97, 526.

133 *Certain Expenses of the United Nations* (Advisory Opinion) [1962] ICJ Rep. 151, para. 167.

134 Ibid. It is possible that this wider power emanates from the ability of the UNSC to make 'recommendations' under Article 39 of the Charter. Although this is arguable, if this had been the intention of the UNSC when adopting authorizing resolutions it is submitted that it would have alluded to this as the basis of its authority and actually used the word itself as it did in Korea, the major previous precedent of collective inter-state use of force. See UNSC Res. 83, supra n. 28.

135 *Reparations for Injuries Suffered in the Service of the United Nations* (Advisory Opinion) [1949] ICJ Rep. 174, para. 182.

136 See supra The United Nations Collective Security System and the Use of Force: 1945–1989.

137 As White points out, 'there are degrees of collective security ... simply because a system does not match an ideal it does not mean that it is not a collective security system'. See White, supra n. 76, 28.

upon Chapter VII generally, the implied powers basis is that which requires the least assumptions to be made. This is not to say that this basis is a good, or even adequate, substitute for the original workings of the Charter, but given the brief analysis above it is perhaps safest to conclude, as Schachter does, that the UNSC acts in these circumstances 'on a liberal construction of its authority derived from its general powers to maintain and restore international peace and security'.[138]

The Impact of the Authorization Technique upon the Sources of the *Jus ad Bellum*

The authorization technique has been instigated at the hands of the US and subsequently embedded as part of the competence of the UNSC. Given that the provisions of the Charter do not expressly provide for the technique, a process of interpretation of the competence of this organ has occurred. This section addresses which of the sources of the *jus ad bellum* have been affected in this process.[139]

A Settled Interpretation of the UN Charter Based Competence of the Security Council

It was noted above that due to the UNSC only ever referencing Chapter VII in its resolutions authorizing the use of force, without assuming more, the technique finds its legal basis in the implied powers possessed by the UNSC in connection with its responsibility for the maintenance of international peace and security. However, the UNSC is only expressly permitted to discharge this responsibility within the 'specific powers' granted to it, none of which specifically grant it the right to *authorize* individual states to use military force, only regional organizations.[140] As Niels Blokker claims, '[i]t is clear that the power to adopt authorization resolutions is not explicitly attributed to the Council by the Charter'.[141]

Nevertheless, in interpreting the Charter, as with all treaties, an integral part of this process is to give sufficient weight to 'any subsequent practice in the application of the treaty which establishes the agreement of the parties regarding its interpretation'.[142] As Anthony Aust rightly points out:

138 Schachter, supra n. 111, 461.

139 For more on the sources of the *jus ad bellum* see Chapter 1.

140 Article 24(2) explicitly states that '[t]he specific powers granted to the Security Council for the discharge of these duties are laid down in Chapters VI, VII, VIII, and XII'. Regional organizations can use force if 'authorized' by the UNSC. See Chapter VIII of the UN Charter.

141 Blokker, supra n. 33, 547.

142 VCLT (1969), Article 31(3)(b). See Chapter 2.

> This is the most important element in the interpretation of any treaty … However precise a text appears to be, the way in which it is actually applied by the parties is usually a good indication of what they understood it to mean, provided the practice is consistent and is common to, or accepted, expressly or tacitly, by both or all parties.[143]

Nigel White is also of this view. He points out that whilst 'it is arguably legally unacceptable to imply a power which goes against the express provisions of the Charter which clearly envisage collective security in the form of the centralization of armed force, there are now, within the UN's terms, several precedents for recommendatory military action, and it is arguable that the Security Council has by its practice established a power to authorize states to take "necessary measures" with regard to a particular conflict or situation'.[144]

The VCLT talks of 'any subsequent practice in the application of *the treaty*' as a whole, not its provisions individually. Therefore, whilst the practice cannot *stricto sensu* be reconciled with the individual provisions, it can be reconciled with the overarching powers and responsibility provided to the UNSC in the UN Charter.[145] However, whilst this subsequent practice has established the agreement of the primary interpretive community of the members of the UNSC as to the correct interpretation of Chapter VII, has it also led to a reinterpretation of the prohibition of force as found in Article 2(4)?

Some may argue against the type of change brought about by the authorization technique due to the *jus cogens* nature of Article 2(4) and the fact the agreement in regards to this change, which would affect this prohibition contained within the UN Charter, cannot be said to be shared by the international community of states as a 'whole' as it has only been witnessed amongst the members of the primary interpretive community of the UNSC. However, this overlooks the fact that the changes that have taken place have been to the *procedural* workings rather than the *substantive* powers of the UNSC contained in Chapter VII. It is still the UNSC that is using force, it is just that it has brought in contractors to do its work. As such, it is a procedural rather than substantive change with no additional exceptions to the prohibition and no substantive changes to the existing ones. Arguably, if the balance had not been struck between the unilateral and multilateral elements of the authorization technique then a widening of the exception to Article 2(4) of collective force under the auspices of the UNSC would arguably have taken place and therefore led to a modification to the prohibition contained within it. As demonstrated above, this balance has been struck.[146]

---

143 A. Aust, *Modern Treaty Law and Practice*, 2nd edn (Cambridge: Cambridge University Press, 2007), 241.

144 White, supra n. 4, 128.

145 That is, primary responsibility for the maintenance of international peace and security. See UN Charter (1945), Article 24(1).

146 See supra *Addressing the balance between unilateralism and multilateralism*.

Whilst it might be tempting to attribute this reinterpretation of the Charter solely to the post-Cold War era, the uses of force during the Cold War, whilst occurring rather sporadically, employing different terminology, and always viewed as somewhat exceptional, highlight that almost from the UN's inception the collective security powers of the UNSC have never been interpreted as envisaged in the provisions of the Charter. This chapter has highlighted not only that the authorization technique has proven to be consistent, but also that it has come to be accepted by those within the primary interpretive community since the end of the Cold War. Consequently, what we have witnessed in the post-Cold War era is rather a settling and embedding of an interpretation tentatively conceived of during the Cold War.[147] Clearly intersubjective agreement emerged that it is necessary to operate outside of the strict confines of the textual Chapter VII provisions. In characterizing this institutional procedural change of the UN, the subsequent and consistent practice of the UNSC, and the agreement between its changing member state composition in the post-Cold War era, is akin to an 'informal modification' of the procedural terms of Chapter VII.[148]

A Modification of Customary International Law Regarding the Security Council's Competence

Although the UN Charter is a treaty and treaties are only binding upon those states which are a party to them,[149] it is possible for a treaty provision to become part of the corpus of general international law if it is of a 'fundamentally norm creating character'.[150] Whilst provisions such as Articles 2(4) and 51 undoubtedly

147 Sarooshi states that 'although the first few instances of Korea and Southern Rhodesia were seen at the time as being exceptional sui generis cases, they only now, however, appear as part of a continuum in this practice'. See Sarooshi, supra n. 81, 167. Gray also notes that these 'early actions set the pattern for more recent action'. See Gray, supra n. 19, 255.

148 T. Gazzini, *The Changing Rules on the Use of Force in International Law* (Manchester: Manchester University Press, 2005), 63. Although a formal modification of the UN Charter is unlikely, the fact that Articles 43 to 50 have fallen into desuetude due to the consistent practice of the authorization technique is recognized to some extent by the High-Level Panel Report recommending the deletion of Article 47, the provision concerning the Military Staff Committee. See Report of the High-Level Panel on Threats, Challenges and Change, 'A More Secure World: Our Shared Responsibility' (2004) UN Doc. A/59/565, para. 300. It may be questioned why the panel stopped there and did not also recommend the deletion of the provisions concerning the Article 43 agreements. However, although authorization by the UNSC is also mentioned in Articles 47(4) and 53(1) in different contexts, it may be too far to suggest inserting provisions formalizing the authorization technique as set out in this chapter.

149 This is the principle of *pacta sunt servanda*. See VCLT (1969), Article 26.

150 *North Sea Continental Shelf Cases (Federal Republic of Germany v Denmark: Federal Republic of Germany v The Netherlands)* [1969] ICJ Rep. 3, para. 71. This is assuming that the other conditions of customary international law formation are fulfilled. See Chapter 2 (n. 34).

reach this threshold and have been held by the ICJ as being of such a character,[151] the provisions of Chapter VII under consideration here cannot be said to be of the same nature. Indeed, these provisions are about the institutional procedural workings of an international organization rather than generally applicable fundamental legal norms.

Nevertheless, virtually all states are party to the Charter and 'the competence of the Security Council to authorize Member states to resort to force has been accepted by virtually the whole membership'.[152] Furthermore, even if the provisions are concerned with UNSC procedure, this procedure constitutes one of the two exceptions to the general prohibition on the use of force that is to be found both within the UN Charter and customary international law. Consequently, it does not follow that simply due to a non-member state not having the *locus standi* to request an authorization to use 'all necessary means'[153] the same state would deny that this is one of the established exceptions to the prohibition of the use of force in either its treaty or customary forms. Whilst none of the primary interpretive communities have expressly addressed this issue, taken together, these factors indicate that the informal modifications to the Charter can be correctly viewed as also having had an impact upon the condition of customary international law. Indeed, in this instance '[t]he emergence of the norm and the simultaneous modification of the Charter can be considered as two dimensions of the same process'.[154]

Although changes to customary international law can be slow, this process of modification can be seen to have occurred relatively quickly. This is arguably due to the institutional, procedural nature of the change. The problems associated with substantiating the agreement as to the legality of a particular practice somewhat dissipate where voting, discursive practices, including the making of assertions and reactions, and the generation of *opinio necessitatis*[155] *or opinio juris* can be

151 See Chapter 2 (n. 33).

152 Gazzini, supra n. 148, 50. As mentioned above, the composition of the UNSC regularly changes and no real objections to the authorization technique *per se* have been seriously pursued.

153 This is probably not without some degree of doubt. For example, the UNSC apparently sees no problem in addressing its resolutions to 'all *states*' rather than 'all members' and directing them towards non-member states and non-state entities. See, for example, UNSC Res. 314 (1972) which also referred to Article 2(6) of the UN Charter. This provision reads: 'The Organization shall ensure that states which are not Members of the United Nations act in accordance with these Principles so far as may be necessary for the maintenance of international peace and security'.

154 Gazzini, supra n. 148, 56. As noted in the above section, the exception to the prohibition has not been substantively widened and therefore the prohibition has remained unchanged.

155 See Chapter 2 (n. 70) for more on this element of customary international law formation.

agreed upon and witnessed by all.[156] Indeed, on this occasion there appears to have been very little dissent to the idea of authorization, more about the incidences in which it should be employed and the controls to be attached. Over the course of the period, '[e]ven adopting the strictest standard, the practice of Member states ... and the United Nations has been sufficiently uniform and general to generate such a norm, even taking into account the magnitude of the change it has introduced in the collective security system'.[157]

The Embedding of a New Common Understanding in Security Council Resolutions

Whilst the regulation of the use of force in terms of the competence of the UNSC to use force has been modified in both its treaty and customary form through the emergence of the authorization technique, it should not be forgotten that the third source of interest in this work, that is, UNSC resolutions, has also witnessed a change. This is in the form of the introduction of a new common understanding between interpretive community members or, in the words of the VCLT, the insertion of a phrase that has been given a 'special meaning'.[158]

Furthermore, subsequent practice set out above confirms that the formula devised by the US provided the template for enforcement actions[159] as '[t]he same (or similar) euphemistic formula has been used in almost all the subsequent resolutions authorizing the use of force by states'.[160] Today, it is regularly employed without comment which confirms the acceptance of the formula in the primary interpretive community of the UNSC and the embedding of a new common understanding.

Conclusion

Although there were precedents for the 'authorization technique' during the Cold War, these consisted of three isolated sporadic measures over a 45-year period and never developed into a settled practice. The US-drafted UNSC Resolution 678 (1990) and the US-led *Operation Desert Storm* 'marked the start of a new era for the UN'[161] so that today, not only has authorization to use 'all necessary means' by

---

156 As Higgins noted, '[w]ith the development of international organizations, the votes and views of states have come to have legal significance as evidence of customary international law'. See Higgins, supra n. 13, 2.

157 Gazzini, supra n. 148, 59.

158 VCLT (1969), Article 31(4).

159 Chesterman, supra n. 45, 164. Christine Gray notes that Resolution 678 (1990) can be seen as 'a model for later authorization of the use of force by member states'. See Gray, supra n. 19, 265.

160 Gray, Ibid., 265.

161 Ibid.

the UNSC become an 'important political aid in justifying the use of force',[162] but also the technique has become so entrenched into the discourse and practice of the primary interpretive community of the UNSC that it is mentioned by those within the secondary interpretive community as one of the exceptions to the prohibition of the use of force without any tribute being paid to the way in which the UNSC has adapted in the post-Cold War era, under the influence of the US, to incorporate this practice.[163] Indeed, it has found a basis within the *jus ad bellum* and has made an impact on all three sources of international law. Consequently, the power of the US, harnessed in the multilateral context and underscored by general positive intersubjective agreement amongst the primary interpretive community concerned with the interpretation of the competence of the UNSC and its resolutions, has made a discernible, necessary, and lasting impact upon the UNSC's ability to use force. This was subsequently refined and employed in different contexts, and involving different states.

However, the granting of authorization is subject to the agreement of the members of the primary interpretive community of the UNSC and, despite the *de facto* power of the US, this cannot always be relied upon. When contemporary authorization has not been provided, or when the US has required more freedom for its actions, it has instead resorted to attempting to coat its actions with the less settled and unsecured legitimacy attached to justifications of a different kind. The following chapters in this Part of the book address these justifications and doctrines and whether, by reference to the primary and secondary interpretive communities, their invocation by the US has had any discernible impact upon the *jus ad bellum*.

---

162 Chesterman, supra n. 45, 162.

163 See, for example, M. Byers, *War Law: International Law and Armed Conflict* (London: Atlantic Books, 2005), 7.

Chapter 4
The Unilateral Determination of Authority to Use Force Under the Auspices of the Security Council (I): The Revival of Authority

a material breach … revives the authority to use force.[1]

Introduction

After the Gulf War military campaign, which had been authorized by Resolution 678 (1990), had come to end in 1991, the UNSC adopted a resolution that contained a ceasefire and imposed obligations upon Iraq to ensure its disarmament.[2] The US subsequently claimed that the express authorization contained in Resolution 678 (1990) which had been used to eject Iraq from Kuwait lay dormant but could be revived to enforce these disarmament obligations upon their breach by Iraq.[3] The claim to revive authority to use force in this way had not been previously made by the US or any other state in the UN era.[4]

The purpose of this chapter is firstly to assess whether these novel interpretive arguments had any validity under the *jus ad bellum* and thus permitted the use of force

---

1 US letter to the UNSC upon the commencement of *Operation Iraqi Freedom*, UN Doc. S/2003/351 (20 March 2003).

2 UNSC Res. 687 (3 April 1991) UN Doc. S/RES/687.

3 Gray, amongst others, has, in previous editions of her book, grouped the revival doctrine under the heading of 'implied' authorization. This was remedied to some extent in the latest edition where the material is grouped under the heading of 'implied (or revived)' authorization. See C. Gray, *International Law and the Use of Force*, 3rd edn (Oxford: Oxford University Press, 2008). As this chapter will demonstrate, there was nothing implicit in the US's arguments. Chapter 5 of this book addresses more accurately the doctrine of implied authorization in the form of the unilateral enforcement of the collective will.

4 The reasons for the US attempts to revive authority can be explained by the coating of legitimacy a justification in international law can provide a state's action. As Krisch notes, 'the reliance on United Nations authority seems motivated by the desire to enhance the appearance of legitimacy'. N. Krisch, 'Unilateral Enforcement of the Collective Will: Kosovo, Iraq, and the Security Council' (1999) 3 *Max Planck Yrbk UN L.* 59, 73.

against Iraq under these circumstances.[5] Under the methodology adopted in this work focus will be placed upon the search for intersubjective agreement between members of the primary interpretive community of the UNSC.[6] In carrying out this analysis, the events and reaction surrounding the revival argument made in the context of Iraq at the macro level will first be addressed before a more detailed assessment of the argument in this context is made at the micro level. Although to date this interpretive doctrine has only been advanced in the specific context of Iraq, this chapter addresses whether it has had an impact upon the *jus ad bellum* more generally. Lastly, some conclusions will be offered on the doctrine's future prospects.

Iraq, the Security Council, and the Use of Force by the United States: 1991–2003

As noted in Chapter 3, 'authorization' to use 'all necessary means' was provided in Resolution 678 (1990) under which states duly forced Iraq out of Kuwait.[7] Following the cessation of military hostilities declared by President George H.W. Bush on 28 February 1991,[8] the UNSC subsequently adopted Resolution 687 on 3 April 1991 which established the conditions for 'a formal ceasefire'[9] including Iraq's disarmament and a UN inspection regime to implement this.[10] However, from the outset Iraq continuously failed to offer full and unconditional cooperation with the inspection regime.[11] In response to Iraq's intransigence the UNSC adopted 12 resolutions[12] and numerous presidential statements[13] between 1991 and 2003. Whilst these were condemnatory of Iraq's behaviour, with some claiming that

---

5 In this respect, this chapter is essentially about the interpretation of UNSC resolutions. As Gazzini claims, the revival doctrine 'is nothing more than a question of interpretation of the relevant resolutions'. T. Gazzini, *The Changing Rules on the Use of Force in International Law* (Manchester: Manchester University Press, 2005), 94.

6 See Chapter 2.

7 See Chapter 3.

8 UN Doc. S/22341 (5 March 1991).

9 UNSC Res. 687, supra n. 2, para. 33.

10 Ibid., paras. 7–14. See also UNSC Res. 707 (15 August 1991) UN Doc. S/RES/707, para. 3; UNSC Res. 715 (11 October 1991) UN Doc. S/RES/715.

11 Gray, supra n. 3, 350.

12 UNSC Resolutions 707 (1991), 715 (1991), 949 (1994), 1060 (1996), 1115 (1997), 1134 (1997), 1137 (1997), 1154 (1998), 1194 (1998), 1205 (1998), 1284 (1999), 1441 (2002).

13 See, for example, UN Doc. S/23609 (19 February 1992); UN Doc. S/23663 (28 February 1992); UN Doc. S/24240 (6 July 1992); UN Doc. S/25081 (8 January 1993); UN Doc. S/25091 (11 January 1993); UN Doc. S/PRST/1996/11 (19 March 1996); UN Doc. S/PRST/1996/28 (14 June 1996); UN Doc. S/PRST/1996/36 (23 August 1996); UN Doc. S/PRST/1996/49 (30 December 1996); UN Doc. S/PRST/1997/49 (29 October 1997); UN Doc. S/PRST/1997/51 (13 November 1997); UN Doc. S/PRST/1997/54 (3 December 1997); UN Doc. S/PRST/1997/56 (22 December 1997); UN Doc. S/1998/PRST/1 (14 January 1998).

Iraq was in 'material breach' of its obligations[14] and others threatening 'serious consequences',[15] none expressly authorized the use of 'all necessary means' to enforce compliance. Nevertheless, the US used, and threatened to use,[16] force against Iraq as a response to its intransigence and based its actions upon previous resolutions of the UNSC.

During a period of intense military action against Iraq[17] and just six days after the UNSC had condemned Iraq's intransigence and determined it to be in 'material breach',[18] on 17 January 1993 the US, acting alone, launched several Tomahawk cruise missiles at a nuclear facility on the outskirts of Baghdad.[19] This was justified as being 'designed to help achieve the goals of United Nations Security Council Resolutions 687, 707, and 715'.[20] Given the subsequent continued intransigence of Iraq this action had patently failed in fulfilling its objective. Indeed, in early 1998 tensions began to rise again which led to the US making threats to use force against Iraq to 'reduce Saddam's capacity to reconstitute his weapons of mass destruction and diminish his ability to threaten Iraq's neighbours and the world'.[21] However, whilst the actual use of force was staved off for a while, US strikes eventually materialized. Immediately after a report by UNSCOM Chief Richard Butler had been given on 15 December 1998,[22] the US, along with the UK, after requesting

14 UNSC Res. 707 (15 August 1991) S/RES/707, preamble and para. 1; UNSC Res. 1441 (8 November 2002) S/RES/1441, para. 1 and para. 4; UN Doc. S/25081 (8 January 1993); UN Doc. S/25091 (11 January 1993). See, generally, infra *Security Council Resolution 1441 (2002): The Concept of 'Material Breach'.*

15 UNSC Res. 1154 (2 March 1998) S/RES/1154, para. 3; UNSC Res. 1441, Ibid., para. 13; UN Doc. S/PRST/1997/49 (29 October 1997); UN Doc. S/PRST/1997/51 (13 November 1997).

16 Whilst it is clear that the use of 'all necessary means' requires the authorization of the UNSC, it is often overlooked that the *threat* to use force carries the same requirement. Threats to use force were made by the US towards Iraq on many occasions in the period 1990–2003. White and Cryer call this 'the stick' offered to Iraq to comply. N.D. White and R. Cryer, 'Unilateral Enforcement of Resolution 687: A Threat Too Far?' (1998–99) 29 *Cal.W.Int'l L.J.* 243, 243. However, this will not be addressed in detail here. It suffices to say that if the use of force would be unlawful then so is the threat to use it. See Chapter 2 (n. 18).

17 Much of which was justified as enforcing the established no-fly zones and in self-defence of the aircraft involved.

18 UN Doc. S/25091 (11 January 1993).

19 *Keesing's* (1993) 39291–92. See also M.R. Gordon, 'Bush Launches Missile Attack on a Baghdad Industrial Park as Washington Greets Clinton' *New York Times* (18 January 1993), A1.

20 'US Press Release: Attack Shows U.S. Fully Backs U.N. Mandate' (17 January 1993), reprinted in M. Weller (ed.), *Iraq and Kuwait: The Hostilities and Their Aftermath* (Cambridge: Grotius, 1993), 746.

21 *Keesing's* (1998) 42096.

22 In this report he informed the UNSC that, although there had been cooperation on many issues, Iraq had failed to resume *full* co-operation with UNSCOM and outlined

UNSCOM personnel to leave Iraq, launched *Operation Desert Fox* which consisted of a series of air strikes against Iraqi military capabilities.[23] The strikes continued until 20 December 1998 when 97 Iraqi sites had been attacked.[24] In justifying its actions the US claimed that the ceasefire contained in Resolution 687 (1991) was conditional upon Iraq's compliance with its disarmament obligations and thus the Iraqi violations meant that the authority to use all necessary means in Resolution 678 (1990) had been effectively revived.[25]

In 2002, tensions over Iraq's disarmament obligations began to rise for what became the last time. Indeed, the issue of Iraq's weapons came very much back on the US's foreign policy agenda beginning with President George W. Bush's State of the Union address on 29 January 2002 in which he identified an 'axis of evil' consisting of Iran, Iraq and North Korea.[26] The rhetoric continued and intensified over the course of the following 12 months. During this time, Congress approved a resolution authorizing the President to enforce existing UNSC resolutions regarding Iraq and to defend the national security interests of the US against the threat posed by Iraq.[27] However, the Congressional approval for the use of force made it clear that attempts to work through the UN and other reasonable diplomatic channels had to be exhausted first.[28] Consequently, the US became a major drafter and sponsor of UNSC Resolution 1441, which was adopted on 8 November 2002.[29] The resolution declared Iraq to be in 'material breach' of its disarmament obligations[30] and gave it one 'final opportunity' to comply.[31] If it failed to take the final opportunity offered it warned of 'serious consequences'.[32] In testing Iraq's resolve to comply with the final opportunity presented, the resolution not only

---

a series of obstructions that had been encountered by the inspectors. He concluded that UNSCOM had not been able to conduct the substantive disarmament work mandated to it by the UNSC. See *Keesing's* (1998) 42697; For the UNSCOM and IAEA reports, see UN Doc. S/1998/1172 (15 December 1998).

23 *Keesings's* (1998) 42697–99; M. Evans, 'US and Britain Strike at Iraq' *The Times* (17 December 1998), 19.

24 *Keesing's*, Ibid. The operation involved more cruise missiles than had been used in *Operation Desert Storm* in 1991. See Gray, supra n. 3, 351.

25 US letter to the UNSC, UN Doc. S/1998/1181 (16 December 1998); UNSC Verbatim Record (16 December 1998) UN Doc. S/PV 3955, 9.

26 President George W. Bush, 'State of the Union Address' (29 January 2002). Available at http://archives.cnn.com/2002/ALLPOLITICS/01/29/bush.speech.txt/ [Accessed: 27 June 2009]; *Keesing's* (2002) 44545–46 and 44591–93.

27 *Keesing's*, Ibid., 44972 and 45028–29; 'Authorization for the Use of Military Force Against Iraq' (10 October 2002) Pub. L. No. 107–243.

28 Ibid.

29 UNSC Res. 1441, supra n. 14.

30 Ibid., para. 1.

31 Ibid., para. 2.

32 Ibid., para. 13.

required Iraq to submit a declaration of its weapons programmes but also set up an enhanced weapons inspection regime.[33]

Whilst Hans Blix, Executive Chairman of UNMOVIC,[34] and Mohamed al-Baradei, Director-General of the IAEA, reported to the UNSC on several occasions in the months after the adoption of Resolution 1441 (2002),[35] and mentioned certain irregularities in the process, neither reported to have uncovered a 'smoking gun'[36] or, significantly, declared Iraq to be in further 'material breach' of its obligations.[37] Neither was there a formal determination of a 'material breach' by the UNSC itself. Nevertheless, after unilaterally determining Iraq to have breached its obligations, the US launched *Operation Iraqi Freedom* on 20 March 2003.[38] This was an air and ground offensive against Iraq, with the support of the military forces of the UK and Australia,[39] and led to the overthrow of the Saddam Hussein regime. In justifying its actions, the US again claimed that on the basis of the material breaches committed by Iraq the authority contained in Resolution 678 (1990) had been revived and thus permitted the actions taken.[40]

The Shifting Boundaries of Intersubjective Agreement and the Use of Force Against Iraq

It has been said that Iraq's aggressive invasion of Kuwait on 2 August 1990 'shaped, forever after, the way the world looked at Saddam Hussein's Iraq'.[41] Indeed, the negative image of Iraq, no doubt confirmed by its previous hostilities with Iran,[42] the incident at Halabja,[43] the suppression of Kurdish and Shia groups

---

33 Ibid., para. 3.

34 UNMOVIC was established on 17 September 1999 to undertake the responsibilities of the former UNSCOM. See UNSC Res. 1284 (17 December 1999) UN Doc. S/RES/1284.

35 See, for example, the reports made on 14 February 2003 (UNSC Verbatim Record (14 February 2003) UN Doc. S/PV. 4708), 28 February 2003 (UN Doc. S/2003/232 (28 February 2003)), and 7 March 2003 (UNSC Verbatim Record (7 March 2003) UN Doc. S/PV 4714).

36 A term used by Hans Blix in UNSC Verbatim Record (27 January 2003) UN Doc. S/PV. 4692. See H. Blix, 'An Update on Inspection' (27 January 2003), 1. Available at http://www.un.org/Depts/unmovic/Bx27.htm [Accessed: 13 December 2009]; See also S.D. Murphy, 'Contemporary Practice of the United States' (2003) 97 *AJIL* 419, 419–21.

37 The significance attached to the term by members of the primary interpretive community is addressed infra at *Security Council Resolution 1441 (2002): The Concept of 'Material Breach'*.

38 *Keesing's* (2003) 45315.

39 Ibid.

40 UN Doc. S/2003/351, supra n. 1.

41 W.H. Taft and T.F. Buchwald, 'Preemption, Iraq, and International Law' (2003) 97 *AJIL* 557, 558.

42 See, generally, E. Karsh, *The Iran-Iraq War 1980–1989* (Oxford: Osprey, 2002).

43 See, generally, J.R. Hiltermann, *A Poisonous Affair: America, Iraq, and the Gassing of Halabja* (Cambridge: Cambridge University Press, 2002).

in Iraq,[44] plus the difficulties in establishing the arrangements under Resolution 687 (1991) as noted above,[45] 'had made it different from other states in terms of the level of threat … that was tolerable'.[46] What could be called the 'Iraq context' was thus established so that in the initial subsequent years there appeared to be intersubjective agreement not only amongst the primary interpretive community of the UNSC but also more widely amongst states within the international community thus permitting limited forcible measures against Iraq both in punishment for its intransigence and in containing the threat posed.

On 13–21 January 1993 a sequence of attacks by the US, some of which were in conjunction with its coalition partners, took place.[47] Whilst, as noted in the above section, only the strike on 17 January 1993 was justified solely to enforce the disarmament obligations, the other uses of force which took place were justified as enforcement of the no-fly zones which had been established and were also often set in the general context of Iraq as a violator of UNSC resolutions. Consequently, the disarmament obligations were mentioned too in these justifications.[48]

This rather muddled justification by the US, along with the fact that the justifications of the other states of the acting coalition often differed to an extent,[49] and the fact that the targets that were struck in enforcing the no-fly zones, that is, missile sites, could quite easily be perceived as actions taken to enforce the disarmament obligations, led to some confusion as to their exact purpose. This confusion was exemplified in a statement made by the UNSG on 14 January 1993, commenting on a raid that had taken place the previous day:

> the forces that carried out the raid have received a mandate from the Security Council, according to resolution 678, and the cause of the raid was the violation by Iraq of resolution 687 concerning the ceasefire. So, as Secretary-General of the United Nations, I can say that this action was taken and conforms to the resolutions of the Security Council and conforms to the Charter of the United Nations.[50]

This is an apparent endorsement of past action taken to enforce the disarmament obligations based upon the revival argument before any action to enforce these

44 For more on this see Chapter 5.

45 See supra Iraq, The Security Council, and the Use of Force by the United States: 1991–2003.

46 D. McGoldrick, *From '9-11 to the 'Iraq War 2003': International Law in an Age of Complexity* (Oxford: Hart, 2004), 52.

47 For more on this see Chapter 5.

48 See, for example, US Press Release: 'US will "deal forcefully" with Iraqi provocations' (17 January 1993), reprinted in Weller, supra n. 20.

49 See, for example, Statement by the UK Secretary of State for Defence (13 January 1993), reprinted in Weller, Ibid.

50 Reprinted in 'UK Materials in International Law' (1993) 65 *BYIL* 736.

obligations had actually been taken[51] and it is ironic that the UNSG made no further statement after the sole operation on 17 January 1993 justified for this purpose. However, this statement, taken in conjunction with the relatively muted response from the primary interpretive community to this period of forcible measures, reflected the general permissiveness regarding such action against Iraq at this time. Indeed, this has even led one commentator to claim that the UNSC in fact had provided an 'informal blessing' for the strikes.[52]

France and Russia, two of the coalition partners and members of the primary interpretive community, appeared to offer mild criticism of the strike undertaken by the US on 17 January 1993 as 'exceeding its UN mandate',[53] thus perhaps signifying cracks in the intersubjective agreement that had formed around this issue. However, in large part, the general perception, both during and since, was that the US appeared to operate, albeit perhaps occasionally on the borders, within the boundaries of the intersubjective agreement existing at the time in regards to the use of force against Iraq. This general view is confirmed by the other forcible actions taken against Iraq in 1993. For example, it was also visible in the context of the enforcement of the no-fly zones established to protect the Kurdish and Shia populations in the north and the south of Iraq[54] and in the reaction to the missile strikes following an alleged assassination plot against the former US President George H.W. Bush.[55]

However, by 1998 the cracks in the intersubjective agreement that were perhaps visible in 1993 had widened. When force was used in *Operation Desert Fox* it was condemned by many as a violation of international law.[56] This condemnation included that of Russia[57] which, given that this state was part of the initial post-

---

51 Indeed, it was 'inconsistent with the justifications proposed by the acting states' themselves. See S. Chesterman, *Just War or Just Peace: Humanitarian Intervention and International Law* (Oxford: Oxford University Press, 2001), 201. However, as Chesterman further notes, it is 'unclear what status should be accorded to such a pronouncement by the Secretary-General'. Chesterman, Ibid., at 201. Indeed, 'the Secretary-General's statements to the press cannot be decisive as to legality'. C. Gray, 'After the Ceasefire: Iraq, the Security Council and the Use of Force' (1994) 65 *BYIL* 135, 167. See Chapter 2 for more on the UNSG as a significant actor of the secondary interpretive community.

52 S.D. Murphy, 'Assessing the Legality of Invading Iraq' (2004) 92 *Geo.L.J.* 173, 232.

53 *Keesing's* (1993) 39292. See also statements made by the Russian Foreign Ministry and the Minister of State for Foreign Affairs of France, reprinted in Weller, supra n. 20, 749 and 751–52 respectively; 'France Says U.S. Raid Exceeded UN Resolutions' *San Diego Union-Tribune* (21 January 1993), A1; P. Lewis, 'US-led Raids on Iraq Strain Unity of Gulf War Coalition' *New York Times* (20 January 1993), A1.

54 See Chapter 5.

55 See Chapter 6.

56 UNSC Verbatim Record (16 December 1998) UN. Doc. S/PV. 3955, Iraq (2), Russia (4), China (5), Costa Rica (7), Sweden (10) and Brazil (11). Some support was expressed by Japan (11).

57 Russia condemned it as an 'unprovoked act of force' and that 'the United States and United Kingdom have grossly violated the Charter of the United Nations, the principles

Gulf War coalition which took measures against Iraq, was an indicator of how the US was now acting outside of the intersubjective agreement.[58] Furthermore, the 'material breach' terminology was noticeably no longer present in the resolutions condemning Iraq's intransigence.[59] Nevertheless, in justifying its use of force the US claimed that 'Iraq has repeatedly taken actions which constitute flagrant, material breaches ... On a number of occasions the Council has affirmed that similar Iraqi actions constituted such breaches, as well as a threat to international peace and security'.[60] Realizing it had overstepped the boundary of tolerated forcible action against Iraq,[61] the US attempted to invoke what it clearly saw as a precedent set by the UNSC determinations, actions taken, and reaction in 1993. However, this was an untenable argument as the boundaries of the intersubjective agreement regarding forcible actions against Iraq had clearly shifted since this time meaning that the US was now acting on the outside of it.

The position of the boundary of intersubjective agreement concerning this issue had shifted even further by 2002. The 'Iraq context' was now no longer about limited forcible measures against a pariah state, but the necessity of weapons inspections in it[62] so that when Resolution 1441 (2002) was adopted it had as its main concern the inspection process. General opposition within the primary interpretive community to any forcible measures taken at this time was palpable.[63] Nevertheless, in justifying its launching of *Operation Iraqi Freedom*, the US again used the 1993 strikes as a precedent for its actions. In its letter to the UNSC, after recalling the confused statement made by the UNSG in 1993 in support, the US declared that '[i]t has been long recognized and understood that a material breach of [the] obligations removes the basis of the ceasefire and revives the authority to use force under resolution 678 (1990) ... Iraq continues to be in material breach of its disarmament obligations'.[64] The invalidity of the 1993 incident as a precedent for the revival argument was demonstrated not only by the considerable rejection of the action taken in 1998 but also now by the general rejection of the legality

of international law and the generally recognized norms and rules of responsible behaviour on the part of states in the international arena'. Ibid., Russia (4).

58 Incidentally, the reaction to the no-fly zones at this time by these states also indicated this. See Chapter 5.

59 Wedgwood notes that 'Russia and France had strenuously resisted a finding of material breach in the 1998 crisis because of a perceived linkage to the use of force'. See R. Wedgwood. 'The Fall of Saddam Hussein: Security Council Mandates and Preemptive Self-Defence' (2003) 97 *AJIL* 576, 580.

60 UN. Doc. S/PV. 3955, supra n. 56, 9.

61 Taft and Buchwald, the US Legal Adviser and Assistant Legal Adviser to the State Department in 2003, concede that '[t]o be sure, that campaign did not lack critics'. See Taft and Buchwald, supra n. 41, 559–60.

62 See infra n. 154 and related text.

63 See infra *Security Council Resolution 1441 (2002): The Concept of 'Material Breach'*.

64 UN Doc. S/2003/351 (20 March 2003).

of the use of force on this occasion.[65] The general consensus appeared to be that, whilst the use of force was not ruled out in the future, the inspection process should have been given more time.[66]

The next section demonstrates that whilst there was definite ambiguity surrounding the language found in Resolution 1441 (2002), given that the primary interpretive community which had adopted that resolution had done so having previously witnessed the interpretations given by the US to the language employed within it in 1993 and 1998, legality of action stands or falls on how it is perceived by the community of actors charged with its interpretation at that time.[67] If there is intersubjective agreement within this community in rejection of a proffered interpretation, then an argument relying on textual ambiguity is not permissible.

Assessing the Revival Argument in the Iraq Context

It was argued in Chapter 3 that through the instigation of the US the UNSC had come to embed the technique of 'authorizing' states to use 'all necessary means' within its culture and practice indicating that the use of force had received the intersubjective support of those within the primary interpretive community associated with this organ.[68] This technique was then employed throughout the decade in various situations and circumstances and in the process became more refined.[69] Once understandings and meanings are embedded within the discourse and practice of the UNSC, these guide its future practice and constrain the interpretation of its resolutions. Consequently, it also applies to, and constrains the arguments of, the US in claiming that the use of force has been authorized on any particular occasion.

In this respect, none of the resolutions passed between 1991 and 2003 concerning Iraq contained the understood formula for the use of force. This was not for the want of trying on the part of the US. Indeed, the US attempted to have

65 See UNSC Verbatim Record (26–27 March 2003) UN Doc. S/PV. 4726, where over 70 states spoke. It was also rejected by many within the secondary interpretive community including the UNSG who claimed that it was 'illegal'. See E. MacAskill and J. Borger, 'Iraq War Was Illegal and Breached UN Charter, says Annan' *The Guardian* (16 September 2004), 1.

66 This was especially stressed in joint memoranda of France, Germany and Russia. See UN Doc. S/2003/214 (24 February 2003); UN Doc. S/2003/253 (3 March 2003). Wedgwood has observed that 'efforts to complete Iraq's disarmament held center stage in a decade of work'. See Wedgwood, supra n. 59, 579.

67 Indeed, '[a] truly international problem cannot be declared as such unilaterally; the states which make up that community must perceive the situation as warranting a response'. G.A. Symes, 'Force Without Law: Seeking a Legal Justification for the September 1996 U.S. Military Intervention in Iraq' (1997–98) 19 *Mich.J.Int'l L.* 581, 601.

68 See, generally, Chapter 3.

69 Ibid.

this formula included in resolutions so as to permit the use of force in 1991,[70] in 1998,[71] and later in 2002.[72] The efforts of the US in this respect, and its failures, provide evidence that both this state and other members of the primary interpretive community realized that this was now the recognized formula for the use of force in UNSC practice.[73] Although apparently contradicted by these earlier attempts at passing resolutions containing the understood formula, further evidence of this recognition was provided at each stage of the crisis examined above, when the US both threatened to use and then ultimately used force after resorting to the argument that Resolution 678 (1990), the sole resolution to contain this formula in the Iraq context, was the basis of the claimed authorization.

Seeing as the version of the revival argument provided at the time of *Operation Iraqi Freedom* in 2003 witnessed the greatest engagement with the legal specifics, this is where the focus for this section will lie.[74] The argument presented at this time can be broken down into the following connected sub-arguments:[75]

---

70 Ian Johnstone, who served as an associate legal officer at the United Nations in 1991, states that 'in a preliminary draft of Resolution 687, the authorization [to use force] was explicitly reaffirmed', but that such language did not make an appearance in the adopted resolution so as to secure support from states who wanted to 'nullify the authorization in Resolution 678 to use force'. See I. Johnstone, *Aftermath of the Gulf War: An Assessment of UN Action* (Boulder, CO: Lynne Rienner, 1994), 39.

71 'Throughout 1998, the United States and the United Kingdom attempted to obtain a resolution authorizing Member States to use force to ensure the observance of Security Council resolutions'. See Gazzini, supra n. 5, 66.

72 'An earlier draft of what became paragraph 4 of Resolution 1441 had stated that "such breach authorizes member states to use all necessary means to restore international peace and security to the area"'. See McGoldrick, supra n. 46, 62.

73 Indeed, '[t]he fact that the final version of [Resolution 1441] left out the words of the original US and UK draft authorizing member states "to use all necessary means to restore international peace and security in the area" is telling'. See N.D. White, 'The Will and Authority of the Security Council after Iraq' (2004) 17 *LJIL* 645, 658. See also McGoldrick, supra n. 46, 62; E. Papastavridis, 'Interpretation of Security Council Resolutions Under Chapter VII in the Aftermath of the Iraqi Crisis' (2007) 56 *ICLQ* 83, 115.

74 Whilst this has been addressed extensively in other works, this section intends to highlight the rejection of the revival argument through specific attention to the response of the primary interpretive community.

75 This argument was also provided by the Attorney-Generals of the UK and Australia. See 'Attorney General's Advice on the Iraq War: Resolution 1441' (2005) 54 *ICLQ* 767 and 'Memorandum of Advice on the Use of Force against Iraq' (2003) 24 *Aust YBIL* 415. The US Legal Adviser and Assistant Legal Adviser to the State Department also provided an account of the US legal position. See Taft and Buchwald, supra n. 41. Similarly, although in contrast to the legal position taken by these three states, the Director of the Legal Department of the Ministry of Foreign Affairs of the Russia Federation also made available his position for publication. See 'Legal Assessment of the Use of Force Against Iraq' (2003) 52 *ICLQ* 1059.

- the US-led coalition gained the authority to use 'all necessary means' against Iraq from the open-ended Resolution 678 (1990) in 1990;
- the ceasefire contained in Resolution 687 (1991) between Iraq and the US-led coalition suspended but did not terminate the authority to use force contained in Resolution 678 (1990);
- a material breach of the ceasefire conditions revives the authority to use force under Resolution 678 (1990);
- Resolution 1441 (2002) determined that Iraq had been and remained in 'material breach' and provided it with a 'final opportunity' to comply or face 'serious consequences';
- because Iraq failed to take the final opportunity presented to it and was in further material breach, the authorization to use force contained in Resolution 678 (1990) was revived; and
- all that was required by Resolution 1441 (2002) was reporting to and discussion by the UNSC of Iraq's failures, but not a further express authorization to use force.

Consequently, from the above elements of the argument it becomes clear that the controversy was not over the form or technique of the UNSC providing its blessing for the use of force in this way, but the extent, or subsequent relevance, of an occasion when this had already occurred. Indeed, the problems arise in determining whether the authorization contained in Resolution 678 of 1990 remained dormant but could be unilaterally revived by the US in 1993, 1998, and 2003. As Lobel and Ratner emphasize, '[t]his position assumed that Resolution 678's authorization to use force remained valid, albeit temporarily suspended – a loaded weapon in the hands of any member nation to use force *whenever it determined* Iraq to be in material breach of the cease-fire'.[76] It is the purpose of this section to critically assess the legal validity of this position of the US, beginning with the arguments connected with the claimed root of the authorization, Resolution 678 (1990).

Security Council Resolution 678 (1990): The Root Authorization

Given the US's revival argument as set out above, the first port of our enquiries is whether the sole resolution expressly to contain the understood formula regarding the use of force in the context of Iraq, Resolution 678 (1990), by its own terms and in the context of its adoption, remained active with the possibility of its revival throughout the period in question.[77]

---

76 J. Lobel and M. Ratner, 'Bypassing the Security Council: Ambiguous Authorizations to use Force, Ceasefires and the Iraqi Inspection Regime' (1999) 93 *AJIL* 124, 124–25 (emphasis added).

77 John Yoo is a leading proponent of the 'open ended' view and argues that it had not expired 12 years after its adoption when Resolution 1441 was adopted in 2002. See J. Yoo, 'International Law and the War in Iraq' (2003) 97 *AJIL* 563, 567. See also C. Greenwood,

An expiration date for the authorization? It has been argued that when an authorization is to be temporally limited by the UNSC a time limit is expressly provided in the authorizing resolution.[78] Resolution 678 (1990) contained no such time limit and, as the previous chapter noted, whilst a few states commented upon the lack of control over the authorization it was not a general issue with those within the primary interpretive community at this time.[79]

The examples given by John Yoo in support of the view that time limits are intended include the authorization resolutions in connection with Bosnia, Somalia, Rwanda and Haiti.[80] However, these were adopted in the years after Resolution 678 (1990) and, as such, cannot be used as precedents for the intentions of the primary interpretive community on this occasion. As Chapter 3 highlighted, Resolution 678 (1990) was to some extent a test case for the authorization technique and left the interpretive community to change and refine its practices and understandings over time, including incorporating certain control mechanisms into the authorizing resolutions of the UNSC.[81] Nevertheless, it has to be conceded that in the text of the resolution no express time limit was set for the authorization. Consequently, one must turn to the mandate contained in this resolution to ascertain whether this limited the time for which the authorization remained open.

The mandate contained in Security Council Resolution 678 (1990) In operative paragraph 2 of Resolution 678 (1990) the UNSC expressly authorized member states to use 'all necessary means' so as 'to uphold and implement Resolution 660 and all subsequent relevant resolutions and to restore international peace and security in the area'.[82] Therefore, there are two parts to the mandate: 'to uphold and implement Resolution 660 (1990) and all subsequent relevant resolutions' and 'to restore international peace and security in the area'.

In connection with the first part of this mandate, the sole demand made in, and object and purpose of, Resolution 660 (1990) was to ensure that 'Iraq withdr[e]w immediately and unconditionally all its forces to the position in which they were located on 1 August 1990'.[83] This was subsequently achieved by *Operation Desert Storm*. However, in determining the identity of the 'subsequent relevant resolutions' referred to and their object and purpose, and whether these included

'The Legality of Using Force Against Iraq' (24 October 2002), memorandum prepared for the House of Commons Select Committee on Foreign Affairs, para. 5.

78 Yoo, Ibid., 567.

79 See Chapter 3.

80 Yoo, supra n. 77, 567. See also Chapter 3 on the authorization of the use of force on these occasions.

81 For more on this see Chapter 3. Furthermore, the more restrictive resolutions in these examples were adopted after the initial indications of the unilateral forcible measures against Iraq by the US.

82 See Chapter 3.

83 UNSC Res. 660 (2 August 1990) UN Doc. S/RES/660, para. 2.

those up to and including Resolution 1441 in 2002, the preamble of Resolution 678 (1990) provides some insight.[84] Here the text clearly notes that 'despite all efforts by the United Nations, Iraq refuses to comply with its obligation to implement Resolution 660 (1990) and *the above-mentioned subsequent relevant resolutions*, in flagrant contempt of the Security Council' (emphasis added). The referred to resolutions were stated as those adopted between Resolution 660 of 2 August 1990 and Resolution 677 of 28 November 1990.

Whilst some scholars within the secondary interpretive community have argued that the difference in wording between operative paragraph 2 and that in the preamble[85] indicates that the resolutions referred to were not one and the same thus permitting the forcible implementation of resolutions beyond Resolution 677 (1990),[86] there is also no obvious reason to believe that the 'subsequent relevant resolutions' differed. In this context it would also be a *reductio ad absurdum* to conclude that the UNSC was giving *carte blanche* authorization to not only implement resolutions which had not even been conceived of at that point[87] but also 'in a crisis completely different from that in which the authorization was originally granted'.[88] As such, the object and purpose of these resolutions was not the disarmament of Iraq, which only became an issue after hostilities ceased, but instead the liberation of Kuwait and the restoration of its territorial integrity.[89]

More controversy lies in interpreting the breadth of the second part of the mandate contained in Resolution 678 (1990) of 'restor[ing] international

84 It is not unusual for the UNSC to recall in the preamble of its resolutions previous resolutions in connection with the same issue. This goes to establishing the context of the resolution. See M. Wood, 'The Interpretation of Security Council Resolutions' (1998) 2 *Max Planck Yrbk UN L.* 73, 87.

85 That is, the preamble restricts itself to the 'above mentioned' resolutions whilst paragraph 2 refers to 'all' resolutions.

86 See, for example, J.D. Fry, 'Remaining Vaild: Security Council Resolutions, Textualism, and the Invasion of Iraq' (2007) 15 *Tul.J.Int'l & Comp.L.* 609, 650–51.

87 Papastavridis notes that 'it is a *non sequitur* that this phrase could mean all the "subsequent Resolutions after 678", so as to embrace also the disarmament obligations laid down in 687 (1991)'. Papastavridis, supra n. 73, 113. 'One obvious problem which emerges is that even if the authority contained in Resolution 678 can be revived, the mandate granted therein, whatever the interpretation placed on it, cannot anticipate enforcement of a resolution that did not exist at the time of adoption of Resolution 678'. See M. Weller, 'The US, Iraq and the Use of Force in a Unipolar World' (1999–2000) 41 *Survival* 81, 90; 'In November 1990, when Resolution 678 authorized member states to use force to oust Iraq from Kuwait, few, if any, of the Council members could have contemplated that the resolution would authorize the bombing of Iraq to secure compliance with an inspection regime – a requirement imposed only after the war's end and the restoration of Kuwaiti sovereignty'. Lobel and Ratner, supra n. 76, 138.

88 Gazzini, supra n. 5, 67. See also Gray, supra n. 3, 361.

89 Murphy, supra n. 52, 181; White and Cryer, supra n. 16, 272; Krisch, supra n. 4, 69; Weller, supra n. 87, 92.

peace and security in the area'. Taken in the context of the situation, including the resolutions passed and the ostensible objective and purpose of the resolution, the mandate was arguably to restore the status quo ante to Resolution 660 of 2 August 1991, that is, the ejection of Iraq from Kuwait. On this interpretation, only if Iraq was to reinvade Kuwait (an option which since 1991 was most unlikely) would this provision have any purpose.[90]

This interpretation is perhaps confirmed by the primary interpretive community upon the adoption of Resolution 678 (1990) when none of its members referred to the resolution as applying to disarmament.[91] In fact, this would have been surprising given that this was not an issue at that point. Indeed, 'member states of the Council voting for Resolution 678 did not interpret the phrase "and to restore international peace and security to the area" as permitting any wider use of force than pushing Iraq out of Kuwait',[92] an aim which was attained by *Operation Desert Storm*, thus rendering any further action unnecessary.[93] Crucially, the US itself recognized the limits of the mandate granted in Resolution 678 (1990) at the time by acknowledging that it did not permit anything beyond the liberation of Kuwait.[94]

The difficulty lies in the fact that this specific purpose would have been covered by the first part of the mandate discussed above. Indeed, taken on the terms of Resolution 678 (1990) it is at least possible to interpret 'to restore international peace and security' more broadly so as to permit the use of force whenever peace and security are not pertaining and need to be restored. Furthermore, because

---

90 As Lobel and Ratner note, 'Resolution 678 clearly authorized force to oust Iraq from Kuwait, but the broad provision on restoring international peace and security ought to be read in the context of that purpose'. See Lobel and Ratner, supra n. 76, 129.

91 See the statements made by members of the UNSC at the adoption of Resolution 678 (1990) in UNSC Verbatim Record (29 November 1990) UN Doc. S/PV. 2963. For example, the UK stated that '[t]here is no ambiguity about what the Council requires in this resolution and in previous resolutions. We require that Iraq comply fully with the terms of resolution 660 (1990) and … withdraw all its forces unconditionally to the positions on which they stood on 1 August'. Ibid., UK (78).

92 White and Cryer, supra n. 16, 272. 'The Council meeting at which 678 was adopted showed that the Member States viewed this as giving the Coalition authority to push Iraq out of Kuwait and to restore peace between the two states, not to take any wider action'. See Papastavridis, supra n. 73, 112 (n. 126); 'The clear intent of the Security Council in 1990 was to provide authority to oust Iraq from Kuwait, not to grant a blanket license for any member state to attack Iraq to enforce inspections mandated after the war'. Lobel and Ratner, supra n. 76, 140.

93 'Necessity' is one of the fundamental principles governing the use of force. See, generally, J. Gardam, *Necessity, Proportionality and the Use of Force by States* (Cambridge: Cambridge University Press, 2004). For more on this requirement in connection with self-defence see Chapter 6.

94 James Baker, US Secretary of State at the time, confirmed in his memoirs that 'the U.N. resolutions did not authorize coalition forces to undertake anything beyond the liberation of Kuwait'. J.A. Baker, *The Politics of Diplomacy* (New York: Putnam, 1995), 436.

the simple ejection of Iraq from Kuwait would not necessarily restore peace and security in the area[95] some have read into this phrase a broader definition of peace and security, in particular the destruction of Iraq's weapons capability as set out in Resolution 687 (1991). It is to this resolution, and the part of the revival argument which it formed, that this chapter addresses next.

Security Council Resolution 687 (1991): The 'Formal Ceasefire'

Whilst the UNSC in Resolution 687 (1991) welcomed the 'restoration' of Kuwait's sovereignty,[96] it also adopted this resolution, which in large part initiated an inspection regime for Iraq's weapons,[97] 'bearing in mind its objective of restoring international peace and security as set out in recent resolutions'.[98] Indeed, this could be interpreted as a clear reference to the latter part of the mandate contained in Resolution 678 (1990) as noted in the above section. Whilst it did not provide express authorization itself to enforce its provisions,[99] there was great debate subsequently as to whether it terminated the authorization provided in Resolution 678 (1990) in the face of Iraqi intransigence with the inspection regime and its disarmament obligations more generally. On the terms of the resolution itself this is not entirely clear.

Textual ambiguity Whilst Resolution 687 (1991) has come to be known as 'the ceasefire resolution',[100] this is a mischaracterization. Resolution 687 (1991) actually contained a 'formal ceasefire'.[101] Indeed, whilst ceasefires in UN parlance are often considered as temporary,[102] the added formal emphasis appears, at least

95 It could be argued that in the context of the conflict this was achieved by the border monitoring unit, UNIKOM, and the creation of the demilitarized zone in paras 2–6 of Resolution 687 (1991). This is perhaps confirmed by the fact that the boundary issue was clearly of primary concern seeing as it appeared so early in the resolution and by the fact that paragraph 4 was the only provision in the whole resolution which mentions 'all necessary measures' to 'guarantee the inviolability of the … international boundary'. However, this is tempered somewhat by the fact that it appears to be mentioned outside of the common understanding in connection with the use of force as no entity as such appears to be authorized to take such measures.

96 UNSC Res. 687, supra n. 2, preamble.

97 See supra Iraq, the Security Council, and the Use of Force by the United States: 1991–2003.

98 UNSC Res. 687, supra n. 2, preamble.

99 Murphy argues that, on the contrary, the consequence of not complying with the provisions of Resolution 687 was of a peaceful nature in the form of the maintenance of the sanction placed upon Iraq in Resolution 661. See Murphy, supra n. 52, 194.

100 See, for example, McGoldrick, supra n. 46, 56.

101 As noted in UNSC Res. 687, supra n. 2, paras 1 and 33.

102 Under international law there are three main modes of halting armed conflicts. 'Peace treaties' permanently halt hostilities and introduce or restore amicable relations

to this author, to indicate something more permanent. However, the ordinary meaning of the phrase does provide a somewhat ambiguous interpretation.

The textual ambiguity of Resolution 687 (1991) is heightened by the fact that the first operative paragraph 'affirms' Resolutions 660 (1990) to 686 (1991), including 678 (1990).[103] Whilst this affirmation could be interpreted as conclusive evidence that the UNSC did not terminate this latter resolution and the authority contained within it, others argue that it was merely recognition of the path the UNSC had been on to get to the formal ceasefire.[104] Indeed, Resolution 660 (1990) was also reaffirmed and any claim that this was still active when it had clearly been fulfilled would be 'nonsensical'.[105]

However, this affirmation of the resolutions had a qualification attached; the resolutions were affirmed 'except as expressly changed below to achieve the goals of this resolution, including a formal ceasefire'.[106] Whilst it is true that at no place in Resolution 687 (1991) is Resolution 678 (1990) expressly changed, paragraph 33 does expressly mention it in regards to the formal ceasefire.[107] To be sure, the UNSC, in paragraph 33:

> *[d]eclare*[d] that, upon official notification by Iraq to the Secretary-General and the Security Council of its acceptance of the provisions above, a formal cease-fire [was] effective between Iraq and Kuwait and the Member States cooperating with Kuwait in accordance with resolution 678 (1990).

It would appear logical that, upon Iraq's acceptance, the formal ceasefire would implicitly change, if not expressly so, the authorization to use force. However, the intentions of the UNSC are not absolutely clear and, as Murphy has correctly pointed out, '[b]y its terms, Resolution 687 of April 1991 neither expressly suspended nor expressly terminated Resolution 678'.[108]

For those who have argued that the resolution merely suspended the authorization, the final phrase of operative paragraph 33 also perhaps raises another aspect of their argument, that is, that the ceasefire was between

---

between the parties. 'Armistices' were traditionally used to suspend hostilities but are now accepted in the current practice of states as denoting a permanent halt with the peace yet to be built. 'Ceasefires' are understood to denote a suspension of hostilities which may be resumed at a later date. See Y. Dinstein, *War, Aggression and Self-Defence* (Cambridge: Cambridge University Press, 2005), 36, 42–47, and 50; Hague Convention [No. IV] Respecting the Laws and Customs of War on Land (18 October 1907), annexed Regulations, Articles 36–41.

103 UNSC Res. 687, supra n. 2, para. 1.

104 Murphy, supra n. 52, 198.

105 Ibid.

106 UNSC Res. 687, supra n. 2, para. 1.

107 Ibid., para. 33.

108 Murphy, supra n. 52, 186.

Iraq and the US-led coalition.[109] This would mean that, under the traditional law of ceasefires, any violation of the ceasefire within would vitiate it thus opening the door to the recommencement of hostilities. However, the current author would argue that, as asserted in Chapter 3,[110] the correct legal basis for *Operation Desert Storm* was action taken under the auspices of the implied powers possessed by the UNSC[111] and, as such, the 'formal ceasefire' contained in Resolution 687 (1991) should be viewed as an agreement between the parties to the conflict, the UNSC and Iraq,[112] and not, as the revival argument goes, the US-led coalition and Iraq.

In context Placing this resolution in context is important.[113] It was adopted at the end of a conflict and remains to this day the most extensive resolution of the UNSC. At the meeting when it was adopted, the primary interpretive community appeared to provide an intersubjective interpretation of it. Ironically, given its negative vote at its adoption, Yemen was the sole member to claim that it was 'only a ceasefire' so that 'the state of war will continue ... until a definitive end is put to the military operations and hostilities'.[114] However, the other members who referred to it termed it a 'permanent ceasefire',[115] a 'proper ceasefire',[116] a 'definitive, formal ceasefire',[117] and a 'final settlement of the crisis'.[118]

---

109 See, for example, Dinstein, supra n. 102, 299; R. Wedgwood, 'The Enforcement of Security Council Resolution 687: The Threat of Force Against Iraq's Weapons of Mass Destruction' (1998) 92 *AJIL* 724, 726; Yoo, supra n. 77, 569.

110 See Chapter 3 for a discussion on the legal basis for the use of force against Iraq in 1991.

111 Even though the US and others could have acted unilaterally in collective self-defence to repel the Iraqi aggression without the authorization which they ultimately received. See Chapter 3.

112 As Krisch correctly notes, 'the cease-fire was not a classical one between states, but was embedded in the collective security system of the United Nations'. Krisch, supra n. 4, 71. See also Gray, supra n. 3, 141; Weller, supra n. 87, 91; J. Quigley, 'The United Nations Security Council: Promethean Protector or Helpless Hostage?' (2000) 35 *Tex. Int'l L.J.* 129, 141. The fact that only Iraq was required to comply with and accept the conditions in Resolution 687, not the US-led coalition, and the fact that Iraq's notification of its acceptance was delivered to the UNSC, enforces the cogency of this view. Lobel and Ratner, supra n. 76, 150.

113 A point made generally about resolutions of the UNSC by Michael Wood, supra n. 84.

114 UNSC Verbatim Record (3 April 1991) UN Doc. S/PV. 2981, Yemen (46). See also Cuba's statement that claimed that the resolution 'still does not categorically or explicitly declare ... the final cessation of hostilities'. Ibid., Cuba (63–5).

115 Ibid., Zaire (53), US (83) and USSR (101).

116 Ibid., France (92).

117 Ibid., India (79–80).

118 Ibid., Cote d'Ivoire (81).

In gauging its true nature, the previous resolution adopted by the UNSC, Resolution 686 (1991), adopted a month before on 2 March 1991, also becomes pertinent.[119] This resolution provided the initial conditions for Iraq to satisfy in order to 'permit a definitive end to the hostilities'.[120] These conditions were essentially in connection with Iraq's invasion of Kuwait, not its disarmament, and during the time required for Iraq to comply with these conditions the 'provisions of paragraph 2 of Resolution 678 (1990) remain[ed] valid'[121] for the sole purpose of fulfilling the conditions. However, in what Sean Murphy has described as 'essentially a provisional cease-fire resolution'[122] the UNSC stressed that it looked forward to 'the rapid establishment of a *definitive end to the hostilities*'.[123] Consequently, 'the Security Council adopted on April 3, 1991 the formal cease-fire embodied in Resolution 687, as the means for definitively ending hostilities'.[124] Although it could be argued that Iraq had, up to 2003, failed to fully comply with all the requirements contained in Resolution 686 (1990), the US did not justify the use of force against Iraq on this basis.[125]

Therefore, through a holistic examination of the extensive text, placed in its context, the collective views of the members of the primary interpretive community, and the views of the secondary interpretive community, despite Resolution 687 (1991) being labelled a 'formal ceasefire', its purpose was more a peace building instrument and hence a *de facto* permanent end to the armed hostilities. This would mean that further authorization was required before force could be used. As Christine Gray submits, 'despite the terminology used in Resolution 687 (1991), it is clearly more than a mere suspension of hostilities. The substance is that of a peace treaty'.[126] Indeed, in the present author's view, Resolution 687 (1991) should be seen as a

---

119 UNSC Res. 686 (2 March 1991) UN Doc. S/RES/686.

120 Ibid., preamble. The conditions for the ceasefire as laid out in Resolution 686 were: the requirement of Iraq to rescind its annexation of Kuwait, accept its liability under international law for loss to Kuwait and third states, release detainees, return Kuwaiti property (para. 2), cease hostile or provocative actions by its forces, designate military commanders to arrange for the military aspects of a cessation of hostilities, arrange the release of all prisoners of war, identify mines and other dangerous weapons in Iraq where coalition forces were present (para. 3).

121 Ibid., para. 4. Paragraph 2 was the paragraph that 'authorized' the use of 'all necessary means'. See Chapter 3. For the two uses of force that took place between the adoption of Resolutions 686 and 687, see Murphy, supra n. 52, 190–91.

122 Murphy, Ibid., 188.

123 UNSC Res. 686, supra n. 119, para. 8.

124 Murphy, supra n. 52, 192.

125 Although James Fry has argued that force could have been used on the basis of Resolution 686 given the 'remain valid' language employed in connection with the authorization to use 'all necessary means'. See, generally, Fry, supra n. 86.

126 Gray, supra n. 3, 144. Peace treaties are no different from other types of treaty and are governed by the law of treaties. Under Article 2(1)(a) of the VCLT (1969) it does not matter what particular name is given to an agreement; a treaty results if the intention is present.

'quasi-peace treaty'; a peace treaty in all but name.[127] However, as noted above, the US revival argument did not take into account its 'formal' nature thus arguing that it provided for recommencement of hostilities should Iraq be found in 'material breach'. It is to this latter key concept of the argument which the chapter now turns and upon which the primary interpretive community has had most to say.

Security Council Resolution 1441 (2002): The Concept of 'Material Breach'

Resolution 1441 (2002), adopted on 8 November 2002, provided Iraq with a 'final opportunity' to comply with its disarmament obligations,[128] and, to that end, established an enhanced inspection regime which would permit UNMOVIC and the IAEA to undertake their assigned duties.[129] The 'final opportunity' phrase is also found in the authorization resolution, 678 (1990).[130] This was arguably inserted by the US to increase the parallels between these two resolutions, given the forcible measures authorized in Resolution 678 (1990).[131] However, during the UNSC meeting debates prior to its adoption it is noticeable that, probably in realization of this, those within the primary interpretive community generally refrained from referring to this particular phrase.[132]

The similarities between Resolution 678 (1990) and Resolution 1441 (2003) go no further than this single phrase and, despite the efforts of the US and the wording of previous drafts of the resolution,[133] Resolution 1441 (2002) did not contain any authorization to use 'all necessary means' if this final opportunity was not seized by Iraq.[134] Instead, after separately recalling Resolutions 678 (1990) and 687

127 Jacobsson talks of Resolution 687 having a 'semi-treaty' character. See M. Jacobsson, 'The Use of Force and the Case of Iraq' in D. Amnéus and K. Svanberg-Topman (eds), *Peace and Security: Current Challenges in International Law* (Sweden: Studentlitteratur, 2004), 373, 383.

128 UNSC Res. 1441, supra n. 14, para. 2.

129 Ibid., paras 5–10. This was the first time that they had entered Iraq after being asked to leave by the US before *Operation Desert Fox* commenced in 1998 and were then subsequently refused re-entry by Iraq.

130 UNSC Res. 678 (29 November 1990) UN Doc. S/RES/678, para. 1.

131 In this respect Taft and Buchwald are correct in claiming that '[t]he language of Resolution 1441 tracked the language of Resolution 678', but they then continue with the incorrect claim that 'the resolution operated in the same way to authorize coalition forces to bring Iraq into compliance with its obligations'. See Taft and Buchwald, supra n. 41, 563. As this section demonstrates, if focus is placed upon the interpretive community, this is incorrect.

132 UN Doc. S/PV. 2963, supra n. 91. Indeed, many states did not refer to the notion at all whilst France referred to a 'last opportunity' (5) and Bulgaria referred to 'one final chance' (9).

133 See supra n. 72.

134 Furthermore, there was no deadline set for Iraq's compliance as in para. 2 of Resolution 678 (1990).

(1991),[135] it held that Iraq 'has been and remains in material breach of its obligations'[136] and that a further 'failure by Iraq at any time to comply with, and cooperate fully in the implementation of, this resolution shall constitute a further material breach'.[137] Whilst it was generally acknowledged that Iraq's cooperation with the inspection process had persistently been found wanting in the past, the focus now would be on its *future* cooperation and behaviour and on the possibility of subsequent material breaches arising. This concept, inserted at the hands of the US, was thus at the core of Resolution 1441 (2002) and consequently the revival argument.[138]

In assessing this final link in the revival argument, the issues that need to be addressed are whether there was intersubjective agreement amongst the primary interpretive community as to the consequences of a material breach, that is, whether such a non-forcible breach provided for the use of force in response, and where the agreement lay as to who was to report such a breach and who possessed the authority for making the final determination of one.

The consequences attached to a 'material breach' The US clearly had it in mind that a material breach in these circumstances could lead to the revival of the forcible means authorized in Resolution 678 (1990).[139] The Legal Adviser and Assistant Legal Adviser to the US State Department, William Taft and Todd Buchwald, used the inclusion of the material breach language in Resolution 707 (1991) and in the two presidential statements in 1993 which preceded the use of force by the

135 UNSC Res. 1441, supra n. 14, preamble.

136 Ibid., para. 1.

137 Ibid., para. 4.

138 Ireland made this point at its adoption by noting that 'the concept of material breach is a key element of this resolution'. UNSC Verbatim Record (8 November 2002) UN Doc. S/PV. 4644, Ireland (7).

139 Whilst the US has never been explicit on the issue, it can perhaps be assumed on the basis of the above justifications that it was making a direct transposition of the 'material breach' concept from the law of treaties, where it is originally to be found. See Article 60 of the VCLT (1969). As Weller notes, '[t]he notion of a material breach is borrowed from the law of treaties'. See Weller, supra n. 87, 90. Indeed, this may be indicated by the US Ambassador to the UN stating in reference to Resolution 1441 that '[t]he resolution confirms what has been clear for years: that Iraq has been and remains in violation of disarmament obligations – *"material breach" in lawyer's language*'. UN Doc. S/PV. 4644, Ibid., 3 (emphasis added). Under Article 60(1) of the VCLT (1969) '[a] material breach of a bilateral treaty by one of the parties entitles the other to invoke the breach as a ground for terminating the treaty or suspending its operation in whole or in part'. However, as argued above, the 'other' party to the 'formal ceasefire' agreement contained in Resolution 687 (1991) was the UNSC, not the US, so that even if this concept was to be transposed from the law of treaties to the law of UNSC resolutions and presidential statements, in the context of the Iraq situation the decision as to whether to suspend or terminate the ceasefire due to a material breach was left to the UNSC.

US[140] to argue that these created an 'understanding that such a determination authorized resort to force'.[141] Consequently, 'it was on this basis that the United States under President Clinton concluded that the Desert Fox campaign against Iraq in December 1998, following repeated efforts by the Iraqi regime to deny access to weapons inspectors, conformed with the Council's resolutions'.[142] Indeed, in its letter to the UNSC upon the launching of *Operation Desert Fox* the US clearly stated that:

> [f]ollowing Iraq's repeated, flagrant and material breaches of its obligations ... the coalition today exercised the authority given by the Security Council resolution 678 (1990) for Member States to employ all necessary means to secure Iraqi compliance with the Council's resolutions and to restore international peace and security in the area.[143]

This alleged understanding that a material breach revived the authority to use force was stated more clearly than ever in its letter to the UNSC upon the launching of *Operation Iraqi Freedom* in 2003:

> It has been long recognized and understood that a material breach of these obligations removes the basis of the ceasefire and *revives* the authority to use force under resolution 678 (1990) ... Iraq continues to be in material breach of its disarmament obligations under resolution 687 (1991), as the Council affirmed in its resolution 1441 (2002) ... In view of Iraq's material breaches, the basis for the ceasefire has been removed and use of force is authorized under resolution 678 (1990).[144]

Furthermore, the penultimate paragraph of Resolution 1441 (2002) expressly recalled that 'the Council has repeatedly warned Iraq that it will face *serious consequences* as a result of its continued violation of its obligations'.[145] The US

140 See supra nn. 12 and 13.

141 Taft and Buchwald, supra n. 41, 559. In 1998, Michael Matheson of the US State Department similarly stated: 'I think that *it is clear on the record* that the Security Council understood that the requirements with respect to the destruction of these weapons and inspection facilities were essential conditions precedent, such that if they were violated, it would be a *material breach* which would lead to the possible use of force'. See M. Matheson, Legal Authority for the Possible Use of Force against Iraq' (1998) 92 *Proceedings of the American Society of International Law* 136, 141 (emphasis added). This was partly based on a statement made by the UNSG at this time. See supra n. 50 and related text.

142 Taft and Buchwald, Ibid., 559.

143 UN Doc. S/1998/1181, supra n. 25.

144 UN Doc. S/2003/351, supra n. 1 (emphasis added). Some scholars agree with this assessment of the consequences of a material breach. Dinstein, for example, argues that a '"material breach" lays the ground for the resumption of hostilities by the other side to a general cease-fire agreement'. Dinstein, supra n. 102, 58. See also Yoo, supra n. 77, 567.

145 UNSC Res. 1441, supra n. 14, para. 13 (emphasis added).

has indicated that it understands the phrase 'serious consequences' to be a term referring to the use of force. The reference to Iraq having been 'repeatedly warned' of such consequences refers back to its usage in the practice of the UNSC in 1997 and 1998.[146] At this time the US claimed that the term was the 'diplomatic code for military action' so 'that military force will ensue' if Iraq violated its obligations.[147] In a less express fashion, the US seemed to equate it with the use of force again in 2002 when it claimed that '*the* most serious consequences for Iraq would follow continued defiance'.[148] Clearly there is no more serious consequence for a state than the use of armed force against it.

It might be thought that the persistency with which the US advocated its views may have had some success given the re-emergence of the concepts of 'material breach' and 'serious consequences' in Resolution 1441 (2002) after such a long absence from the UNSC resolutions regarding Iraq.[149] Indeed, their inclusion could be interpreted as an indicator that the primary interpretive community had come to accept that a 'material breach' opened the door to the use of forcible measures or 'serious consequences'.[150] This may have indicated either a shift in common understandings amongst the primary interpretive community thereby replacing the embedded phrase 'all necessary means' or alternatively, it constituted an additional common understanding indicating the same thing. As Dominic McGoldrick has noted, this would be determined by the primary interpretive community concerned: 'If the members of the SC were agreed that the SC resolutions could be interpreted this way then, in principle, the terms

146 In a presidential statement issued on 29 October 1997, the UNSC warned 'of the serious consequences of Iraq's failure to comply immediately and fully with its obligations under the relevant resolutions' (UN Doc. S/PRST/1997/49 (29 October 1997)). This warning was recalled in a further presidential statement on 13 November 1997 (UN Doc. S/PRST/1997/51 (13 November 1997)). Later, in similar although not identical wording, the UNSC stressed in Resolution 1154 (1998), para. 3, that 'any violation would have severest consequences for Iraq'.

147 This was stated by the United States Assistant Secretary of State James P. Rubin on 3 March 1998 regarding the inclusion of the phrase 'severest consequences' in Resolution 1154 (1998). See B. Gelman, 'U.S. Avoids Military Threat After Iraqi Defiance: Stress is Placed on Economic Sanctions' *Washington Post* (7 August 1998), A1.

148 UN Doc. S/PV. 4644, supra n. 138, 3 (emphasis added).

149 These concepts have also not been employed in UNSC resolutions in other contexts.

150 The UK Attorney-General also stated in 2002 that '"serious consequences" is accepted as indicating the use of force'. See 'Attorney-General's Advice', supra n. 75, 770. This view of accepted understanding has also received limited support from the secondary interpretive community. For example, Kirgis has noted that '[t]he phrase "serious consequences" has been widely understood to include the use of force'. See F.L. Kirgis, 'SC Resolution 1441 on Iraq's Final Opportunity to Comply with Disarmament Obligations' (November 2002) *American Society of International Law Insights*. Available at http://www.asil.org [Accessed: 16 April 2004].

"material breach" and "serious consequences" could be added to "all necessary means" and be equally understood as authorising the use of force'.[151]

The problem here is that those within the primary interpretive community have generally avoided making any reference to either of the terms 'material breach'[152] or 'serious consequences'. Consequently, any distinct common understanding in the context of UNSC resolutions is not discernible. Although there was a lack of express reference to these concepts, in light of the generally negative reaction to the operations against Iraq in 1998 and 2003 as noted above and as the focus of the primary interpretive community in 2002 was placed on peaceful measures,[153] such as a continuation of inspections[154] and on the fact that force should be a last recourse,[155] it can perhaps be concluded that there were no discernible modifications or additions to the common understandings existing between the members of this primary interpretive community to indicate that the use of force had been authorized. Indeed, whilst their inclusion in Resolution 1441 (2002) represented a degree of ambiguity, perhaps intentional given the clarity with which the US expressed its views as to their forcible meaning in 1998 and 2002, very few members of the community ever referred to them, making it hard to argue under these circumstances, as the US appeared to do, that they had become embedded concepts within UNSC procedure with the interpretations attached to them that the US argued they had.[156]

---

151 McGoldrick, supra n. 46, 66.

152 Only three members of the primary interpretive community, including the US and the UK, even mentioned it in the debates prior to the adoption or Resolution 1441. The other was Ireland who also noted its basis in the VCLT (1969). See UN Doc. S/PV. 4644, supra n. 138, 7–8. There was no doubt concern regarding the concept in light of the US's previous reliance on it to justify the use of force in 1993 and 1998. Indeed, the Russian delegate noted that 'the wording is not ideal' (8) and in a previous French draft of the resolution the concept was intentionally absent owing to concerns that the words might be used again as a trigger for the use of force (see T. Weiner, 'Threats and Responses' *New York Times* (28 October 2002), A2).

153 Cameroon was clear that the UNSC had 'just adopted unanimously a resolution on the peaceful disarmament of Iraq'. UN Doc. S/PV. 4644, Ibid., 11. See also France (5), Mexico (6), Russia (8), Bulgaria (9), Norway (10), Guinea (11), Mauritius (12) and China (12).

154 Ireland noted that '[t]his is … a resolution about disarmament, not war. It is about removing all threat of war'. Ibid., 7. See also Russia (8) and China (13).

155 Ibid., in particular France (5), Ireland (7) and Mexico (6).

156 As White correctly notes, '[i]n the United Nations there is consensus that the phrase "all necessary measures" or "all necessary means" in combination with an "authorization" "under Chapter VII" signifies that military enforcement action is being sanctioned. Other language will not do. For example US and UK attempts to interpret Security Council resolutions condemning Iraq for non-compliance with weapons inspections during 1998, when "serious consequences" were indicated by the Security Council, failed because there was no support for that position from Russia and China and many other members of the Security Council. Failure to secure the necessary authorizing language in a resolution

Whilst Taft and Buchwald, the Legal Adviser and Assistant Legal Adviser to the State Department in 2003, have asserted that in the negotiations leading up to the adoption of Resolution 1441 (2002) 'all agreed that a Council determination that Iraq had committed a material breach *would* authorize individual member states to use force to secure compliance with the Council's resolutions' this is a misrepresentation of the intersubjective agreement on the issue.[157] In fact, whilst none of the members of the primary interpretive community expressly ruled out that a UNSC determination of a material breach *could* eventually lead to the authorization of member states to use force, it would be for the UNSC to so determine such a breach and either authorize the use of force or permit the revival argument to be used. In short, the main point of contention was not what the ultimate consequences of a material breach were, but the process of determining such a state of affairs and where the authority lay for determining the immediate consequences. Indeed, it was in connection with the issue of 'automaticity' that the strongest views were expressed and which it addressed next.

The issue of automaticity Those within the primary interpretive community did not wish for Resolution 1441 (2002) to be the final word on the matter before the resort to force. Indeed, the predominant theme in both 1998 and 2002–03 was the lack of any 'automaticity'[158] in the act of passing the resolutions and in the text of the resolutions themselves. On this issue the intersubjective agreement among the primary interpretive community was clear, with the majority of states opting for what became known as the 'two-stage approach'.[159] This can be broken down into two separate yet sequential steps: the authority to report a suspected material breach and the authority to make the final determination as to one and the subsequent consequences.

The issue of preliminarily reporting a material breach was addressed in paragraphs 4 and 11 of Resolution 1441 (2002). After '*[d]ecid*[ing] that, in order to begin to comply with its disarmament obligations, … the Government of Iraq shall provide to *UNMOVIC, the IAEA, and the Council*, … a currently accurate, full, and complete declaration of all aspects of its [weapons] programmes',[160] the UNSC, in paragraph 4:

---

signifies a lack of consensus over military action, it is disingenuous for certain states to then claim that they can unilaterally interpret resolutions as sanctioning military action. All there is then is an unjustified claim to take military action'. See N.D. White, 'The Legality of Bombing in the Name of Humanity' (2000) 5 *JCSL* 27, 32.

157 Taft and Buchwald, supra n. 41, 560 (emphasis added).

158 This was how the issue came to be termed in the UNSC.

159 See UN Doc. S/PV. 4644, supra n. 138, France (5), Mexico (6), Ireland (7) and China (12).

160 UNSC Res. 1441, supra n. 14, para. 3 (second emphasis added).

> *[d]ecid*[ed] that false statements or omissions in the declarations submitted by Iraq pursuant to this resolution and failure by Iraq at any time to comply with, and cooperate fully in the implementation of, this resolution *shall constitute a further material breach of Iraq's obligations* and *will be reported to the Council for assessment* in accordance with paragraphs 11 and 12 below.[161]

Paragraph 11 then:

> *[d]irect*[ed] the *Executive Chairman of UNMOVIC and the Director-General of the IAEA* to report immediately to the Council any interference by Iraq with inspection activities, as well as any failure by Iraq to comply with its disarmament obligations, including its obligations regarding inspections under this resolution.[162]

At first glance it appears that paragraph 4 does not indicate who is permitted to report a preliminary finding of a material breach whilst paragraph 11 directs UNMOVIC and the IAEA to make such a report in connection with the inspections. The US interpreted, and arguably drafted, paragraph 4 so as to permit member states to report a material breach.[163] This interpretation was made explicit in the meeting where Resolution 1441 (2002) was adopted when the US declared that:

> [i]f there is a further Iraqi breach, reported to the Council by UNMOVIC, the IAEA *or a Member State*, the matter will return to the Council for discussions as required in paragraph 12.[164]

The US subsequently made such a report in the form of an address to the UNSC by Secretary of State Colin Powell on 5 February 2003.[165]

However, other members of the primary interpretive community approached the issue differently, with many stressing that it was UNMOVIC and the IAEA that were to make the reports without any mention of member states possessing this right.[166] Indeed, the first stage of the 'two-stage approach' was for UNMOVIC and the IAEA to carry out the inspections as stated in Resolution 1441 (2002) and, if necessary, report a material breach. This is a logical approach, as the members of the UNSC made clear, as it is UNMOVIC and the IAEA who are carrying out the inspections

161 Ibid., para. 4 (second emphasis added).

162 Ibid., para. 11 (second emphasis added).

163 Indeed, there is nothing in the text of this provision to expressly preclude them doing so.

164 UN Doc. S/PV. 4644, supra n. 138, 3 (emphasis added).

165 See UNSC Verbatim Record (5 February 2003) UN Doc. S/PV. 4701.

166 Mexico clearly stated that 'the resolution stipulates that should Iraq fail to comply, it will be the inspectors who will report to the Council'. UN Doc S/PV. 4644, supra n. 138, Mexico (7). See also France (5), Ireland (7), Russia (8) and China (13).

and thus it is for them to make reports on their findings, including the existence of any material breaches. Given that member states were not directly involved in the inspection process, they would not have had any experience or knowledge to make such a determination, including on the declaration submitted by Iraq.

The inspection agencies did not report a material breach and, in presenting their regular reports, steered well clear of such language.[167] Furthermore, any interference or failure to comply by Iraq was to be reported 'immediately'. There were no reports delivered with a sense of urgency and no meetings of the UNSC urgently convened.

In regards to the Iraqi declaration of its weapons programmes, if it is clearly stated that it should be provided to 'UNMOVIC, IAEA, and the Council', it should be for these bodies collectively to report any breaches contained within it. Just as a single inspector of the inspection teams would not have had the authority to report a material breach, the same goes for member states of the UNSC.

However, regardless of who had the authority to make a preliminary determination that a material breach had occurred and report it to the UNSC, the most important issue appeared to be who possessed the ultimate authority to make the final determination of such a breach and the ensuing consequences. Again, the US consistently took the position that states themselves possessed this authority, even in the context of violations of ceasefires or material breaches of obligations contained in resolutions of the UNSC, an organ of an international organization.

Whilst the UNSC did not make a determination of a 'material breach' prior to the launching of *Operation Desert Fox* in 1998,[168] the US appeared to argue that as long as the Iraqi actions at this time were similar in nature to previous actions which the UNSC had branded as material breaches, this was sufficient to revive the authority to use force.[169] In a clear reference back to the determinations made in 1991 and 1993, and in furthering its unilateralist approach, the US stated in justifying *Operation Desert Fox* in December 1998 that 'the Council need not state these conclusions on every occasion'.[170] Indeed, the Legal Adviser to the State Department in 2003 confirmed that at the time of *Operation Desert Fox* '[t]he U.S. view was that whether there had been a material breach was an *objective fact*, and it was not necessary for the Council to so determine or state'.[171]

---

167 See supra Iraq, the Security Council, and the Use of Force by the United States: 1991–2003. Indeed, 'the Reports afford no warrant for the assertion that a contextual interpretation of the said Resolution could give a different meaning to 1441, so as to imbue the Operation with legitimacy, since they steered clear from condemning Iraq for another "material breach" of its obligations'. Papastavridis, supra n. 73, 115.

168 The UNSC instead described the actions of Iraq as a 'flagrant violation'. UNSC Res. 1205 (5 November 1998) UN Doc. S/RES/1205, para. 1.

169 See supra Iraq, the Security Council, and the Use of Force by the United States: 1991–2003.

170 UN Doc. S/1998/1181, supra n. 25, 2.

171 Taft and Buchwald, supra n. 41, 560 (emphasis added).

However, as noted above, the reaction of the primary interpretive community suggested that this view placed the US once again outside of the intersubjective agreement that existed between the other members. Indeed, the response to these strikes in 1998 and the discourse which took place in the debates regarding the resolutions adopted in the 12 months preceding them clearly shows that those in the UNSC had rejected the possibility of automaticity. For example, it was stressed that 'any hint of automaticity with regard to the application of force has been excluded; that would not be acceptable for the majority of the Council's members'.[172] The fact that this had been assured by the sponsors of Resolution 1154 (1998), including the US, was a noted factor in its adoption.[173]

In connection with this, another major theme present amongst the interpretive community in 1998 was the importance of maintaining the authority of the UNSC. Indeed, it was stressed that '[i]t is the Security Council that must evaluate the behaviour of a country, if necessary to determine any possible violations, and to take the appropriate decisions'.[174] It was emphasized that 'this very important principle'[175] was embedded in each of its resolutions where the text of the last paragraph determined that the UNSC 'will remain seized of the matter'.[176] Furthermore, many members stressed at this time, as they did in 2002, the futility of the use of force under these circumstances,[177] and the necessity of the resolution of conflicts through peaceful, political, and diplomatic means.[178]

Nevertheless, regardless of the fact that the US was no longer operating within the intersubjective agreement, it maintained its 'objective fact' approach to the

172 UNSC Verbatim Record (2 March 1998) UN Doc. S/PV. 3858, Russia (17). See also Brazil (7), Kenya (10), Japan (11), China (14), France (15) and Gambia (18).

173 Ibid., Russia (17) and Brazil (7).

174 UN Doc. S/PV. 3858, supra n. 172, France (15). See also Russia (17), Brazil (7), Costa Rica (5), Sweden (9), Kenya (10), Slovenia (12) and Egypt (22); UNSC Verbatim Record (12 November 1997) UN Doc. S/PV. 3831, France (10); UNSC Verbatim Record (5 November 1998) UN Doc. S/PV. 3939, France (3) and Sweden (6); UNSC Verbatim Record (16 December 1998) UN Doc. S/PV. 3955, Russia (4), Costa Rica (7), Sweden (10), Brazil (11) and Kenya (12). As Lobel and Ratner note, '[s]uch authorization cannot be revived by the contractees unilaterally; it is for the Security Council to consider whether a breach of that cease-fire justifies a reauthorization of force'. See Lobel and Ratner, supra n. 76, 144.

175 UN Doc. S/PV. 3939, Ibid., Sweden (6).

176 UN Doc. S/PV. 3858, supra n.172, Brazil (7), Sweden (9), Japan (11) and Slovenia (12); UN Doc. S/PV. 3939, Ibid., Russia (4), Sweden (6), Brazil (6) and Kenya (7); UN Doc. S/PV. 3955, supra n. 174, Russia (4).

177 UN Doc. S/PV. 3831, supra n. 174, Russia (13); UN Doc S/PV. 3858, supra n. 172, Bahrain (8), Pakistan (19), Malaysia (20) and Egypt (21); UN Doc. S/PV. 3939, supra n. 174, Russia (4).

178 UN Doc. S/PV. 3831, supra n. 174, Russia (13) and China (15); UN Doc. S/PV. 3858, supra n. 172, China (14), Mexico (19) and Malaysia (20); UN Doc. S/PV. 3939, supra n. 174, Russia (4), Bahrain (7), Costa Rica (8), China (9); UN Doc. S/PV. 3955, supra n. 174, Russia (4), Sweden (10) and Brazil (11).

existence of a 'material breach' in 2002–03.[179] In an astute piece of drafting, paragraph 12 of Resolution 1441 (2002) stated that the UNSC:

> *[d]ecide*[d] to convene immediately upon receipt of a report in accordance with paragraphs 4 or 11 above, in order to *consider* the situation and the need for full compliance with all of the relevant Council resolutions in order to secure international peace and security.[180]

In the meeting where Resolution 1441 (2002) was adopted, the US, in interpreting this provision and asserting that 'this resolution contains no "hidden triggers" and no "automaticity" with respect to the use of force',[181] nevertheless asserted its claimed right of unilateral determination more fervently than ever:

> one way or another, Iraq will be disarmed. *If the Security Council fails to act decisively* in the event of further Iraqi violations, this resolution does not constrain any Member State from acting to defend itself against the threat posed by Iraq *or to enforce relevant United Nations resolutions* and protect world peace and security.[182]

Therefore the US accepted that, as required by paragraph 12, the UNSC should convene to *consider* the situation, but if the Council failed to come to a *decision* to authorize the use of force in the face of Iraqi violations it reserved the right to use force either under the UNSC resolutions or in self-defence. Ultimately, not only did the US claim to have the authority to determine a material breach but it also claimed to have the authority to determine the consequences of a finding of one. This claim was only supported in the UNSC by the UK which, whilst stating that '[t]here is no "automaticity" in this resolution', went on to claim that:

> [i]f there is a further Iraqi breach of its disarmament obligations, the matter will return to the Council *for discussion* as required in paragraph 12. We would expect the Security Council then to meet its responsibilities.[183]

Whilst none of those within the primary interpretive community on this occasion took direct issue with the US over its particularly bellicose claim, the consensus in the meeting was clear and differed little to that adopted in 1998. Indeed, whilst the US and UK acknowledged that the other members of the primary interpretive community should be consulted, the other members themselves emphasized the

---

179 Significantly, this was rejected by the UK Attorney-General. See supra n. 75.
180 UNSC Res. 1441, supra n. 14, para. 12 (second emphasis added).
181 UN Doc. S/PV. 4644, supra n. 138, US (3) (emphasis added).
182 Ibid., 3 (emphasis added).
183 Ibid., 5 (emphasis added).

'central role' of the UNSC[184] so as to 'ensur[e] that the Security Council would maintain control of the process at each stage'.[185] In expressly rejecting 'automaticity' or the 'automatic' use of force,[186] the primary interpretive community made it clear that should the inspection agencies report a breach to the UNSC, it was for that body to decide 'what is appropriate'[187] or on 'any ensuing action'.[188] Any subsequent determination on the propriety of force should be either through 'explicit *agreement* of the Council'[189] *or* through 'prior explicit *authorization*'.[190] Indeed, '[t]he resolution should not be interpreted, through certain paragraphs, as authorizing any state to use force'.[191]

It is surprising that despite clearly differing positions on what automaticity meant – a mere *discussion* or an actual *decision* before force could be resorted to – the members of the primary interpretive community appeared to be either oblivious to those differences or to intentionally ignore them for the sake of the adoption of the resolution. Indeed, after two strong statements of interpretation as to the meaning of 'automaticity' from the US and the UK it was surprising that France then 'welcome[d] the fact that all ambiguity on this point and all elements of automaticity ha[d] disappeared from the resolution'.[192] Furthermore, Ireland 'welcom[ed] the unity that the Council ha[d] shown in the adoption of this resolution'.[193] Additionally, a number of states expressly stated that it was the assurances from the sponsors as to the draft resolution's lack of a basis for the use of force which permitted them to vote in favour of it.[194]

However, perhaps to pre-empt the foreseeable interpretation given to the resolution by the US and UK so as to permit the use of force, Russia succinctly summarized the interpretive methodology which the other members of the primary interpretive community had stated expressly to be in agreement over:

> Implementation of the resolution will require *goodwill* on the part of all those involved in the process of seeking a settlement of the Iraq question. They must have the willingness to concentrate on moving forward towards the *declared*

184 Ibid., Syria (10). See also Ireland (7), Bulgaria (9), Colombia (11), Cameroon (11), Guinea (11) and Mauritius (12).

185 Ibid., France (5).

186 Ibid., France (5), Mexico (6), Ireland (7), Russia (8), Syria (10), Bulgaria (9), Colombia (11), Cameroon (11) and China (13).

187 Ibid., Mexico (7).

188 Ibid., Ireland (7). This state claimed that previous UNSC debates had 'made it clear that this is the broadly held view within the United Nations'. Ibid., Ireland (7).

189 Ibid., Mexico (6) (emphasis added).

190 Ibid.

191 Ibid., Syria (10).

192 Ibid., France (5).

193 Ibid., Ireland (7). Additionally, two states welcomed the 'consensus' of the UNSC on this occasion. See Bulgaria (9) and Guinea (11).

194 Ibid., Ireland (7), Russia (8) and Syria (10).

> *common goals*, not yielding to the *temptation of unilateral interpretation* of the resolution's provisions and preserving the *consensus* and unity of all members of the Security Council.[195]

In contrast to the drafting of Resolution 678 (1990) and the insertion of the authorization technique the fact that the US had drafted Resolution 1441 (2002) to be interpreted in a certain way did not guarantee that it would be by the community responsible for its interpretation and application. As Gray correctly summarizes, '[t]he USA and the UK have based their case for force on the words of particular resolutions and have discounted the drafting history which showed an unwillingness by other states to accept that the resolutions in question could be interpreted to authorize force'.[196] This highlights the fact that regardless of what the terms of a text may be taken to mean, they must be interpreted within the boundaries of the intersubjective agreement of the other members of the primary interpretive community.[197] In this case, despite some apparent confusion as to how the US and the UK had interpreted the terms used in the resolution and the general purpose of the resolution as a whole, the intersubjective agreement on the issue by the primary interpretive community was clear.[198] Indeed, this episode indicates that whilst 'the lack of such a authorization did not keep the United States from taking military action against Iraq', 'the United States did not hold total sway over the Security Council'.[199] However, the question remains as to whether the arguments and justifications of the US have had an impact upon the *jus ad bellum* in the years since 2003.

The Revival Doctrine: Life After *Operation Iraqi Freedom*

The US revival argument has not since been witnessed in the practice or discourse of the interpretive communities outside of the context of *Operation Iraqi Freedom*. The UN reports which were inspired by the divisions caused over this incident did not raise the issue of the revival argument[200] and neither did the World Summit

195 Ibid., Russia (9) (emphasis added).

196 Gray, supra n. 3, 369.

197 See Chapter 2.

198 Furthermore, the introduction of a draft resolution in February 2003 which would have enhanced the revival argument was withdrawn before being put to the vote when it became clear that it would not even gain enough votes to secure even a 'moral' victory, that is, nine votes in favour regardless of a veto from one or more of the P5. See *Keesing's* (2003) 45264 and 45315.

199 Quigley, supra n. 112, 142.

200 Report of the High-Level Panel on Threats, Challenges and Change, 'A More Secure World: Our Shared Responsibility' (2 December 2004) UN Doc. A/59/565; Report of the UN Secretary-General, 'In Larger Freedom: Towards Security, Development and Human Rights for All' (21 March 2005) UN Doc. A/59/205.

Outcome document in September 2005 which provided members of the primary interpretive community of the UN Charter and general customary international law with the opportunity to collectively have their say on this issue.[201] Furthermore, resolutions adopted by the UNSC since Resolution 1441 (2002) indicate that 'other states are ... exercising even more caution with respect to the language of new Security Council resolutions'.[202] For example, the resolutions adopted in connection with post-invasion Iraq fairly soon after *Operation Iraqi Freedom* had been declared over were 'very tightly worded so as to leave little scope for arguments that [they] provided *ex post facto* authorization of the war'[203] or endorsement of the revival argument.[204]

This caution can also be witnessed in the subsequent resolutions adopted by the UNSC in other contexts. Indeed, the key terms associated with the revival argument, that is, 'material breach', 'serious consequences', and perhaps 'final opportunity', have not made an appearance in any resolution by the UNSC since Resolution 1441 (2002), let alone any resolution authorizing the use of force. Significantly, the final paragraph of Resolution 1718 (2006),[205] adopted in response to the DPRK testing a nuclear weapon on 9 October 2006, stressed that 'further *decisions* will be required should additional measures be necessary'.[206] Although no previous authorization to use 'all necessary means' had been granted in respect of this situation and so there was no authorization to revive, the express reference to the taking of a 'decision' as opposed to merely 'convening' to 'consider' the situation as employed in Resolution 1441 (2002) is notable.[207]

Whilst the UNSC has since *Operation Iraqi Freedom* mostly authorized states to use 'all necessary means' in the context of the extension of peace keeping mandates,[208]

201 2005 World Summit Outcome Document (15 September 2005) UN Doc. A/60/L.1.

202 M. Byers, 'Agreeing to Disagree: Security Council Resolution 1441 and Intentional Ambiguity' (2004) 10 *Global Governance* 165, 181.

203 Byers, supra n. 202, 181. Gray also notes that 'Security Council Resolutions on Iraq passed after the start of *Operation Iraqi Freedom* took the pragmatic approach of simply accepting the status quo without any express or implied observation on the legality of the military operation'. Gray, supra n. 3, 365.

204 See, for example, UNSC Resolutions 1472, 1483, 1500, and 1511 (2003).

205 UNSC Res. 1718 (14 October 2002) UN Doc. S/RES/1718.

206 Ibid., para. 16 (emphasis added).

207 Gray, perhaps overstating the significance, claims that '[t]his was clearly designed to avoid the type of argument made by the USA and the UK in the case of Iraq; they had claimed that because Resolution 1441 (2002) did not expressly require a further Security Council *decision*, but said only that the Security Council should *consider* the situation if Iraq committed further material breaches of its obligations, therefore it was open to them to resort to force even without a further Security Council resolution'. Gray, supra n. 3, 367.

208 See, for example, UNSC Res. 1493 (28 July 2003) UN Doc. S/RES/1493, para. 26 (UN Mission in Democratic Republic of Congo); UNSC Res. 1773 (24 August 2007) UN Doc. S/RES/1773, para. 1 (UN Interim Force in Lebanon).

there is no indication that the technique for such authorization has changed in any way as a result of the US's revival argument in Iraq. In other words, no discernible negative impact to the UNSC procedure has been witnessed. Indeed, one could plausibly argue that if the revival argument has had, and will have, any impact it is in fact a positive one in the form of the adoption of sharper worded, less ambiguous resolutions with more restricted possibilities for the same kind of abuse and bad faith interpretations demonstrated by the US in the 'Iraq context' to be used again.

Conclusion

To dismiss the episodes in 1993, 1998, and 2003 as simple violations of international law is to overlook the fact that the US recognized the embedded common understanding regarding the use of force and consequently advanced a 'sophisticated' legal argument for its actions which was both 'legally tenable and defensible'.[209] Given the US's instrumental role in establishing this understanding in the practice of the UNSC the making of these arguments was perhaps to some extent unavoidable.[210] However, as a sign of the robustness of the *jus ad bellum* against the coercive pressures of even the most powerful state, this understanding then denied its maker the full-jacket of legitimacy that it required. Consequently, seeing as it could not get its way, certain terms were inserted into UNSC resolutions to muddy the waters and bring an element of ambiguity into the interpretive process.[211]

Nevertheless, it was the collective interpretation placed upon these terms that ultimately mattered. Whilst the first part of this chapter demonstrated that from 1998 the US was clearly operating outside of the intersubjective agreement within the UNSC as to permissible action against Iraq, the chapter went on to demonstrate in more detail that this was not due simply to reasons of the actions taken being disproportionate.[212] Instead, the cause of condemnation related directly to the fundamental unilateral elements of the revival doctrine based upon these terms.

On this point, if the doctrine had have been accepted thus permitting states to be able to unilaterally revive authority to use force then, due to the balance shift towards unilateralism, this would be a widening of the exception of collective security to the prohibition of the use of force and would therefore require the intersubjective agreement of the primary interpretive community connected

209 McGoldrick, supra n. 46, 66. Gray also recognizes that the argument was 'impressively concise and cleverly argued'. See Gray, supra n. 3, 359.

210 See Chapter 3.

211 As Lobel and Ratner point out, '[t]he refusal of the United States to accept limitations on its power by the Security Council thus depended on creatively interpreting the Council's resolutions to accord authority'. See Lobel and Ratner, supra n. 76, 124–5.

212 Proportionality is one of the fundamental principles governing the use of force. See, generally, Gardam, supra n. 93. For more on this requirement in connection with self-defence see Chapter 6.

with this prohibition. However, due to the argument having clearly not made any headway with the primary interpretive community of the UNSC, it was not relevant to see whether this was present.

Furthermore, life for the revival doctrine after *Operation Iraqi Freedom* has proved rather bleak with no real discernible signs of impact upon the *jus ad bellum*. Whilst all actions and justifications by the acting state, have the potential of at least widening the terms of the debate with the potential for future modifications of the law, the final section of this chapter demonstrated that even this has not occurred. Indeed, one can conclude that the proposed trigger concepts of 'material breach' and 'serious consequences' have not displaced or supplemented the current common understanding for the permission to use force within the primary interpretive community of the UNSC.[213]

Furthermore, it is most unlikely that the doctrine will make an impact upon the *jus ad bellum* in the future. This is essentially due to the *sui generis* nature of the 'Iraq context' in which it has been solely invoked. Indeed, as noted above, with Iraq's overall behaviour, and particularly its invasion of Kuwait and the extensive obligations and inspection regime imposed, it was viewed in rather a unique way by the international community.[214] This set of circumstances is unlikely to be repeated and consequently the general and consistent practice required for any modifications to the law will not be generated.[215] For example, even though problems are currently being witnessed in connection with the disarmament of Iran and North Korea,[216] the revival argument could not play a role given the lack of any prior authorization in connection with these states.[217]

It has been said that the actions by the US over this time were taken because 'Iraq's action was inconsistent with the "will" of the Council'.[218] Whereas on this occasion the US relied on a legal argument tracing back to explicit authorization provided by the UNSC, it has employed the argument on other occasions that it was simply enforcing the 'collective will' of the UNSC. This is perhaps an even more controversial argument and is the subject of the next chapter.

213 Byers, supra n. 202, 172.

214 See supra *The Shifting Boundaries of Intersubjective Agreement and the Use of Force Against Iraq*.

215 As Byers points out, 'what matters is the behaviour of states over time. For the moment, all that can be conclusively said is that that there was a sufficient absence of agreement over the interpretation of Resolution 1441 to indicate that the interpretive approach preferred by the United States and the United Kingdom has not yet become legally required'. Byers, supra n. 202, 179.

216 See also Chapter 5.

217 Instead, the US may argue it was acting under the collective will doctrine or in pre-emptive self-defence. See Chapters 5 and 7 respectively.

218 Weller, supra n. 87, 88. Krisch includes the material of this chapter under the heading of 'unilateral enforcement of the collective will'. See Krisch, supra n. 4.

Chapter 5
The Unilateral Determination of Authority to Use Force Under the Auspices of the Security Council (II): Enforcing the Collective Will

armed force shall not be used, save in the common interest.[1]

Introduction

It was highlighted in Chapter 3 that, as part of a practice instigated by the US, states may have express and contemporary authorization granted to them by the UNSC to use force to achieve the will of that organ. However, it was demonstrated in Chapter 4 that given the general acceptability of this practice amongst those within the interpretive communities the US began to argue that the authority granted to it in Resolution 678 (1990) remained open and active beyond the forcible evacuation of Iraq from Kuwait in 1991 so as to permit it to enforce the obligations contained within the ceasefire agreement without the intersubjective agreement of the primary interpretive community of the UNSC that this was acceptable.[2]

This chapter examines the arguably more controversial doctrine implicitly advanced by the US that it had the authority to resort to forcible measures to implement the will of the international community in the absence of any authorization having been granted by the UNSC in the context in which the measures are taken. Although this is first and foremost about the right to unilaterally enforce, or take action in support of, UNSC resolutions and the obligations and sentiments contained within them, due to these actions having arisen in the context of human rights violations in Iraq and the Kosovo region of the FRY, the right to use unilateral force for humanitarian

---

1 UN Charter (1945), preamble.

2 Of course, the revival of authority could be said to be a form of unilaterally enforcing the collective will. Indeed, Krisch includes it as such in his study of the topic whilst acknowledging that this 'general tendency was to some degree hidden behind more detailed arguments'. See N. Krisch, 'Unilateral Enforcement of the Collective Will: Kosovo, Iraq, and the Security Council' (1999) 3 *Max Planck Yrbk UN L.* 59, 90. See also N.D. White, 'The Legality of Bombing in the Name of Humanity' (2000) 5 *JCSL* 27, 27; C. Stahn, 'Enforcement of the Collective Will After Iraq' (2003) 97 *AJIL* 804, 805.

purposes is also considered. Before a discussion can commence on the US's enforcement of the collective will and whether, through reference to the primary and secondary interpretive communities, this has had any discernible impact upon the *jus ad bellum*, some explanation needs to be given as to the meaning of this concept.

Defining the Collective Will

There are certain issues of general concern within the international community the regulation and enforcement of which present no, or very little, direct and immediate benefit to the elites at the helm of states.[3] Nevertheless, perhaps because of domestic political pressure, pressure from elements within the international community, or just the perceived benefits of being seen to be 'doing the right thing', they become involved in their regulation and resolution. For example, the emergence of concern over the protection of the environment and the prevention of climate change has become an issue which states are currently collectively attempting to regulate and resolve.[4] Similarly, the issue of global terrorism, although of a much more immediate interest to states, has received much attention, particularly after the events of 11 September 2001.[5] However, arguably the first of such areas of general concern to rise to prominence in the UN Charter era was the protection of human rights.

Human Rights

It is clear that at the end of the Cold War serious violations of human rights were a matter of international concern and their prevention and punishment in international law had gained momentum since the adoption of the UN Charter in 1945.[6] This has led to the perception, particularly amongst those within the secondary interpretive community, that the obligation on states to respect and protect the basic rights of all human persons is owed *erga omnes*.[7] Other relevant actors connected with this

---

3 Krisch, Ibid., 59.

4 As Martin Shaw has observed, 'an extensive range of environmental problems is now the subject of serious international concern'. See M. Shaw, *International Law*, 6th edn (Cambridge: Cambridge University Press, 2008), 844.

5 See, in particular, what many deem to be a 'legislative act' by the UNSC on the issue of terrorism, UNSC Res. 1373 (28 September 2001) UN Doc. S/RES/1373.

6 This began with the Universal Declaration of Human Rights in 1948. Other important instruments include the Genocide Convention in 1948, the Torture Convention in 1984, the International Covenant on Economic, Social and Cultural Rights in 1966, and the International Covenant on Civil and Political Rights in 1966.

7 A. Cassese, *International Law*, 2nd edn (Oxford: Oxford University Press, 2005), 262. An obligation *erga omnes* is one that concerns all states and 'all states can be held to have a legal interest in their protection' and include 'the principles and rules concerning the basic rights of the human person …'. See *Barcelona Traction, Light and Power Company Limited (Belgium v Spain)* [1970] ICJ Rep. 3, 32. Article 33(1) of the ILC Articles on

concern are NGOs, pressure groups and, within the UN itself, the Human Rights Council and Social and Economic Council. However, amongst this network of rights and obligations, institutions and actors, means of enforcement are limited.[8]

The rights being of a community concern, one would expect a collective response if force was to be employed in their enforcement, as opposed to one based on self-defence, which is concerned with protecting immediate individual state interests.[9] Although the UNSC does not have as its primary responsibility the protection of human rights, it has, through the back door, also become concerned with internal repression and human rights violations and has on occasion condemned them, demanded their cessation, and also authorized the use of force to prevent them.[10] Although there have been murmurings of discontent at this within the interpretive communities it has become an accepted part of the competence of the UNSC in the post-Cold War era.[11] However, as Chapter 4 demonstrated, sometimes the UNSC withholds granting such authorization even though it has concerned itself with a situation. Nevertheless, it is arguable that the determinations and decisions contained in the existing resolutions on these situations represent the 'collective will'.

Security Council Resolutions

In various meetings of the UNSC those within this primary interpretive community have claimed that the UNSC represents the international community[12] and that

---

Responsibility of States for Internationally Wrongful Acts (2001) talks of 'obligations ... owed to ... the international community as a whole'.

8 However, Krisch correctly notes that 'in international law many rights are lacking an appropriate remedy, and that only very few can be forcibly implemented'. See N. Krisch, 'Review Essay: Legality, Morality and the Dilemma of Humanitarian Intervention after Kosovo' (2002) 13 *EJIL* 323, 327. See also White, supra n. 2, 35.

9 Although Wedgwood talks of 'embracing a right of "collective self-defence" against a government's armed attacks on its own population'. See R. Wedgwood, 'Unilateral Action in the UN System' (2000) 11 *EJIL* 349, 356. For a more recent invocation of the right of self-defence in this context see, generally, G.P. Fletcher and J.D. Ohlin, *Defending Humanity: When Force is Justified and Why* (New York: Oxford University Press, 2008). If the human rights violations are connected with citizens of the intervening states this more appropriately comes under the conceptual heading of self-defence. See R.B. Lillich, 'Forcible Self-Help by States to Protect Human Rights' (1967) 53 *Iowa L.Rev.* 325, 332.

10 See Chapter 3. As Krish notes, '[i]n the 1990s, the Council ... extended its competences considerably to internal situations and especially to humanitarian concerns'. Krisch, supra n. 2, 64. See also G. Symes, 'Force Without Law: Seeking a Legal Justification for the September 1996 US Military Intervention in Iraq' (1997–98) 19 *Mich.J.Int'l L.* 581, 593. Indeed, 'the increasing legitimacy of humanitarian intervention in sovereign nations has occurred primarily in the context of multilateral action'. Symes, Ibid., 594.

11 See Chapter 3.

12 See, for example, UNSC Verbatim Record (29 November 1990) UN Doc. S/PV. 2963, Kuwait (7), UK (79–80) and USSR (94–95); UNSC Verbatim Record (8 November 2002) UN Doc. S/PV. 4644, Ireland (8) and Mauritius (12).

UNSC resolutions represent the will of the international community.[13] This is a view which has also been found in the secondary interpretive community.[14] Whilst any purely unilateral claim to be acting in the interests of the international community are of course subjective and open to divergent views, if the UNSC has previously expressed concern over a situation and determined it to be a 'threat to the peace', any claims of unilaterally acting to enforce the interests in the resolutions are arguably enhanced. As Lobel and Ratner note, '[w]hen a group of states act to enforce a Security Council resolution that the Council itself is unwilling to enforce ... the argument can be made that those states are not acting unilaterally, but on behalf of a clearly articulated community mandate'.[15] In this way 'states rely on Security Council authority in order to prove the common interest involved, and purely unilateral justifications are avoided even when possible'.[16]

Consequently, as the incidents of the use of force by the US under discussion in this chapter have occurred after and in the same context as the UNSC expressing humanitarian concern and demanding a halt to occurrences of human rights violations, although stopping short of authorizing the use of force, it could be said that the actions were taken to enforce the 'collective will' of the international community. Before assessing this claim further, these incidences will first be set out.

The Unilateral Enforcement of the Collective Will in the Post-Cold War Era

The Establishment and Defence of the Safe Havens and No-Fly Zones in Iraq: 1991–2002

After the defeat of Iraq by the US-led coalition in late February 1991, and after a call by President George H.W. Bush for the 'Iraqi people to take matters into their own hands – to force Saddam Hussein, the dictator, to step aside ...',[17] Iraqi civilians and opposition groups began to rise up against the government of

---

13 UN Doc. S/PV. 2963, Ibid., Ethiopia (49–50), UK (81) and USSR (91).

14 White notes that the UNSC represents 'the UN when taking action in the field of peace and security. The international community has granted the Security Council this function'. White, supra n. 2, 29. Seeing as membership of the UN is virtually universal, it could then be said that the UNSC represents the international community.

15 J. Lobel, and M. Ratner, 'Bypassing the Security Council: Ambiguous Authorizations to Use Force, Ceasefires and the Iraqi Inspection Regime' (1999) 93 *AJIL* 124, 130–31.

16 Krisch, supra n. 2, 64.

17 President George H.W. Bush, 'Remarks to the American Association for the Advancement of Science' (1991) 1 *Bush Papers* 145. However, President Bush later denied that this was a suggestion that the US would be there to support them. See President George H.W. Bush, 'Remarks on Assistance for Iraqi Refugees and a News Conference' (1991) 1 *Bush Papers* 380.

Saddam Hussein, particularly the Kurdish groups in the north of Iraq and the Shia groups in the south.[18] However, the coalition stopped short of supporting such an uprising with the possibility of deposing Saddam Hussein. Indeed, President Bush stated that 'it was not an objective of the coalition or the US to overthrow Saddam Hussein'.[19] Consequently, Iraqi armed forces were successful in crushing the uprisings and the US-led coalition forces did not intervene.[20]

On 5 April 1991, just a few days after the adoption of Resolution 687 (1991),[21] the UNSC adopted Resolution 688 (1991).[22] This resolution condemned and demanded an end to the 'repression of the Iraqi civilian population in many parts of Iraq ... the consequences of which threaten international peace and security'.[23] Although the resolution called upon Iraq to 'allow immediate access by international humanitarian organizations to those in need of assistance',[24] and appealed to all member states and to all humanitarian organizations 'to contribute to these humanitarian relief efforts',[25] it was not adopted under Chapter VII and made no provision for the use of force to compel the Iraqi government to halt its campaign of repression against the Kurdish and Shia groups.[26]

Nevertheless, President Bush announced on 16 April 1991 a reversal of his policy of military non-intervention and stated that US troops would enter northern Iraq to establish safe havens.[27] Although no justification of an established legal basis was provided, the safe havens were, according to the President, 'consistent with' Resolution 688 (1991) and 'motivated by humanitarian concern' and that this humanitarian concern was 'so overwhelming that there will be a lot of understanding about this'.[28] The day after, on 17 April 1991, the US, UK,

---

18 *Keesing's* (1991) 38081.

19 *Keesing's* (1991) 38127.

20 *Keesing's* (1991) 38081. For a good historical account of this crisis see P. Malanczuk, 'The Kurdish Crisis and Allied Intervention in the Aftermath of the Second Gulf War' (1991) 2 *EJIL* 114, 114–23.

21 See Chapter 4 for more on this resolution and the 'formal ceasefire' which it contained.

22 UNSC Res. 688 (5 April 1991) UN Doc. S/RES/688.

23 Ibid., preamble.

24 Ibid., para. 3.

25 Ibid., para. 6.

26 That is, it did not contain 'authorization' to use 'all necessary means'. For more on the 'authorization technique' see Chapter 3.

27 President George H.W. Bush, 'The United States President's News Conference' (16 April 1991) *Weekly Compilation of Presidential Documents* 716 quoted in M. Weller (ed.), *Iraq and Kuwait: The Hostilities and Their Aftermath* (Cambridge: Grotius, 1993), 717. President Bush also openly espoused the US intention of regime change. See Ibid., 718.

28 Ibid. The UK also claimed to be acting 'in support of UNSCR 688'. See 'Statement in the House of Commons by the UK Secretary of State' (18 January 1993) quoted in Weller, Ibid., 748–49. France also claimed that 'in all instances involving France, her action in this

and France, with the support of Russia, moved into northern Iraq and forced Iraqi military to leave as part of what became known as *Operation Provide Comfort*.[29] Later, an 'air exclusion zone' (commonly known as the 'no-fly zone') was also created above the 36th parallel so as to prevent further attacks by the Iraqi Government.[30] Although the US-led coalition pulled their ground troops out of Iraq on 15 July 1991, the no-fly zones were still enforced in the form of *Operation Poised Hammer*, a multinational rapid deployment air force based in Turkey and on ships in the Gulf.[31]

On 26 August 1992, after a critical report by the Human Rights Commission,[32] the US announced that it was establishing 'surveillance missions' and a 'no-fly zone' in southern Iraq.[33] The US claimed that *Operation Southern Watch* was established because 'Iraq [was] failing to meet its obligations under UN Security Council resolution 688'.[34] On the same day, the coalition itself, including the US, the UK, France and Russia, made a similar joint announcement.[35]

The justifications of the US for these actions centred on both the concerns expressed in UNSC Resolution 688 (1991) and on general humanitarian concerns. The primary interpretive community in connection with the first part of the justification was the UNSC. If, however, this community was to accept that unilateral determinations could be made that its resolutions are to be enforced, this would be a narrowing of the prohibition of the use of force which would thus require the consultation of the primary interpretive communities connected with interpreting this prohibition in both its textual and customary forms, that is, the parties to the UN Charter and the international community more generally. These latter primary interpretive communities were also relevant in connection with the second part of the justification. This is because if a doctrine of unilateral humanitarian intervention is to emerge this would not simply be a procedural change to the competence of the UNSC but a distinct additional exception to the prohibition of the use of force found in the UN Charter and customary international law.

However, at various subsequent UNSC meetings no member of this particular primary interpretive community condemned the actions, or even mentioned them,

---

respect has been strictly confined by the texts of the United Nations and we do not operate outside of the framework of the United Nations'. See 'Official Declaration issued by the Ministry for Foreign Affairs of France' (21 January 1993) quoted in Weller, Ibid., 752.

29 *Keesing's* (1991) 38127.

30 Ibid.

31 C. Haberman, 'Allied Strike Force Aimed at Iraq Forms in Turkey' *New York Times* (25 July 1991), A1. See also *Keesing's* (1991) 38307–08.

32 UN Doc. S/24386 (5 August 1992).

33 'US Press Release: Coalition to Impose "No-Fly" Zone in Southern Iraq' (26 August 1992) quoted in Weller, supra n. 27, 724–25.

34 Ibid.

35 See 'Statement Issued by the Members of the Coalition at New York' (26 August 1992) quoted in Weller, Ibid., 725.

and there was no official condemnation by this organ.[36] Consequently, it appeared that the participating states had been provided with the blessing of those charged with interpreting the competence and resolutions of the UNSC. Furthermore, there was no official condemnation by the UNGA for the creation and enforcement of the safe havens and no-fly zones and little audible dissent from members of the primary interpretive community concerned with interpreting the UN Charter and customary international law. Indeed, the US-led coalition, in setting up these enforcement measures, appeared to be acting within the general intersubjective agreement of the primary interpretive communities connected with both arms of the US's justification at this time.

Subsequent actions that were taken were equally greeted with what appeared to be positive intersubjective agreement. Whilst on occasion incursions into the no-fly zones by Iraq did not result in a forcible response from the US,[37] this was generally the exception with the US-led coalition shooting down Iraqi aircraft[38] and striking at missile sites[39] and air-defence installations[40] with some frequency, especially in 1993. Russia, a member of the primary interpretive community of the UNSC, was generally supportive of this action. Indeed, the reliance on Resolution 688 (1991) in the US justification for the actions was expressly supported by this state: 'The action of the coalition forces in Iraq was taken in the context of the international community's efforts to ensure the observance of a decision jointly adopted under UN aegis to alleviate the consequences of Iraqi aggression'.[41]

However, in response to Iraqi forces entering the northern no-fly zone to intervene in a conflict between two rival Kurdish groups,[42] the US launched *Operation Desert Strike* on 3–4 September 1996 which consisted of cruise missile attacks against military targets in southern Iraq.[43] The US stated that it was in response to the Iraqi army's attack on, and seizure of, Kurdish-controlled areas 'despite clear warnings from the United States and the international community'.[44]

These strikes appeared to be a turning point in the support for the actions taken by the US in enforcement of the collective will. Indeed, whilst no meeting was

36 See, for example, UNSC Verbatim Record (11 August 1992) UN Doc. S/PV. 3105; UNSC Verbatim Record (23 November 1992) UN Doc. S/PV. 3139.

37 See, for example, *Kessing's* (1992) 38886.

38 See, for example, the incidents on 27 December 1992 (*Keesing's* (1992) 39247) and 17 January 1993 (*Keesing's* (1993) 39291).

39 See, for example, the incidents on 13 January 1993 (*Keesing's* (1993) 39291) and 19 August 1993 (*Keesing's* (1993) 39616).

40 See, for example, the incidents on 13 January 1993 (*Keesing's* (1993) 39291) and 18 April 1993 (*Keesing's* (1993) 39439).

41 See 'Press Release: Statement by the Russian Foreign Ministry' (14 January 1993) quoted in Weller, supra n. 27, 744–45.

42 *Keesing's* (1996) 41246.

43 *Keesing's* (1996) 41296–97.

44 UN Doc. S/1996/711 (3 September 1996).

held to discuss this issue by the UNSC or the UNGA, Russia, in letters to the UNSC, now denounced the action as unilateral, as a threat to Iraqi sovereignty and territorial integrity, and as a violation of international law.[45] It also labelled the air strikes 'an inappropriate and unacceptable reaction to the latest events in northern Iraq'.[46] There was reportedly further condemnation from those within the primary interpretive communities concerned with the UNSC, the UN Charter, and customary international law. For example, China,[47] the Arab League,[48] and even the normally pro-US states in the Arab world, such as Egypt, Jordan and Saudi Arabia expressed their disagreement with the action.[49] Indeed, this reaction from these states was a significant indicator of negative intersubjective agreement regarding the US's actions. Only the UK appeared to give its unreserved support for the US's response.[50]

The US further isolated itself from the consensus within the primary interpretive communities by announcing an extension of the southern no-fly zone from the 32nd to the 33rd parallel in 1999.[51] This led initially to France, the lead sponsor of Resolution 688 (1991), a key ally in establishing the safe havens and no-fly zones, and a member of the primary interpretive communities associated with the UNSC, the UN Charter and customary international law, refusing to patrol the extended area[52] and later to completely withdraw from the patrols.[53] Not only was France reportedly upset at the lack of consultation[54] but also that the original humanitarian purpose was no longer present.[55]

Although the US and UK were now isolated, they continued to take actions to such an extent that President George W. Bush in 2001 described them as 'a routine mission'.[56] Nevertheless, others within the primary interpretive communities

---

45 UN Doc. S/1996/712 (3 September 1996); UN Doc. S/1996/715 (4 September 1996).

46 C.R. Whitney, 'From Allies, U.S. Hears Mild Applause or Silence' *New York Times* (4 September 1996), A1.

47 Ibid.

48 A. Darwish, 'Arabs Refuse to Back US Strike' *The Independent* (4 September 1996), 22.

49 Ibid.

50 Ibid.

51 Ibid. For condemnation by the Arab League of the extension of the no-fly zone see UN Doc. S/1996/796 (26 September 1996).

52 *Keesing's* (1996) 41297. See also B. MacIntyre, 'France Refuses to Patrol Widened Iraq No-Fly Zone: Split Allies' *The Times* (6 September 1996), 15.

53 C. Truehart, 'French Military to Quit Patrols Over N. Iraq' *Washington Post* (28 December 1996), A1.

54 Whitney, supra n. 46.

55 C.R. Whitney, 'France to Pull its Planes out of Patrols Over Northern Iraq' *New York Times* (28 December 1996), A1.

56 J. Borger and R. Norton-Taylor, 'Allied Planes Bomb Baghdad' *The Guardian* (17 February 2001), 1. For the further actions taken see, for example: 3 November 1996

continued to condemn these actions taken in unilateral enforcement of the collective will all the way up to the invasion of Iraq in 2003.[57]

Operation Allied Force *in the Federal Republic of Yugoslavia: 1998–1999*

Although the background to the crisis was extensive,[58] in response to the killing of four Serb police officers by the Kosovo Liberation Army (KLA) in the disputed province of Kosovo in February 1998, Serb forces launched a violent crackdown against the Kosovo Albanians.[59]

In response to the crisis unfolding in Kosovo, the UNSC adopted resolutions 1160,[60] 1199,[61] and 1203.[62] They were all adopted under Chapter VII of the

---

(*Keesing's* (1996) 41393); 30 June 1998 (*Keesing's* (1998) 42369; 30 December 1998 (*Keesing's* (1998) 42700; J. Borger, 'New Iraqi Attack Brings US Strike' *The Guardian* (31 December 1998), 2); 7 January 1999 (*Keesing's* (1999) 42754–55; S. Myers, 'U.S. Jet Fires Missiles at an Iraqi Batter After Being Targeted' *New York Times* (8 January 1999), A8); 13 August 2000 (*Keesing's* (2000) 43723; B. Whitaker and J. Aglionby, 'US and Britain Resume Iraq Raids' *The Guardian* (14 August 2000), 2); 16 February 2001 (*Keesing's* (2001) 44026–27; M. Dejevsky, 'US and British Aircraft Bomb Iraqis' *The Independent* (17 February 2001), 1); 6 September 2002 (*Keesing's* (2002) 45005; J. Borger, 'One Year On: Strategy: Air Strikes On Iraq Rise Sharply: Increase Seen As Preparation For Winter Attack' *The Guardian* (7 September 2002), 4).

57 For example, strikes undertaken on 16 February 2001 received particularly widespread condemnation. See *Keesing's* (2001) 44026–27; J. Burke, K. Ahmed and E. Vulliamy, 'Blair and Bush Defy World Fury: Fresh Raids on Iraq Threatened as Outrage Grows' *The Observer* (18 February 2001), 1; R. Norton-Taylor and J. Borger, 'Saudi Arabia Denounces Iraq Strikes' *The Guardian* (22 February 2001), 15.

58 For a brief account of the background to this conflict see R. Wedgwood, 'NATO's Campaign in Yugoslavia' (1999) 93 *AJIL* 828, 828–29.

59 *Keesing's* (1998) 42156–57.

60 UNSC Res. 1160 (31 March 1998) UN Doc. S/RES/1160, calling for a political solution to the issue of Kosovo (para. 1), imposing an arms embargo on Yugoslavia (para. 8), and claiming that additional measures would be considered if progress was not made towards the peaceful resolution of the situation (para. 19).

61 UNSC Res. 1199 (23 September 1998) UN Doc. S/RES/1199, expressing concern regarding the intense fighting, the flow of refugees, the humanitarian situation, the impending humanitarian catastrophe, and the increasing violations of human rights and international humanitarian law (preamble), determining that the deterioration of the situation in Kosovo constituted a threat to peace and security in the region (preamble), demanding an end to hostilities (para. 1), and setting out measures to be taken by Yugoslavia (para. 4) that if were not taken would lead to the consideration of further action and additional measures (para. 16).

62 UNSC Res. 1203 (24 October 1998) UN Doc. S/RES/1203, reaffirming that primary responsibility for the maintenance of international peace and security is conferred on the UNSC (preamble), expressing concern at the continuing violation of Resolution 1160 (preamble), and the grave humanitarian situation and the impending humanitarian catastrophe (preamble), reaffirming that the situation constitutes a continuing threat to

UN Charter and condemned both the excessive use of force by Serbian forces and acts of terrorism by the KLA. Resolutions 1199 (1998) and 1203 (1998) also determined that the situation constituted a threat to peace and security in the region.[63] However, like Resolution 688 (1991), none of these resolutions authorized member states to use 'all necessary means' against the FRY in order to halt the humanitarian catastrophe that was unfolding in Kosovo. Nevertheless, the US, the UK, and NATO issued threats to use force against the FRY throughout 1998 and early 1999.[64]

Due to the negative stance of certain members of the UNSC towards the possible use of force against the FRY,[65] the focus moved to NATO. On 13 October 1998, the North Atlantic Council, NATO's decision-making body, issued activation orders for a phased air campaign in the FRY and limited air operations.[66]

A period of intense diplomatic pressure and peace talks followed which ended without the FRY signing a proposed peace agreement.[67] Furthermore, the FRY also appeared to intensify its offensive operations in Kosovo against the Kosovar Albanians, this intensification culminating in a tragedy in the market town of Raçak when 45 civilians were killed and 5,500 fled.[68]

Following this 'final warning bell',[69] and with the prospects for a peaceful resolution to the conflict diminishing, armed forces from member states of NATO began to assemble in the region[70] and, on 24 March 1999, commenced *Operation Allied Force*.[71] This was an air campaign against military targets within the FRY

---

peace and security in the region (preamble), and demanding full implementation of the agreements reached with NATO and the OSCE on the 15 and 16 October respectively concerning verification mechanisms established to monitor compliance with Resolution 1199 (para. 2).

63 UNSC Res. 1199, supra n. 61, preamble; UNSC Res. 1203, Ibid., preamble.

64 See, for example, W. Dinyon and G. Bone, 'Yeltsin Veto Threat Stalls Kosovo Raids' *The Times* (7 October 1998), 15; I. Butcher, 'NATO Warns Milosevic of Kosovo Air Strikes' *The Daily Telegraph* (25 July 1998), 19; D. Kritsiotis, 'The Kosovo Crisis and NATO's Application of Armed Force Against the Federal Republic of Yugoslavia' (2000) 49 *ICLQ* 330, 330–31. See Chapter 2 (n. 18) for more on threats to use force.

65 See infra *The Federal Republic of Yugoslavia: Security Council Resolutions 1160, 1199, and 1203.*

66 See the statement made to the press by the NATO Secretary-General. Available at http://www.nato.int/docu/speech/1998/s981013a.htm [Accessed: 15 January 2010]. See also http://www.nato.int/docu/speech/1999/ s990130a.htm [Accessed: 15 January 2010].

67 See, generally, M. Weller, 'The Rambouillet Conference on Kosovo' (1999) 75 *International Affairs* 211.

68 T. Whitaker, 'Belgrade's Link to Massacre' *The Independent* (29 January 1999), 13.

69 R.A. Falk, 'Kosovo, World Order, and the Future of International Law' (1999) 93 *AJIL* 847, 849.

70 K. Buchen and C. Dinmore, 'US Steps Up Pressure on Serbs and Ethnic Albanians' *The Financial Times* (22 February 1999), 14.

71 *Keesing's* (1999) 42845–49. S. Davisch, 'Massive Bombardment by NATO Smashes into Serb Air Defences' *The Independent* (25 March 1999), 3. For an account

with the aim of forcing Slobodan Milošević, the Yugoslav President, to halt the repression of the Kosovo Albanians and withdraw his troops from Kosovo. The bombing continued throughout April and May.[72] After Milošević accepted an EU proposed peace agreement on 4 June 1999 and began to withdraw troops from Kosovo,[73] the NATO Secretary-General, Javier Solana, announced a suspension of the 78-day operation on 10 June 1999.[74]

There was some ambivalence in the justifications offered by NATO and its member states as to the legal basis for the actions. At the UNSC meeting held on the day *Operation Allied Force* commenced, whilst only two of the acting or supporting states expressly claimed that the action was legal,[75] most deemed it 'necessary'[76] either to avert a 'humanitarian catastrophe'[77] or because of the FRY's refusal to act in compliance with UNSC resolutions.[78]

A justification for the actions of NATO of an established legal nature was never provided by the US. Like those of the majority of other NATO states, the US's justification revolved more around moral and political considerations as opposed to those of a legal nature. At the first UNSC meeting, the US asserted that:

> such action is necessary to respond to Belgrade's brutal persecution of Kosovar Albanians, violations of international law, excessive and indiscriminate use of

---

of the events leading up to the launching of *Operation Allied Force* see S.D. Murphy, 'Contemporary Practice of the United States' (1999) 93 *AJIL* 167–70 and 628–30.

72 *Keesing's* (1999) 42899–903 and 42955–61. No NATO ground troops were ever deployed.

73 *Keesing's* (1999) 43007. For the acceptance letter see UN Doc. S/1999/646 (4 June 1999).

74 UN Doc. S/1999/663 (10 June 1999); *Keesing's*, Ibid., 43013.

75 UNSC Verbatim Record (24 March 1999) UN Doc. S/PV. 3988. The Netherlands noted that 'the legal basis ... we have available in this case is more than adequate'. Ibid., Netherlands (8); the UK also stated that '[t]he action being taken is legal. It is justified as an exceptional measure to prevent an overwhelming humanitarian catastrophe'. Ibid., UK (12).

76 For example, the UK claimed that 'on the grounds of overwhelming humanitarian necessity, military intervention is legally justifiable'. Ibid., UK (12). See also US (4), Slovenia (6), Gambia (7), Netherlands (8), France (9), Malaysia (10), Argentina (11) and Slovenia (19).

77 The US claimed that '[w]e have begun today's action to avert this humanitarian catastrophe and to deter further aggression and repression in Kosovo'. Ibid., US (3). See also Canada (6), Bahrain (7), Netherlands (8), Malaysia (9), Argentina (11), Slovenia (6), UK (12), EU (16) and Albania (18).

78 A leading proponent of this basis was France which stated that '[t]he actions that have been decided upon are a response to the violation by Belgrade of its international obligations, which stem in particular from the Security Council resolutions adopted under Chapter VII of the United Nations Charter'. Ibid., France (9). See also Canada (5), Slovenia (6) and UK (11). Furthermore, Slovenia claimed that 'the action which is being undertaken will be carried out strictly within the substantive parameters established by the relevant Security Council resolutions'. Ibid., Slovenia (7).

> force, refusal to negotiate to resolve the issue peacefully and recent military build-up in Kosovo – all of which foreshadow a humanitarian catastrophe of immense proportions.[79]

Although the consensus among the acting and supporting states speaking in the primary interpretive community of the UNSC was that whilst the action was not strictly in conformity with the requirements of the collective security system the action was necessary nonetheless, some members of the community opposed the action and condemned it as 'aggression',[80] 'completely illegal',[81] and 'unlawful'.[82] Russia stated that it was 'profoundly outraged' at *Operation Allied Force* which was 'carried out in violation of the Charter of the United Nations and without the authorization of the Security Council'[83] whilst China, which was 'strongly opposed' to the action also clearly stated it viewed the action as 'a blatant violation of the United Nations Charter and of the accepted norms of international law'.[84] However, two days later at the UNSC meeting on 26 March 1999, a draft resolution sponsored by Russia condemning the use of force by NATO as a 'flagrant violation' of the UN Charter and which called for an immediate return to negotiations was heavily defeated.[85] Ultimately, although the general intersubjective agreement appeared to be favourable to the use of force on this occasion, this excluded two permanent members of the UNSC.

On 29 April 1999, the FRY had initiated proceedings in the ICJ against 10 NATO states demanding provisional measures to stop immediately the NATO air strikes.[86] The FRY essentially argued that the NATO states had violated the prohibition of the use of force and intervention in the internal affairs of a state in commencing *Operation Allied Force*.[87] Furthermore, it argued that there was no doctrine of humanitarian intervention in international law but, even if there was, the air strikes undertaken would not qualify.[88]

In responding to these charges, the NATO states did not venture into legal specifics in justifying their actions with most relying on the fact the FRY had

---

79 Ibid., US (4). See also the press briefing by US Department of State spokesman James P. Rubin (16 March 1999).

80 Ibid., Serbia (13) and Belarus (15).

81 Ibid., India (16) and Russia (3).

82 Ibid., Belarus (15).

83 Ibid., Russia (2).

84 Ibid., China (12).

85 See UN Doc. S/1999/328 (26 March 1999) (3(China, Namibia, Russia)-12(Argentina, Bahrain, Brazil, Canada, France, Gabon, Gambia, Malaysia, Netherlands, Slovenia, UK, US)-0).

86 *Legality of Use of Force Case* (Provisional Measures) [1999] ICJ Rep. 124. See, generally, C. Gray, 'Legality of Use of Force: Provisional Measures' (2000) 49 *ICLQ* 730.

87 Ibid.

88 Ibid.

initiated a 'humanitarian catastrophe'.[89] This was with the exception of Belgium which whilst maintaining that the operation was 'based on' the UNSC resolutions also went into some detail in setting out a doctrine of humanitarian intervention.[90] The US, after claiming the exhaustion of peaceful remedies, argued that *Operation Allied Force* was justified because of the humanitarian catastrophe, the acute threat posed to the security of neighbouring states, the serious violation of international humanitarian law and human rights, and the violation of the resolutions of the UNSC.[91] Ultimately, however, the FRY's request for provisional measures was refused on the ground of a lack of *prima facie* jurisdiction on the merits of the case thus preventing the ICJ, a significant actor within the secondary interpretive community, from pronouncing on the issue.[92]

The Unilateral Enforcement of the Collective Will Under International Law

Whilst the revival doctrine examined in Chapter 4 of this work was possessed of a detailed legal argument with intricate interpretive strategies linking the actions taken with prior express authorization and subsequent precedents, on this occasion the justification was far simpler, yet with the possibility of also having a far greater transformative, and perhaps destructive, impact upon the collective security system and the *jus ad bellum* more generally. Indeed, a clear picture emerged so that 'despite different ways of justification in detail, the acting states in principle claimed a right to unilateral enforcement of [the] collective will'.[93] This claimed right to enforce the collective will, both in terms of unilaterally enforcing the demands and obligations contained in UNSC resolutions and taking action to prevent a 'humanitarian catastrophe' will be examined in this section.

Unilateral Enforcement of Security Council Resolutions

The very basis of the doctrine of unilateral enforcement of the collective will is that the UNSC has not granted express permission for such enforcement action in a resolution. Indeed, '[n]one of the resolutions on which military actions against Iraq and the FRY were, in whole or in part based, provided authority for those actions'.[94] In this case, 'the intervening states have invoked the argument that they are acting on behalf of the "international community". The Security Council

89 Ibid.

90 Ibid.

91 Statement of David P. Andrews, Legal Adviser, US Department of State, 'Legality of the Use of Force (*Yugoslavia v United States of America*)' CR 99/24 (11 May 1999).

92 The Court later decided that it had no jurisdiction to determine the case. See [2004] ICJ Rep. 279.

93 Krisch, supra n. 2, 60.

94 White, supra n. 2, 32.

resolutions represent the will of the international community and the states are enforcing that will'.[95] The problem with this doctrine is that it contradicts the now embedded technique and procedure within the UNSC whereby when it is to delegate its collective powers of enforcement to individual member states this is done so through the adoption of a resolution authorizing the use of 'all necessary means'.[96] This technique possesses a common understanding and agreement among the interpretive communities that the will of the UNSC is to be enforced.[97]

Consequently, in examining the text of the resolutions more generally it is hard to make the claim that other provisions or language contained within them provided similar authority. For example, an argument based upon their adoption under Chapter VII of the UN Charter or their determination of either a 'threat to the peace', a 'breach of the peace' or an 'act of aggression' is untenable.[98] Such a determination is to affirm the UNSC's role in the situation and remove the barrier of the domestic jurisdiction clause contained in Article 2(7) of the UN Charter rather than to provide a basis for making the argument of authorization. In any case, none of the acting states or members of the primary interpretive community in any of the incidents discussed in this chapter made the argument that a determination of a 'threat to the peace' should be interpreted as an authorization of the use of force, thus confirming no shift in, or additions to, the embedded common understandings regarding the use of force under the auspices of the UNSC.

However, under the methodology adopted in this work, whilst it has been demonstrated that common understandings of certain terms can become embedded in the practice and discourse of the UNSC, it is not the text of a resolution or the language of the aims contained within it which is of paramount importance but rather the intersubjective interpretation provided to it by the primary interpretive community. This is where the focus of this chapter will turn to.

Iraq: Security Council Resolution 688 (1991) Whilst it might be thought that the US resorted to the doctrine of unilateral enforcement of the collective will on this occasion due to the impossibility of obtaining a resolution authorizing the use of all necessary means stemming from a threat to veto such a proposal,[99] at the meeting where Resolution 688 (1991) was adopted the use of force to enforce its provisions was not something that those within the primary interpretive

95 Ibid., 34. See supra n. 13 for an occasion where members of the primary interpretive community have made this claim in the UNSC.

96 See, generally, Chapter 3.

97 Ibid.

98 These are determinations under Article 39 – the 'gateway' provision to Chapter VII of the UN Charter. See Chapter 3. As Lobel and Ratner note, '[i]mplied Security Council authorization to use force is often inferred from the Council's condemnation of a nation's action as a threat to the peace'. See Lobel and Ratner, supra n. 15, 134.

99 Most significantly from China. See supra *The Establishment and Defence of the Safe Havens and No-Fly Zones in Iraq: 1991–2002.*

community of the UNSC were concerned with.[100] Indeed, the main concern was more in connection with the general intervention by the UNSC in the internal affairs of Iraq, hence the resolution not being expressly adopted under Chapter VII,[101] than about any fears regarding the utilization of the resolution by individual states to justify the use of force. Much of the debate centred on whether this was a situation that genuinely posed a threat to international peace and security,[102] the applicability of Article 2(7) of the UN Charter,[103] and the competence of the UNSC to handle a situation which concerned human rights issues.[104] Indeed, upon the resolution's adoption, no member of the primary interpretive community raised the issue of enforcement of its provisions.[105]

However, subsequent practice under the resolution in the years after its adoption in some respects blurred the line between an express authorization and an implied authorization. As described above, no member of the UNSC which had voted for Resolution 688 (1991) publicly challenged the view advanced by the US that the basis for *Operation Provide Comfort* was that it was 'consistent with' this resolution.[106] Although there was much initial support for the enforcement of the of the resolution through forcible means on this occasion, given that this occurred after the embedding of the common understanding regarding the authorization technique, those offering this support were arguably aware of the formal illegality of the actions undertaken. That is, it is unlikely that members of the primary interpretive community connected with interpreting the competence and resolutions of the UNSC believed that an

100 See UNSC Verbatim Record (5 April 1991) UN Doc. S/PV. 2982.

101 Although it has been asserted that for a Chapter VII resolution to come into existence this does not have to have been expressly stated and the fact the UNSC has determined a threat to international peace and security is sufficient. See Malanczuk, supra n. 20, 128.

102 UN Doc. S/PV. 2982, supra n. 105, Turkey (4–5), Pakistan (9), Iran (13–15), Romania (23), Yemen (27), Ecuador (36), Zaire (38), France (53), China (56), US (57), USSR (59–60), UK (64–5), Belgium (67), Italy (69–70), Germany (71), Luxembourg (74–75), Denmark (78), Spain (81), Sweden (82), Netherlands (86) and Canada (92).

103 Ibid., Turkey (6), Pakistan (9), Iraq (17), Romania (23), Yemen (27), Zimbabwe (31), Ecuador (33–35), Zaire (38), Cuba (42), China (56), US (58), USSR (61), India (63), UK (64–65) and Sweden (83).

104 Ibid., Yemen (28–30), Zimbabwe (31), Ecuador (36), Cuba (46) and India (63).

105 Krisch notes that 'no intention to use force was expressed … during the debates in the Council, and therefore no argument is available for an interpretation in favour of its authorization'. See Krisch, supra n. 2, 78.

106 N. Rodley, 'Collective Intervention to Protect Human Rights and Civilian Populations: The Legal Framework' in N. Rodley (ed.), *To Loose the Bands of Wickedness: International Intervention in Defence of Human Rights* (London: Brassey's, 1992), 14, 33. See supra *The Establishment and Defence of the Safe Havens and No-Fly Zones in Iraq: 1991–2002*. Although Iraq did explicitly reject the contention 'that Resolution 688 authorized them to engage in such obvious military intervention in the internal affairs of Iraq and to violate its territorial integrity. This claim could not be further from the truth, and the resolution does not grant any party any such authorization'. UN Doc. S/22599 (14 May 1991).

express right existed under the *jus ad bellum* which permitted the acting states to use force on this occasion, perhaps reflected in the fact that no claim was made that the actions were lawful under the *lex lata.*[107]

From this reaction, it is arguable that the primary determinant of initial acceptability of action, and thus a potential impact upon the law, is not simply the text of a resolution, but the intersubjective understanding connected with its aims and overall general purpose in the context in which it was adopted and in which the actions are taken. It must be remembered that the UNSC is a political, not a legal, organ with no *stare decisis*. As Georg Nolte has claimed, the question of whether UNSC resolutions provide the basis for the use of force 'must, in the absence of another decision by the Council, be determined by the traditional means of dialogue within the community of member states'.[108] Certainly, whilst no statements were made at its adoption that the resolution, or certain terms contained within it, authorized the use of force, as was the case with Resolution 678 (1990), this does not mean that an understanding could not have begun to emerge that it did. For example, whilst 'much depends on the preservation of "shared understandings", i.e. how a representative group of states interprets the Charter and individual Security Council resolutions',[109] this does not mean that they are fixed. Rather, they are open to change.[110]

Under the methodology adopted in this work, due to the US operating within the intersubjective agreement of the primary interpretive community of the UNSC at this time, it was arguably not acting unilaterally, that is, at this time the US was not engaging in a *unilateral* enforcement of the collective will. Indeed, although it did not have an authorizing resolution it was still acting with the unofficial permission of this organ. However, maintaining this position and opening up the possibility of an impact upon the *jus ad bellum* by the subsequent practice embedding new common understandings depended upon the acting states continuing to operate in good faith. The presence of good faith essentially comes down to there being a general consensus that action is necessary between the acting state(s) and the primary interpretive community.[111] This, however, is easily lost once the

107 The necessity surrounding the actions no doubt stemmed from the fact that they were taking place within the 'Iraq context' which was prevailing at the time. See Chapter 4 for more on what has been described in this work as the 'Iraq context'. Even though Iraq 'opposed' the intervention, it appeared to accept the necessity by claiming that it was 'not opposed to the provision of humanitarian assistance to Iraqi citizens who are in need of it'. UN Doc. S/22513 (22 April 1991).

108 G. Nolte, 'The Limits of the Security Council's Powers and its Functions in the International Legal System: Some Reflections' in M. Byers (ed.), *The Role of Law in International Politics* (Oxford: Oxford University Press, 2000), 315, 319.

109 Ibid.

110 An analogy can be made here with how domestic law changes with changing values or the common law evolves to meet new situations.

111 As Symes notes, '[a] truly international problem cannot be declared as such unilaterally; the states which make up that community must perceive the situation as warranting a response'. Symes, supra n. 10, 601.

community perceives a shift in the objectives of the acting state(s) from enforcing the collective will to enforcing its own subjective will, even if the acting state(s) believes that its actions are sincere and necessary.

In this case, by the time of *Operation Desert Strike* and the extension of the southern no-fly zone in 1996 '[t]he international community clearly viewed the situation differently than the United States'.[112] Indeed, any general consensus of necessity as to enforcement of the collective will on this occasion, despite technical illegality, started to wane once action began to be taken solely by the US, that is, when the US began to resort to unilateral tendencies rather than operating and consulting with the coalition partners in taking collective action that was the hallmark of the initial years of the safe havens and no-fly zones.[113] This meant that the US went 'from unity to polarization' in its claims to enforce the collective will[114] and had consequently overstepped the boundaries of intersubjective agreement thus dissolving the collective basis under which it had acted.

Whilst up to this point the US was not acting unilaterally, the fact that it was seen to have begun to act outside of the boundaries of intersubjective agreement also highlights that a right to *unilaterally* enforce the collective will was not something that the primary interpretive community of the UNSC was willing to endorse. This was about whether the primary interpretive community was willing to permit resolutions of this organ to be enforced without its agreement. If it had emerged that they were willing to permit this to become a right and a principle under the *jus ad bellum* then this would have widened the prohibition of the use of force due to an additional exception having arisen rather than simply the procedure of the UNSC by which it uses force having changed. That is, the balance would have swung too far in favour of unilateralism as the decision of when to use force would have been entirely in the hands of individual states. Had the primary interpretive community of the UNSC demonstrated positive intersubjective agreement as to this possibility it would not have ended there. Indeed, given the substantive widening of

---

112 Ibid., 601. The fear is that if states are consistently seen to act in bad faith this leads to the removal of incentives for cooperation in the UNSC and general mistrust amongst its members. Indeed, 'it would be very difficult for the Security Council to adopt any sort of resolution at all, if the very fact of the expression of the "will" of the Council were taken to imply a mandate to enforce it militarily'. See M. Weller, 'The US, Iraq and the Use of Force in a Unipolar World' (1999–2000) 41 *Survival* 81, 89. See also Krisch, supra n. 2, 94; White, supra n. 2, 654–55.

113 The importance of 'consultation' in measures taken for the maintenance of international peace and security in the UN system without the agreement contained in Article 43 in place that would have provided the UNSC with its own standing army is stressed by Article 106 of the Charter. In this situation the provision provides that the five permanent members of the UNSC shall 'consult with one another and … with other Members of the United Nations with a view to such joint action on behalf of the Organization as may be necessary for the purpose of maintaining international peace and security'.

114 An idea put forward by Christine Gray in 'From Unity to Polarisation: International Law and the Use of Force against Iraq' (2002) 13 *EJIL* 1.

the exception of the use of force under the auspices of the UNSC and therefore the potential impact upon the prohibition of the use of force, this would have required the intersubjective agreement of the primary interpretive communities connected with the UN Charter and customary international law. However, given the negative intersubjective agreement of the primary interpretive community of the UNSC on this occasion as to this possibility, it was not necessary to look further. The question is whether NATO's intervention in Kosovo a few years later was to change this.

The Federal Republic of Yugoslavia: Security Council Resolutions 1160, 1199 and 1205 (1998) In the first meeting on the situation in March 1998 when Resolution 1160 (1998) was adopted, many within the primary interpretive community on this occasion stressed that the human rights violations that had taken place brought the situation onto the international stage and was thus a threat to *international* peace and security.[115] Whilst the possible use of force was not an issue at this point, this had changed six weeks later at the adoption of Resolution 1199 (1998). In the meeting of the primary interpretive community before its adoption only Russia, China, the UK and the US spoke, that is four of the five permanent members. Russia made it clear that it favoured a 'settlement of the conflict in Kosovo exclusively through peaceful and political means'[116] and that '[n]o use of force and no sanctions [were] being imposed by the Council at the present stage'.[117] In contrast, the US asserted the necessity of action, if not the legality, by claiming that '[p]lanning at the North Atlantic Treaty Organization for military operations if these efforts do not succeed is nearing completion. The international community will not stand idly by as the situation in Kosovo deteriorates'.[118]

This division over the possible use of force continued and, just a month later, in the meeting before the adoption of the final resolution before the commencement of *Operation Allied Force*, Resolution 1205 (1998), the issue of the use of force received much attention from the primary interpretive community.[119] Whilst the US now maintained that '[t]he NATO allies, in agreeing on 13 October to the use of force, made it clear that they had the authority, the will and the means to resolve this issue'[120] it was not so clear where it gained the stated authority from.

Although some considered NATO to be a regional organization, or as Brazil put it, a 'non-universal organism', and therefore one that required UNSC authorization prior to resorting to force,[121] others simply claimed that that this threat to use

115 UNSC Verbatim Record (31 March 1998) UN Doc. S/PV. 3868, Japan (3), Costa Rica (3), France (4), Sweden (5), Slovenia (7), Portugal (10), UK (12), US (13), EU (14), Germany (19), Turkey (21), Hungary (25) and Bosnia and Herzegovina (28). Those opposing this view were Russia (10), China (11), Serbia (16) and Ukraine (29).

116 UNSC Verbatim Record (23 September 1998) UN Doc. S/PV. 3930, Russia (3).

117 Ibid.

118 Ibid., US (5).

119 UNSC Verbatim Record (24 October 1998) UN Doc. S/PV. 3937.

120 Ibid., US (15).

121 Ibid., Brazil (10–11).

force 'violated the purposes, principles and relevant provisions of the United Nations Charter, as well as international law and widely acknowledged norms governing relations between states' as the 'decision was made unilaterally, without *consulting* the Security Council *or* seeking its *authorization*'.[122] Indeed, as described above in connection with Resolution 688 (1991), it appeared that the decisive issue was not simply that none of the resolutions authorized the use of force, but that there had been a lack of consultation and no intersubjective agreement amongst the primary interpretive community including these members that the use of force was necessary as was the case in the earlier stages of the establishment and defence of the safe havens and no-fly zones in Iraq.[123] Furthermore, Russia and China, two permanent members of this community, were clear that the text of Resolution 1205 (1998), and the agreement within the UNSC as to its interpretation, was such that it did not contain any provisions which could or should be interpreted as providing authority for the use of force.[124]

What is clear from the debates over the resolutions and the commencement of *Operation Allied Force* is that, whereas in the Iraq context the intersubjective agreement within the primary interpretive community shifted over time, in the context of the use of force in Kosovo although there was a majority in agreement over the use of force this did not include two of the five permanent members. Indeed, the idea of force, and the use of force itself, proved to be divisive within this community.[125] However, whilst a sharp break was being proposed to the collective security system, and the relatively new authorization technique, it was done so by NATO and the US was not alone at one pole of a polarized community as it was in the second half of the decade-long period of forcible measures against Iraq. Indeed, in this incident, some of the states that opposed the latter enforcement of the no-fly zones were in fact supportive of the operations in Kosovo.[126]

---

122 Ibid., China (14) (emphasis added). See also Russia (12). For threats see Chapter 2 (n. 18).

123 See supra *The Establishment and Defence of the Safe Havens and No-Fly Zones in Iraq: 1991–2002.*

124 Russia confirmed that '[e]nforcement elements have been excluded from the draft resolution, and there are no provisions in it that would directly or indirectly sanction the automatic use of force'. UN Doc. S/PV. 3937, supra n. 119, Russia (11). See also Russia (12). China similarly asserted that '[w]e believe that the resolution just adopted does not entail any authorization to use force or to threaten to use force against the Federal Republic of Yugoslavia, nor should it in any way be interpreted as authorizing the use of force or threatening to use force against the Federal Republic of Yugoslavia'. Ibid., China (14).

125 Although on the basis of the debates within the UNSC and the failed draft resolution proposed by Russia it could be claimed that 60 per cent were in favourable agreement over the action taken. See Chapter 2 for more on discerning intersubjective agreement within the UNSC.

126 A notable example was France.

Given this position from the outset, with a majority in agreement over the necessity of action but clear statements from some permanent members ruling out a forcible interpretation of the resolutions, questions arise as to whether the UNSC was functioning as originally intended by not authorizing the use of force on this occasion, or whether, on the contrary, it had failed to act in the face of a humanitarian catastrophe. Indeed, whilst none of the acting or supporting states expressly argued that the actions found a legal basis in the resolutions preceding them, the argument was framed more in terms of the fact that given the situation, the UNSC had failed in its responsibility to maintain international peace and security in failing to enforce these previous resolutions.

Question marks also surrounded whether this incident was to have an impact upon future occasions of the use of force under the auspices of the UNSC. As Vera Gowlland-Debbas noted at the time, the key question is 'whether, in the face of the inadequacy or paralysis of such mechanisms, there is room for non-collectively authorized unilateral action for the execution of collective *decisions*, and the extent to which such unauthorized unilateral measures can constitute precedents which impact upon the evolution of the United Nations Charter'.[127]

It is clear that the UN Charter grants the UNSC primary responsibility for maintaining international peace and security.[128] Indeed, the importance of this organ was stressed by the primary interpretive community in the UNSC meetings.[129] The fact that resolutions of this organ to this day almost always clearly state that it has decided to 'remain seized of the matter' could be described as an indirect reflection of the intersubjective agreement regarding this issue.[130] Whilst some scholars within the secondary interpretive community have previously argued that a failure by the UNSC to act provides grounds for states to take unilateral action,[131] on this occasion attempts at diluting the authority of the UNSC as it is found in the UN Charter were made by some of those within the primary interpretive community. For example, it was argued that '[t]he responsibility of the Security Council for international peace and security is a primary responsibility ... not an exclusive responsibility' so that its authority in this field depended 'on its ability to develop

127 V. Gowlland-Debbas, 'The Limits of Unilateral Enforcement of the Community Objectives in the Framework of Peace Maintenance' (2000) 11 *EJIL* 361, 366.

128 UN Charter (1945), Article 24(1). See also Chapter 3.

129 UN Doc. S/PV. 3937, supra n. 119, Brazil (11) and Costa Rica (7). UN Doc. S/PV. 3988, supra n. 75, Malaysia stressed that the use of force should be 'sanctioned by the Security Council, which has been vested with primary responsibility for the maintenance of international peace and security'. See Malaysia (9–10). See also Belarus (15), India (16), Russia (3), Gambia (7), China (12) and Serbia (13).

130 Two states referred to this in the FRY context. See UNSC Verbatim Record (31 March 1998) UN Doc. S/PV. 3868, Slovenia (9) and Bosnia and Herzegovina (28). This phrase formed the last paragraph of the resolutions in connection to Kosovo. See UNSC Res. 1160, supra n. 61, para. 20; UNSC Res. 1199, supra n. 62, para. 17; UNSC Res. 1205, supra n. 63, para. 6.

131 See, for example, W.M. Reisman, 'Coercion and Self-determination: Construing Charter Article 2(4)' (1984) 78 *AJIL* 642.

policies that will make it worthy of the authority it has under the Charter'.[132] On this occasion, it was claimed the organ had not proved its worth.

However, under the system as it stood at the time of *Operation Allied Force*, the fact that even a single permanent member disagreed with the proposed action was sufficient to prevent an authorizing resolution from being adopted. As Nigel White remarked, at the time of *Operation Allied Force*, even '[a]ssuming that the Security Council was being blocked by an illegitimate threat of the veto in a situation that clearly warranted Security Council authorized military action, it is still not legally permissible for states to take it upon themselves, whether in the forum of another organization or not, to enforce those resolutions'.[133] As the UN Charter expressly requires, 'decisions' by the UNSC to use force must have the agreement of the permanent members.[134] It would therefore be disingenuous to argue that simply because there is agreement amongst a majority in the UNSC in favour of the use of force that this can override the wishes of a single permanent member.

Not all resolutions are meant to be enforced and if they are this is for the UNSC to determine and to delegate its powers accordingly in the form of an authorizing resolution or, on the precedent of the early stages of the safe havens and no-fly zones in Iraq, for clear positive intersubjective agreement to be present regarding their enforcement. The whole point behind the contemporary collective security system as envisaged was to grant certain states the ability to prevent actions which they disagreed with from proceeding. This is perfectly lawful under the system established in 1945 and still pertained at the time of launching *Operation Allied Force*. Consequently, under the system as it stood, any arguments that *Operation Allied Force* had a legal basis in the resolutions of the UNSC had no standing *lex lata*.

However, the support for this operation has to be acknowledged. Intersubjective agreement emerged among a majority within the primary interpretive community that force was necessary on this occasion based partly upon the resolutions that had been passed. It is arguable if it had not have been for the objection of Russia and China forcible action would have received a green light through the invocation of the authorization technique. Consequently, the question remains as to whether *Operation Allied Force* left the door open to future uses of force to enforce UNSC resolutions outside of the agreement of the permanent members.

Given the permanent status of the objecting members of the primary interpretive community on this occasion, an express formal modification of the UN Charter text to reflect such a change would not be possible.[135] However, as Chapter 3 demonstrated, there are ways of informally modifying the UN Charter. The

132 UN Doc. S/PV. 3988, supra n. 75, Slovenia (19). For a more restrained version of this argument see Netherlands (8).

133 White, supra n. 2, 41.

134 UN Charter (1945), Articles 27(3) and 39–42.

135 Article 108 of the UN Charter states: 'Amendments to the present Charter shall come into force for all Members of the United Nations when they have been adopted by a vote of two thirds of the members of the General Assembly and ratified in accordance

development of the authorization technique was not strictly speaking in accordance with the provisions of Chapter VII of the Charter. Indeed, these provisions are largely based around the UNSC having a standing army and a fully functioning Military Staff Committee.[136] When it was realized that these elements of the envisaged collectively security system were not going to be a reality, a functional interpretation of the procedural competence of the UNSC was provided to enable this organ to carry out its primary responsibility.[137]

Changing interpretations of international law often emerge through its violation. One cannot rule out that a similar, albeit more groundbreaking, functional interpretation will be made in the future so that whilst the use of force will still be under the auspices of the UNSC through the intersubjective agreement of the members of this community, the agreement of the permanent members will no longer be required in decisions to use force. Such a development would of course destroy 'the legal right to control the use of force on behalf of the UN through the exercise of the veto in the Security Council'.[138] Given that the US is one of the gendarmes of this right, its demise may be one of the unintended consequences of its actions in *Operation Allied Force*. However, if this procedure is to change, settled positive general intersubjective agreement must be discernible. As the final section of this chapter demonstrates, as yet there is no evidence to suggest such agreement has emerged in any of these communities in this respect. Furthermore, as Chapter 4 noted in connection with the 'revival' doctrine, the UNSC has taken care to tighten up the wording of its resolutions to prevent a further occasion from arsising when this form of the unilateral enforcement of the collective will could be employed. Overall, the procedures of the UNSC, including the necessity of the agreement of the permanent members, have remained intact.

In any case, if the UNSC is prevented from taking action through an authorizing resolution or positive intersubjective agreement, the power to act arguably falls upon the General Assembly.[139] In fact, the point has been made that the UNGA actually has greater claim to represent the collective will than the UNSC, especially in the field of human rights: 'if any forum can legitimately claim to represent or indeed embody the international community, then it has to be the General Assembly of the UN. The General Assembly not only has subsidiary competence in the field of collective security, it has primary competence in issues of human rights'.[140]

---

with their respective constitutional processes by two thirds of the Members of the United Nations, *including all the permanent members of the Security Council*' (emphasis added).

136 UN Charter (1945), Articles 43–47.

137 See, generally, Chapter 3.

138 Weller, supra n. 112, 89.

139 Ibid. Indeed, 'the reference to "primary responsibility" for peace and security in article 24(1) relates to the division of competence within the UN – it is the General Assembly, and also to a lesser extent, the International Court of Justice, two other principal organs of the UN, that have subsidiary competence in the field of international peace and security, not states acting unilaterally or multilaterally'. White, supra n. 2, 29.

140 White, Ibid., 38.

The fact that the members of the primary interpretive community of the UNSC which were in favour of the use of force on this occasion did not resort to the body which has primary competence in the field of human rights and which arguably represents the true collective will is questionable. Indeed, the procedure to utilize the UNGA in this respect, under the Uniting for Peace resolution, has been in place since 1950.[141] However, the fact that they did not utilize it is perhaps indicative of an emerging belief amongst these states that they themselves outside of the context of any organ of the UN or resolutions adopted by them now have the authority to take such forcible action in protection of human rights so that that the resolutions of the UNSC were merely supportive of the invocation of a right of unilateral humanitarian intervention on this occasion. It is to this possibility that this chapter now turns.

The Unilateral Use of Force for Humanitarian Purposes

From a reading of the preamble and the purposes and principles of the UN in Articles 1 and 2 of the UN Charter, it becomes clear that the two priorities of the Organization are the prevention of war and the protection of human rights. It is not, however, immediately apparent which should take priority and no form of hierarchy appears to have been established.[142] However, upon further reading it is noticeable that whereas the prohibition of the use of force is of a clear and obligatory character, the human rights provisions are more hortatory, promotional, and aspirational in nature.[143] Furthermore, it is traditionally contended by actors within the secondary interpretive community that countermeasures in response to violations of human rights obligations must not involve the unilateral threat or use of force.[144] However, as this is not expressly stated in the Charter but is the way in which it has been traditionally interpreted it is possible that with subsequent practice by the primary interpretive community of all states, and in light of an increasing concern over human rights, these provisions may be reinterpreted

141 Ibid., 38–41. See also A. Pellet, 'Brief Remarks on the Unilateral Use of Force' (2000) 11 *EJIL* 385, 390.

142 Indeed, Valek argues that '[t]he text and structure of the Charter ... do not provide any basis for the hierarchy, except that the maintenance of international peace and security is mentioned first'. See P. Valek, 'Is Unilateral Humanitarian Intervention Compatible with the UN Charter' (2004–05) 26 *Mich.J.Int'l L.* 1223, 1239.

143 For example, whilst Article 2(4) requires all member states to 'refrain' from the threat or use of force, Article 1(3) talks of 'promoting and encouraging respect for human rights' and Article 55 states that the UN 'shall promote universal respect for, and observance of, human rights'. For more on Article 2(4) see Chapter 2.

144 The ICJ stated in the *Nicaragua* case that 'the use of force could not be the appropriate method to monitor or ensure ... respect for [human rights]'. See *Case Concerning Military and Paramilitary Activities in and against Nicaragua (Nicaragua v United States of America)* (Merits) [1984] ICJ Rep. 14, para. 268. See also B. Simma, 'NATO, the UN and the Use of Force: Legal Aspects' (1999) 10 *EJIL* 1; J. Charney, 'Anticipatory Humanitarian Intervention in Kosovo' (1999) 93 *AJIL* 834, 835.

along with a modification of customary international law. However, whilst it is possible that the prohibition of the use of force may give way to forcible unilateral countermeasures in response to massive human rights violations, subsequent practice between 1945 and 1989 was not indicative of such a change.

The main candidates as examples of forcible unilateral intervention for humanitarian purposes in the period between the adoption of the UN Charter and the end of the Cold War include India's intervention in East Pakistan (Bangladesh) in 1971,[145] Vietnam's intervention in Cambodia (Kampuchea) in 1978–79,[146] and Tanzania's intervention in Uganda in 1979.[147] Although humanitarian concerns found their way into the justifications of the acting states on these occasions, an express and independent right to intervene for humanitarian purposes was not specifically advanced. Whilst any '*reliance* by a state on a novel right or an unprecedented exception to the principle might, if shared in principle by other states, tend toward a modification of customary international law',[148] reliance in these cases was placed more upon the justification of self-defence, the principle exception to the prohibition of the use of force.[149] This reliance on an established exception limits any impact the invocation of humanitarian concerns may have had upon the law.[150] Consequently, whilst it is at least arguable that the actions had a positive humanitarian outcome, a new interpretation of the prohibition of the use of force or the development of a distinct exception to it did not appear to be the aim of the acting states. Indeed, practice in this context has not been nearly as clear and unambiguous as would be necessary to reinterpret or modify the prohibition of the use of force.[151]

Nevertheless, '[t]he absence of the express invocation of the right by states did not, however, deter some writers from arguing that all or some of the above

145 See (1971) *UNYB* 146.

146 See *Keesing's* (1979) 29613.

147 See *Keesing's* (1979) 29669–73.

148 See *Nicaragua Case*, supra n. 144, para. 207 (emphasis added).

149 See Chapter 6 for more on this right.

150 The ICJ in the *Nicaragua* case hinted at such a proposition: 'The Court concludes that the argument derived from the preservation of human rights in Nicaragua cannot afford a legal justification for the conduct of the United States, and cannot in any event be reconciled with the legal strategy of the respondent state, which is based on the right of collective self-defence'. See *Nicaragua Case*, supra n. 144, para. 268. Indeed, such absence of reliance 'speaks volumes' for the legal quality attributed to the doctrine by states. See P. Hilpold, 'Humanitarian Intervention: Is There a Need for a Legal Reappraisal?' (2001) 12 *EJIL* 437, 444–45.

151 Krisch has noted that 'states indeed do not appear to have consistently claimed a right to humanitarian intervention, although this would have been indispensable in order for such a right to emerge'. Krisch, supra n. 2, 63. Sean Murphy also found little or no support for the doctrine in his extensive study of the issue. See S. Murphy, *Humanitarian Intervention: The United Nations in an Evolving World Order* (Philadelphia: University of Pennsylvania Press, 1996), 366 and 387.

episodes were actually part of state practice supporting a legal right to humanitarian intervention because the states using force *should have* or *could have* used this justification'.[152] Whilst some writing within the secondary interpretive community have indeed used these as precedents for the emergence of such a right under discussion,[153] for the reasons outlined above it is clear that their claims lie more in *lex ferenda* than *lex lata* and based more upon ideology than upon law. Indeed, in 1986, many years after the occurrence of these incidences, the UK rejected the existence of such a right under international law:

> … the *overwhelming* majority of contemporary legal opinion comes down against the existence of a right of humanitarian intervention, for three main reasons: first, the UN Charter and the corpus of modern international law do not seem specifically to incorporate such a right; secondly, state practice in the past two centuries, and especially since 1945, at best provides only a handful of genuine cases of humanitarian intervention, and, on most assessments, *none at all*; and finally, on prudential grounds, that the scope for abusing such a right argues strongly against its creation. … In essence, therefore, the case against making humanitarian intervention an exception to the principle of non-intervention is that its doubtful benefits would be heavily outweighed by its costs in terms of respect for international law… the best case that can be made in support of humanitarian intervention is that it cannot be said to be unambiguously illegal.[154]

Whilst not publishing a similar statement, this position has been echoed by the US which 'has consistently rejected the idea that [humanitarian intervention] is a sufficient, independent basis for using force other than in hostage rescues'.[155]

It appears that the reticence amongst states to rely on a doctrine of humanitarian intervention has been maintained since. Indeed, whilst the US claimed that it was 'motivated by humanitarian concerns' in establishing the safe-havens in Iraq and resorted to similar arguments in subsequently defending the no-fly zones[156] and had what appeared as the aversion of a 'humanitarian catastrophe' as one of its principle justifications for *Operation Allied Force*, the fact that the US resorted to vague and multiple justifications for its uses of force was a clear indicator that it still believed that humanitarian intervention was not an independent legal

---

152 C. Gray, 'The Legality of NATO's Military Action in Kosovo: Is There a Right of Humanitarian Intervention' in W. Tieva and S. Yee (eds), *International Law in the Post-Cold War World* (London: Routledge, 2000) 240, 252.

153 See, for example, R. Wedgwood, 'NATO's Campaign in Yugoslavia' (1999) 93 *AJIL* 828, 833; A. D'Amato, 'Trashing Customary International Law' (1987) 81 *AJIL* 101, 101.

154 UK Foreign Office Policy Document No. 148. See 'UK Materials in International Law' (1986) 57 *BYIL* 614, 619 (emphasis added).

155 A. Sofaer, 'International Law and Kosovo' (2000) 36 *Stan.J.Int'l L.* 1, 18.

156 Indeed, '[t]he primary justifications for the intervention put forth by the United States were grounded in humanitarian concerns'. See Symes, supra n. 10, 592.

basis for using force. Whilst other coalition partners and members of the primary interpretive community argued for the *legality* as opposed to the *necessity* of humanitarian intervention, this was a minority view, at least expressly.[157] The fact that even the acting states did not rely on this expressly as a 'right' and under what appeared fertile grounds to do so, militates against a finding of *opinio juris* as to this as a legal basis. Indeed, it is unclear how these justifications can modify the prohibition of the use of force in both its treaty and customary forms.[158] As Casten Stahn correctly notes:

> even if one refuses to recognize Article 2(4) as a norm of *jus cogens* ... recourse to the Council has not become optional. The practice of the permanent Council members in the cases of Kosovo and Iraq may have special significance for the development and future interpretation of the Charter framework. But it has been neither widespread nor consistent enough to crystallize criteria that would be so broadly accepted as to permit the enforcement of the collective will without explicit Council authorization under customary international law.[159]

Furthermore, even if one was to take the invocation of humanitarian concern as an implicit claim to a right of humanitarian intervention, the fact remains that it was not thought sufficient to support the use of force in its pure form. Indeed, it was only relied upon in conjunction with the fact that the UNSC had already expressed concern about the situation and imposed obligations upon the delinquent state concerned. Just as any claim to the emergence of a right of humanitarian intervention in light of the interventions during the Cold War era is stymied by the fact that the states relied on self-defence as the legal basis for their actions, in the context of Iraq and the FRY, the joint reliance on sentiments expressed in UNSC resolutions undermines the argument for a new right to humanitarian intervention.[160] Indeed, it could be argued that claims to such a right are in fact less tenable after the Iraq and Kosovo crises than before them. As Nico Krisch remarks, '[t]hese claims to a right to use force in order to ensure compliance with Security Council resolutions imply

---

157 A leading proponent of this view was the UK which has, since making the statement in 1986, reverted to arguing for the legality of the doctrine. However, this again appears to be a claim of *lex ferenda*. For example, in the UK Attorney-General's advice on the war in Iraq in 2003 he noted cautiously that '[t]he use of force to avert an overwhelming humanitarian catastrophe *has been emerging* as a further, and exceptional, basis for the use of force'. See 'Attorney General's Advice on the Iraq War: Resolution 1441' (2005) 54 *ICLQ* 767, para. 4 (emphasis added). He also concedes that '[t]he doctrine remains controversial'. Ibid. Belgian was not so coy in its arguments before the ICJ in the *Legality of the Use of Force* cases. See supra Operation Allied Force *in the Federal Republic of Yugoslavia: 1998–1999.*

158 See Gowlland-Debbas, supra n. 127, 377; Gray, supra n. 152, 251. See Chapter 2.

159 Stahn, supra n. 2, 814.

160 White, supra n. 2, 32–33; Krisch, supra n. 2, 93; Gowlland-Debbas, supra n. 127, 373; Gray, supra n. 152, 253.

the rejection of a legal necessity to obtain clear authorization, but likewise that of a purely unilateral right of action'.[161]

However, despite the difference in chosen emphasis, what unites the justifications of the acting states and the views of the supporting states is the fact that, regardless of the procedural irregularities, the actions were necessary nonetheless. Whilst many members of the primary interpretive community in the UNSC on the occasions when it met emphasized the importance of human rights, the acting states went further and claimed a 'humanitarian necessity' for forcible measures.[162] Indeed, most states, and NATO itself, did not argue that their actions were lawful under an established right of humanitarian intervention but instead focused on the pure necessity of averting a 'humanitarian catastrophe'.

Consequently, although the *usus* and *opinio juris* elements of customary international law formation are clearly lacking in sufficient quantity and quality to be able to claim the emergence of a new right, '*opinio necessitatis* has been forcefully and loudly proclaimed by the states engaging in military action'.[163] Whilst such *opinio* may be the seed of change,[164] on this occasion some of the acting states expressed a preference that the events in Kosovo should not set a precedent[165] and, even more significantly, there was notable opposition to the actions taken and the utilization of humanitarian concern as a basis for action.[166]

Nevertheless, whilst there was *opinio necessitatis* expressed by many states towards the intervention for humanitarian purposes on these occasions, it is only in

161 Krisch, Ibid., 91. In discussing *Operation Desert Strike* of 1996, Symes takes up this view: 'Perhaps recognizing the appeal and legitimacy of multilateralism and the difficulties inherent in justifying unilateral humanitarian military intervention, the State Department apparently attempted to split the difference by portraying the intervention as a unilateral action undertaken in the interests of international law and the international community'. See Symes, supra n. 10, 599.

162 A. Cassese, 'A Follow-Up: Forcible Humanitarian Countermeasures and *Opinio Necessitatis*' (1999) 10 *EJIL* 791, 797–98.

163 Ibid., 797.

164 See Chapter 2 (n. 70) for more on this.

165 As Cassese claims, '[a]rguably, they shared the *opinio necessitatis*, but were probably not prepared to extend it to similar future actions'. Cassese, supra n. 162, 798.

166 Indeed Russia made it quite clear that '[a]ttempts to justify the NATO strikes with arguments about preventing a humanitarian catastrophe in Kosovo are completely untenable. Not only are these attempts in no way based on the Charter or other generally recognized rules of international law, but the unilateral use of force will lead precisely to a situation with truly devastating humanitarian consequences'. UN Doc. S/PV. 3988, supra n. 75, Russia (2–3). Symes, a supporter of this view within the secondary interpretive community, also states that 'humanitarian concern is unacceptable under international law as a justification for unilateral military intervention'. See Symes, supra n. 10, 598. On this point, Cassese, rather optimistically, notes that 'the contention can be made that, at least to some extent, the opposition or reservations of some of the aforementioned states may also be due to the conduct of hostilities by the armed forces of NATO and the heavy casualties they caused'. See Cassese, supra n. 162, 798.

their aftermath and with subsequent practice that it was to become clear whether this was to solidify into *opinio juris* thus indicating a change in the *jus ad bellum*.[167]

Unilateral Enforcement of the Collective Will: Life After *Operation Allied Force*

Unlike other areas of the *jus ad bellum* examined in this work, the US has not expressly claimed new rights to either the unilateral enforcement of UNSC resolutions or the use force for humanitarian purposes. Instead, the US has acted with the claim that its actions on those occasions were necessary. This claim has been shared and found some support at different times and from different states but proved insufficient by itself to create any new rights at the time.

The purpose of this section is to examine the subsequent practice of the key actors within the primary and secondary interpretive communities to determine whether what were described as 'context-breaking' incidents at the time have ultimately merited this title.[168]

Events at the United Nations

Activity within the UN, as part of both the primary and secondary interpretive communities, began soon after *Operation Allied Force* came to an end and therefore it seems appropriate to address it first in this section. Whilst no direct mention was made of the unilateral enforcement of UNSC resolutions or the possibility of reinterpreting the competence of the UNSC to permit it to use force despite the objections of a permanent member, arguably a sign of the obvious illegality and dubious prospects for collective security posed by such possibilities, much was said, or not said at significant moments, on the issue of the use of force for humanitarian purposes. Whilst not wishing to put the cart before the horse and address the secondary interpretive community prior to the primary interpretive community, given the way that the debate has evolved it seems logical to address this activity in a chronological order.

The International Law Commission's Draft Articles on Responsibility of States for Internationally Wrongful Acts (2001) In 2001, less than two years after the end of *Operation Allied Force*, the ILC published its *Draft Articles on Responsibility of States for Internationally Wrongful Acts*.[169] Whilst these articles are essentially

---

167 As Cassese correctly notes, '[i]n order to establish whether a new rule may have emerged, it thus seems judicious to await any repetition of such actions under the same conditions and exigencies'. See Cassese, Ibid., 797.

168 White, supra n. 2, 27.

169 ILC, 'Draft Articles on Responsibility of States for Internationally Wrongful Acts' (21 April–3 June 2001 and 2 July–10 August 2001) UN Doc. A/56/10 (hereafter

concerned with 'injured states', to which they make provision for non-forcible countermeasures and self-defence,[170] they also entitle '[a]ny state other than an injured state … to invoke the responsibility of another state' if '[t]he obligation breached is owed to the international community as a whole'.[171] However, the response to such violations is restricted to demanding '[c]essation of the internationally wrongful act, and assurances and guarantees of non-repetition'[172] and '[p]erformance of the obligation of reparation',[173] not countermeasures of *any* type. Indeed, what is of significance for the purposes of this work is that the articles were published and endorsed *after* the Iraq and Kosovo interventions yet did not include the right of *forcible* unilateral countermeasures in response to serious breaches of obligations *erga omnes*. Arguably, this portrays a rather limited impact of the US's actions and justifications on the position of forcible countermeasures in response to human rights violations.

The United Nations Millennium Summit (2000) In September 2000, just over a year after *Operation Allied Force* had ended, the UN met for the Millennium Summit. Although the Millennium Declaration did not say a great deal in connection with either unilateral enforcement or humanitarian intervention it did 'reaffirm … faith in the Organization and its Charter as indispensable foundations of a more peaceful, prosperous and just world'.[174] Whilst this statement is not clear and direct enough to be taken as a significant indicator of negative intersubjective agreement within the primary interpretive community associated with the UN Charter as to a right to take unilateral forcible actions to prevent humanitarian catastrophes, by reaffirming faith in the Charter, including the general prohibition of the use of force in Article 2(4) and the Chapter VII provisions on collective action, this was similarly not a ringing endorsement of such a right.

The Report of the International Commission on Intervention and State Sovereignty (2001) After the UN Millennium Summit the International Commission on Intervention and State Sovereignty was established. Whilst not strictly an activity at the UN, it was formed in response to the UNSG's challenge to the international community shortly after *Operation Allied Force* had come to an end to act upon future violations of human rights and humanitarian law and trigger subsequent debate within the UN.[175]

DASR 2001). See, generally, J. Crawford, *The International Law Commission's Articles on State Responsibility* (Cambridge: Cambridge University Press, 2002).

170 DASR 2001, Ibid., Chapter II.

171 Ibid., Article 48(1)(b).

172 Ibid., Article 48(2)(a).

173 Ibid., Article 48(2)(b).

174 UN Millennium Declaration, UNGA Res. 55/2 (8 September 2000) UN Doc. A/RES/55/2, para. 1.

175 This challenge was made in his Annual Report to the General Assembly. See UN Doc. SG/SM7136 (20 September 1999).

The Commission subsequently published its report, *The Responsibility to Protect*, in December 2001[176] in which it set out its conception of a 'responsibility to protect'. This, it described, is 'the idea that sovereign states have a responsibility to protect their own citizens from avoidable catastrophe – from mass murder and rape, from starvation – but when they are unwilling or unable to do so, that responsibility must be borne by the broader community of states'.[177]

Whilst the report stressed that the 'Security Council should be the *first port of call* on any matter relating to military intervention for human protection purposes',[178] the Commission left open whether an 'intervention not authorized by the Security Council or [the] General Assembly' would be lawful.[179] Indeed, it has been suggested that '[t]he report of the Commission managed to gather broad support because it avoided taking a final stance on the question of the legality/legitimacy of unauthorized interventions'.[180] However, the concept of a 'responsibility to protect' was picked up and given different treatment by the other subsequent reports issued by the High-Level Panel, the UNSG, and the 2005 UN World Summit Outcome.

The High-Level Panel Report on Threats, Challenges and Change (2004) This report of December 2004 incorporated the notion of a 'responsibility to protect' which had emanated from the Report of the International Commission on Intervention and State Responsibility.[181] However, the panel saw this responsibility within the context of strengthening the collective security system under the UN Charter.[182] Indeed, it acknowledged:

> the emerging norm that there is a collective international responsibility to protect, *exercisable by the Security Council authorizing military intervention as a last resort*, in the event of genocide and other large-scale killing, ethnic cleansing or serious violations of international humanitarian law which sovereign Governments have proved powerless or unwilling to prevent.[183]

As Chapter 3 demonstrated, this authorization is largely based on the UNSC determining the existence of a threat to international peace and security in such circumstances and has already become an embedded part of UNSC practice in

176 The report is available at http:www.iciss.ca/report-en.asp [Accessed: 29 January 2009].

177 Ibid., VIII.

178 Ibid., para. 6.28 (emphasis added).

179 Ibid., para. 6.37.

180 C. Stahn, 'Responsibility to Protect: Political Rhetoric or Emerging Legal Norm?' (2007) 101 *AJIL* 99, 104.

181 Report of the High-Level Panel on Threats, Challenges and Change, 'A More Secure World: Our Shared Responsibility' (2 December 2004) UN Doc. A/59/565, para. 203.

182 Stahn, supra n. 180, 105.

183 High-Level Panel Report, supra n. 181, para. 203 (emphasis added).

the post-Cold War era.[184] It was in regards to unilateral action on which it took a clearer line than the Commission on State Sovereignty and Intervention. Indeed, whilst 'the possibility of individual Member States bypassing the Security Council' was recognized,[185] 'the panel did not envisage that an international responsibility to protect could be invoked by coalitions of the able and willing or regional organizations in the absence of Security Council authorization'.[186]

The Report of the United Nations Secretary-General: In Larger Freedom (2005) In his report of March 2005, the UNSG also expressly recognized the 'responsibility to protect' principle[187] and claimed to be 'aware of the sensitivities involved in this issue'.[188] However, whilst the report 'did not expressly rule out the possibility of unilateral action in any circumstances (e.g., where the veto is used to block action in a case of genocide)',[189] there was a distinct emphasis on peaceful means. Indeed, in rubber-stamping the already developed authorization technique embedded within the UNSC, the UNSG posed the rhetorical question whether 'genocide, ethnic cleansing and other such crimes against humanity, are … not also threats to international peace and security, against which humanity should be able to look to the Security Council for protection?'[190] The position adopted was, therefore, like the High-Level Panel's, concerned more about strengthening the collective security system than endorsing any unilateral rights.

The United Nations World Summit Outcome Document (2005) Whilst the above reports, with the exception of the UN Millennium Summit, have emanated from those within the secondary interpretive community, the primary interpretive community got to have its say on this issue at the World Summit held at the UN in September 2005.[191] As a result, the states expressed their preparedness:

> to take collective action, in a timely and decisive manner, *through the Security Council, in accordance with the Charter, including Chapter VII*, on a case-by-case basis and in cooperation with relevant regional organizations as appropriate, should peaceful means be inadequate and national authorities are manifestly failing to protect their populations from genocide, war crimes, ethnic cleansing and crimes against humanity.[192]

---

184 See Chapter 3. See also Ibid., para. 202.

185 Ibid., paras 206, 196, and 197.

186 Stahn, supra n. 180, 106.

187 Report of the UN Secretary-General, 'In Larger Freedom: Towards Security, Development and Human Rights for All' (21 March 2005) UN Doc. A/59/205, para. 135.

188 Ibid.

189 Stahn, supra n. 180, 107.

190 Report of the UN Secretary-General, supra n. 187, para. 125.

191 2005 World Summit Outcome Document, UNGA Res. A/60/L.1 (15 September 2005) UN Doc. A/60/L.1.

192 Ibid., para. 139 (emphasis added).

It is true that 'the text of the Outcome Document does not firmly state that UN collective security action constitutes the *only* option for responding to mass atrocities through the use of force'.[193] Consequently, this is not a clear enough statement to be taken as a significant indicator of negative intersubjective agreement by the primary interpretive community concerned with interpreting the UN Charter and customary international law in regards to the unilateral enforcement of the collective will. Nevertheless, through this direct reference of preparedness 'to act through the Security Council' but not one to take unilateral action, it appears that this was the favoured approach.

All in all, whilst from this brief summary of the various reports' handling of the issues it is clear that the 'responsibility to protect' idea may have become firmly embedded within the discourse of the UN,[194] in all practical senses it has been in the form of the UNSC taking collective action, not states individually, thereby militating against any development of a doctrine of unilateral enforcement of the collective will through either unilateral enforcement of UNSC resolutions or unilateral humanitarian intervention. This next section examines whether the result of this discourse during this period has been reflected in the practice of states outside of the UNGA and the response by the UNSC to situations on the ground.

State and Security Council Practice

The Group of 77 On 24 September 1999, just a few months after *Operation Allied Force* had come to an end, a Ministerial Declaration was produced by the meeting of Foreign Ministers of the Group of 77 in New York.[195] Paragraph 69 of this Declaration stated that '[t]he Ministers stressed the need to maintain clear distinctions between humanitarian assistance and other activities of the United Nations. They rejected the so-called right of humanitarian intervention, which has no basis in the UN Charter or international law'.[196]

This rejection is significant for two reasons. Firstly, given the temporal proximity to *Operation Allied Force*, it was arguably meant as a reaction to that particular use of force. Secondly, this group represents the opinion of 132 developing states including 23 Asian, 51 African, 22 Latin American and 13 Arab states. Such a large and representative rejection of the doctrine can be taken as a clear and significant indicator of negative intersubjective agreement regarding the use of unilateral forcible measures for humanitarian purposes and discounts any arguments that a general *opinio juris* had formed as a result of the actions of the US in Iraq and Kosovo.

193 Stahn, supra n. 180, 109 (emphasis added).

194 See, for example, UNSC Res. 1674 (28 April 2006) UN Doc. S/RES/1674, para. 4, which reaffirmed paras. 138 and 139 of the 2005 World Summit Outcome Document regarding the responsibility to protect.

195 Quoted in I. Brownlie, *Principles of Public International Law* 7th edn (Oxford: Oxford University Press, 2008), 744.

196 Ibid.

Sudan (Darfur) Since 2003, the Janjaweed Arab–African militia, supported by the Government of Sudan, has killed at least 200,000 black Africans (although also Muslim) in Darfur and also displaced 2 million.[197] This was to suppress a rebellion by some of Darfur's black agricultural tribes who had risen up against the Sudanese Government in February 2003.[198]

The African Union in its *Constitutive Act* of 2000 established '[t]he right of the Union to intervene in a Member State pursuant to a decision of the Assembly in respect of grave circumstances, namely: war crimes, genocide and crimes against humanity'.[199] Whilst this has been described as providing support to 'a regional right of humanitarian intervention'[200] the fact that this was not relied upon to take action against the genocide which was taking place in Darfur is telling as to the reality of such a right. Indeed, '[t]he AU was not willing to intervene in the absence of consent by the government of Sudan'.[201] Although it did establish a force to monitor the ceasefire which subsequently became a peacekeeping force, this was with the consent of the Sudanese Government.[202]

Furthermore, the UNSC endorsed the initial deployment of the AU force, AMIS, in Resolution 1556 (2004), its first resolution adopted on the situation and under Chapter VII.[203] This resolution also deemed the situation a 'threat to international peace and security',[204] a determination which has been repeated in many resolutions concerning the situation since.[205] Additionally, the resolution expressed the UNSC's 'grave concern at the ongoing humanitarian crisis and widespread human rights violations'[206] and imposed obligations upon the Sudanese Government to disarm the Janjaweed.[207] In this respect, the resolution was similar in tone to those adopted before *Operation Allied Force* commenced.[208]

197 Report of the UN Secretary-General (30 August 2004) UN Doc. S/2004/703.

198 See (2004) *UNYB* 233.

199 The AU *Constitutive Act* (2002), Article 4(h). Available at http://www.africa-union.org/root/au/AboutAu/Constitutive_Act_en.htm [Accessed: 20 June 2009]. However, it is not expressly stated that this 'intervention' would take the form of the use of force and, confusingly, follows the AU's adherence to the prohibition of the use of force (4(f)) and the non-interference in the internal affairs of another member state (4(g)).

200 C. Gray, *International Law and the Use of Force*, 3rd edn (Oxford: Oxford University Press, 2008), 53.

201 Ibid., 55.

202 Ibid., 380.

203 UNSC Res. 1556 (30 July 2004) UN Doc. S/RES/1556, para. 2. See, generally, A. Abass, 'The UN, the AU, and the Darfur Crisis' (2007) 54 *NILR* 416.

204 UNSC Res. 1556, Ibid., preamble.

205 See, for example, UNSC Res. 1593 (31 March 2005) UN Doc. S/RES/1593.

206 UNSC Res. 1556, supra n. 203, preamble.

207 Ibid., para. 6.

208 See supra Operation Allied Force *in the Federal Republic of Yugoslavia: 1998–1999.*

With violations of the ceasefire agreement and the AU force unable to maintain peace there were calls, notably from the UNSG,[209] for the UNSC to take action. However, 'states were not willing to intervene through the Security Council in the absence of [Sudan's] consent, nor did they assert the right of any unilateral action'.[210] The UNSC subsequently set out proposals for a hybrid AU/UN force in Resolution 1706 (2006) but again merely invited Sudan's consent for such a deployment.[211] It was only at the end of 2007 that consent was given for such a force.[212] As Gray correctly concludes, '[t]he problems involved in the implementation of the "responsibility to protect", whether through the UN or, more controversially, through regional or unilateral humanitarian intervention, were all too apparent with regard to the humanitarian catastrophe in Darfur (Sudan)'.[213] Whilst the responsibility to protect is fine in principle, an obligation upon states to intervene has not as yet proved workable in practice and has been caught up with the problem of selectivity. Furthermore, the justifications advanced by the US for its intervention in Kosovo could have been deployed to justify a forcible intervention in this context. The US's unwillingness to intervene or to set out its reasons for its failure to do so under these circumstances is a significant indicator of negative intersubjective agreement as to the existence or emergence of any general right of unilateral enforcement of the collective will.

Outside of the humanitarian context: Iran and North Korea Like human rights, the issue of nuclear non-proliferation is another issue which has been of collective concern to various actors within the international community. The difficulties surrounding Iran and the DPRK's nuclear ambitions have been prominent on the agenda of the UNSC and on the conscience of the international community. Whilst much of the debate within the secondary interpretive community has focused on the possibility of the invocation of pre-emptive self-defence against such states who pose a threat,[214] the fact that the UNSC has been involved and expressed concern in adopting several resolutions also raises the issue of the possibility of unilateral enforcement of the collective will.

However, there are signs, possibly as a result of the events in Iraq and Kosovo, that the UNSC is being more deliberate and precise in its choice of language in this context. For example, in response to the testing of long-range ballistic missiles and the withdrawal from the nuclear non-proliferation treaty on 5 July 2006 by the DPRK, the UNSC responded with Resolution 1695 (2006).[215] This expressed grave

209 See, for example, UN Press Releases SC/8196 (24 September 2004) and SC/8823 (11 September 2006).

210 Gray, supra n. 200, 53.

211 UNSC Res. 1706 (31 August 2006) UN Doc. S/RES/1706, para. 1.

212 See UN Doc. SG/SM/10945 (16 April 2007).

213 Gray, supra n. 200, 53.

214 See Chapter 7 for more on the doctrine of pre-emptive self-defence.

215 UNSC Res. 1695 (15 July 2006) UN Doc. S/RES/1695.

concern at these events[216] and demanded that the DPRK suspend all activity related to its ballistic missile programme,[217] but neither was it passed under Chapter VII of the UN Charter nor did it determine a threat to international peace and security. Whilst the next resolution, 1718 (2006),[218] adopted by the UNSC in response to a nuclear weapons test on 9 October 2006 by the DPRK was adopted under Chapter VII,[219] it did not determine a threat to international peace and security. Furthermore, it was, unusually, clear in stating to be acting under Article 41[220] and that 'further decisions will be required should additional measures be necessary'.[221] Lastly, the use of force in its enforcement was on the minds of the members of the primary interpretive community and, in the debate prior to its adoption, China made clear that it was firmly opposed to such use of force.[222]

This specificity and caution has also been witnessed in the UNSC resolutions in connection with Iran's nuclear ambitions. Whilst Iran has stated that its nuclear enrichment is solely for peaceful domestic energy purposes, due to its lack of full compliance with the IAEA, suspicions have been raised that its ambitions are more sinister. In Resolution 1696 (2006),[223] in demanding that Iran suspend its enrichment processes and cooperate with the IAEA,[224] the UNSC again expressly stated to be acting under Article 40 of the UN Charter.[225] In the antepenultimate paragraph it again also stated that 'further decisions will be required should such additional measures be necessary'.[226] Again, the possible use of force was an issue with some members of the primary interpretive community with Russia this time 'rule[ing] out the use of military force'.[227] Resolutions 1737 (2006)[228] and 1747 (2007)[229] then imposed sanctions upon Iran under Article 41. Furthermore, both called for reports on Iran's compliance with the IAEA but clearly stated that if these reports confirm that Iran has not complied then it is the UNSC that 'shall adopt further measures under Article 41'.[230] Russia, again, ruled out the use of force.[231]

216 Ibid., preamble.
217 Ibid., para. 2.
218 UNSC Res. 1718 (14 October 2006) UN Doc. S/RES/1718.
219 Ibid., preamble.
220 Ibid.
221 Ibid., para. 16.
222 UNSC Verbatim Record (14 October 2006) UN Doc. S/PV. 5551.
223 UNSC Res. 1696 (31 July 2006) UN Doc. S/RES/1696.
224 Ibid., para. 2.
225 Ibid., preamble.
226 Ibid., para. 9.
227 UNSC Verbatim Record (13 October 2006) UN Doc. S/PV. 5550.
228 UNSC Res. 1737 (27 December 2006) UN Doc. S/RES/1737.
229 UNSC Res. 1747 (24 March 2007) UN Doc. S/RES/1747.
230 See para. 24(c) and para. 13(c) respectively.
231 See UNSC Verbatim Record (23 December 2006) UN Doc. S/PV. 5612; UNSC Verbatim Record (24 March 2007) UN Doc. S/PV. 5647.

Whilst unilateral military measures against either state are perhaps unlikely at the present time, it can only be hoped that by expressly stating to be acting under Article 41 and that *decisions* should be taken by the UNSC before any further measures could be taken, this will prevent any arguments that action can be taken unilaterally to enforce the collective will. Indeed, the UNSC has made it clear that it alone has the possibility of enforcing this.

Conclusion

The incidents in this chapter involving the US have demonstrated that while uses of force may not possess a strictly legal basis under either the correct procedures or the common understandings in interpreting resolutions of the UNSC they may nonetheless be accepted by the primary interpretive community as being necessary in the context in which they are taken. Indeed, when the US has taken actions which appear to have a humanitarian goal, positive intersubjective agreement has been witnessed in the primary interpretive community in regards to them.

However, maintaining this agreement amongst members of the primary interpretive community was a delicate exercise. When the actions were perceived to have moved beyond pure enforcement of the collective will to satisfying other more subjective or unilateral motives then the unity broke down leading to accusations of illegality and with the diminishment of any possibility of a precedent forming which would have had an impact upon the *jus ad bellum*. Enforcing the collective will within the boundaries of intersubjective agreement but without an authorizing resolution has been acceptable on occasions, but *unilateral* enforcement has not. Indeed, this was confirmed by the stark disagreements over this controversial basis during the crisis over the possible intervention in Iraq in 2003.[232]

However, this is not to suggest that the events in Iraq and the FRY have not left a mark. Indeed, the final section demonstrated that, with 10 years to assess the impact of *Operation Allied Force*, it appears that these incidences of unilateral enforcement of UNSC resolutions have in fact, if anything, had a positive impact with the UNSC tightening the wording of its resolutions and making it clear where authority lies for decision making under them in an attempt to rule out such unilateral enforcement.

Furthermore, the terms of the debate regarding the use of force for humanitarian purposes appear to have changed and widened. The notion of a 'responsibility to protect', if perhaps without much practical substance at this stage, has now become a part of UN discourse. However, even this humanitarian principle has been interpreted in its forcible form as one relating to collective measures under the auspices of the UNSC as opposed to having any unilateral meaning. Whether this remains the case awaits to be seen due to the principle still being in its early stages of life. However, the crisis in Darfur is a tragic example, if one were

232 Chapter 4.

needed, of the emptiness of the rhetoric regarding putting such a principle into practice. Indeed, the principle has not been invoked in either its collective or, more controversially, unilateral form and the desire to obtain Sudan's consent to any operation highlights that the principle of state sovereignty is deemed a powerful one when there is reluctance to intervene.

The difficulties these concepts present have also been faced by scholars within the secondary interpretive community. Indeed, '[d]espite the many attempts in legal doctrine, commentators have still not arrived at a canon of commonly accepted criteria for humanitarian intervention. Even less agreement has been reached in the definition of the much broader category of "enforcement of the collective will."'[233]

For those who observed a right of humanitarian intervention emerging as a result of the Kosovo intervention, this is not perceived as a 'pure' right. Indeed, in making such an observation Cassese notes that one of the necessary criteria to be satisfied before force can be resorted to is that 'the situation must be considered by the Security Council to constitute a threat to peace and security'.[234] In any case, '[t]he lawfulness of humanitarian intervention not authorized by the Security Council is still strongly contested by the Non-aligned Movement, China and Russia at every opportunity. Unless states and commentators are willing to ignore the position of these states, it is difficult to see how events in Iraq and Kosovo have changed the law'.[235] As the final section of this chapter has demonstrated, these interventions and the discourse engaged in have not had such an impact.

---

233 Stahn, supra n. 2, 816.

234 Cassese, supra n. 162, 798.

235 Gray, supra n. 114, 20.

PART II
The Use of Force in Self-Defence

Chapter 6
Self-Defence and Terrorism: The Harbouring Standard of Attribution

> From this day forward, any nation that continues to harbour or support terrorism will be regarded as a hostile regime.[1]

Introduction

Being the sole unilateral right of states to use force under both the UN Charter regime and traditional customary international law, the right of self-defence holds a special place in the *jus ad bellum*.[2] As Christine Gray emphasizes, 'states using force against another state almost invariably invoke self-defence'.[3] Indeed, the fact that states rely on it so frequently to justify their uses of force can be attributed to its accepted legal basis. However, that is not to say that there is agreement on its interpretation. In fact, given the auto-interpretative nature of the right, disagreement on its acceptable boundaries has arisen in a number of areas, for example whether it can be used in the protection of nationals abroad.[4]

The US, with its possibilities for greater action than other less powerful states, has been especially active in its attempts to widen the boundaries of this right. These attempts have occurred most significantly since the terrorist attacks of 9/11 and the commencement of the proclaimed 'war on terror'.[5]

---

1 President George W. Bush, 'Address Before a Joint Session of the Congress on the United States Response to the Terrorist Attacks of September 11' (2001) 37 *Weekly Compilation of Presidential Documents* 1347, 1349.

2 See UN Charter (1945), Article 51. The customary form of the right was affirmed in *Case Concerning Military and Paramilitary Activities in and against Nicaragua (Nicaragua v United States of America)* (Merits) [1986] ICJ Rep. 14, para. 34.

3 C. Gray, *International Law and the Use of Force*, 3rd edn (Oxford: Oxford University Press, 2008), 114.

4 Whilst the US has rescued nationals abroad in the time period under discussion in this book these were largely uncontroversial. Christine Gray goes as far as to label this 'a topic of mainly historical interest' as 'there have been no significant instances of the use of force to rescue nationals in the last ten years'. Ibid., 160. As the purpose of this book is to focus on the objects of controversy and change, attempted or otherwise, these are not examined.

5 As Gray notes, '[t]he massive terrorist attacks ... led to a fundamental reappraisal of the law on self-defence. The US response was to announce "a different kind of war against a different kind of enemy", a global war on terrorism'. Ibid., 193. For a critique of the

Indeed, this has occurred in two main areas: the use of force in self-defence in response to the attacks of non-state entities and the use of force in pre-emptive self-defence.

Whilst the invocation of self-defence for these two purposes is not new, the US, under the administration of President George W. Bush, has attempted changes to the law in these areas with particular vigour since 9/11 and these are consequently the focus of the second Part of this book.[6] This first chapter of Part II does not attempt to examine the whole of the debate on the use of force against terrorism. Instead, it takes as its focus the main attempted change to the law by the US, that is, a shift in the rules regarding the practical elements of undertaking actions in self-defence against non-state terrorist attacks. After setting out the traditional view on the law of self-defence for this purpose, the chapter addresses how the US has taken actions which have attempted to widen the standard for attributing the actions of non-state entities to territorial states, in particular the introduction of the 'harbouring' standard of attribution. Finally, it examines the subsequent practice of the interpretive communities since in an attempt to discern any impact in light of the US invoking this standard.

The Traditional Law Governing Responses in Self-Defence Against International Terrorism

In Theory

Unilateral responses in self-defence are governed first and foremost by Article 51 of the UN Charter which provides that:

> Nothing in the present Charter shall impair the inherent right of individual or collective self-defence if an armed attack occurs against a Member of the United Nations, until the Security Council has taken measures necessary to maintain international peace and security. Measures taken by Members in the exercise of this right of self-defence shall be immediately reported to the Security Council and shall not in any way affect the authority and responsibility of the Security Council in order to maintain or restore international peace and security.

However, this key provision of the Charter does not contain the whole of the law governing self-defence. Instead, it has been informed by, and interpreted in light

---

applicability of the term 'war' in fighting international terrorism see, generally, F. Mégret, 'War? Legal Semantics and the Move to Violence' (2002) 13 *EJIL* 361.

6 Not only are these two areas selected because this is where most activity and controversy have arisen but also for reasons of brevity as a complete study of self-defence would constitute an entire book in itself.

of, the customary international law principles of necessity,[7] proportionality,[8] and immediacy.[9] These principles are traditionally referenced as emanating from the correspondence in the *Caroline* incident of 1841.[10] Although Sir Robert Jennings described this incident as the '*locus classicus*' of self-defence,[11] due to the use of force not being legally prohibited at the time, the incident *in itself* did not have an impact upon contemporary customary international law.[12] Nevertheless, these principles have since been regularly invoked by members of the primary interpretive community connected with the source of the right in both its textual and customary forms[13] and by scholars[14] and the ICJ[15] within the secondary interpretive community in gauging whether actions taken in self-defence are lawful.

---

7 The use of force should be the only option for a state to defend itself against an armed attack. M. Shaw, *International Law*, 6th edn (Cambridge: Cambridge University Press, 2008), 1142. See also C. Greenwood, 'International Law and the United States Air Operation Against Libya' (1986–87) 89 *W.Va.L.Rev.* 933, 945. Although, taken to its extreme, peaceful means can always be attempted by the state attacked, '[i]t would be unreasonable to lay down such a principle that armed action in self-defence is never permissible as long as peaceful means are available'. See O. Schachter, 'The Right of States to Use Armed Force' (1984) 82 *Mich.L.Rev.* 1621, 1637.

8 The force used should be reasonable and do no more than repel the attack. See I. Brownlie, *International Law and the Use of Force by States* (Oxford: Clarendon Press, 1963), 434. In gauging proportionality, although some claim that '[t]he use of force in self-defence must be proportionate to the wrongful act to which it is a response' (Greenwood, Ibid., 946. See also Y. Dinstein, *War, Aggression and Self-Defence*, 4th edn (Cambridge: Cambridge University Press, 2005), 225), proportionality more accurately refers to what is required to halt or repel the attack. See T. Gazzini, *The Changing Rules on the Use of Force in International Law* (Manchester: Manchester University Press, 2005), 148. In any case, conclusions as to this can only be drawn *a posteriori*. See Dinstein, Ibid., 237.

9 There must not be an undue time lag between the armed attack and the exercise of self-defence. See Dinstein, Ibid., 210. See also Gazzini, Ibid., 143. However, Thomas Franck has claimed that the application of this principle to traditional self-defence 'comes from a misunderstanding of the *Caroline* decision which deals only with *anticipatory* self-defence'. See T.M. Franck, 'Terrorism and the Right of Self-Defence' (2001) 95 *AJIL* 839, 840.

10 For more on this incident, including the facts, see Chapter 7.

11 R. Jennings, 'The *Caroline* and McLeod Cases' (1938) 32 *AJIL* 82, 92.

12 J.A. Green, 'Docking the *Caroline*: Understanding the Relevance of the Formula in Contemporary Customary International Law Concerning Self-Defence' (2006) 14 *Cardozo J.Int'l & Comp.L.* 429, 475.

13 For example, in the debates in the UNSC after the Osiraq incident in 1981, several delegations referred to the *Caroline* formulation of the right of anticipatory self-defence as an accepted statement of customary international law. UNSC Verbatim Record (15–19 June 1981) UN Docs. S/PV. 2285–2288.

14 See, for example, supra nn. 7, 8 and 9. See, generally, K. Trapp, 'Back to Basics: Necessity, Proportionality, and the Right of Self-Defence against Non-State Terrorist Actors' (2007) 56 *ICLQ* 141.

15 *Nicaragua Case*, supra n. 2, para. 176; *Legality of the Treat or Use of Nuclear Weapons* (Advisory Opinion) [1996] ICJ Rep. 226, para. 141; *Case Concerning Oil*

When the UN Charter was drafted the permissibility of any forcible measures contained within it was in the context of inter-state conflicts. Non-state entities, especially in the context of global terrorism, were not a consideration.[16] Consequently, given the essentially inter-state nature of international law, the right of self-defence has traditionally been interpreted as excluding measures in response to attacks undertaken purely by non-state entities.[17]

However, Article 2(4) only prohibits the threat or use of force *against* 'any state' and although Article 51 requires an 'armed attack' against a member of the UN before the right of self-defence becomes operational nothing is said about the entity from which such an attack must emanate from and thus the target of any self-defense measures in response.[18] In theory, so long as a response, taken in the context in which it arises, is necessary, proportionate and immediate, there is nothing in this provision to prevent a state from carrying out an act of self-defence in response to an attack regardless of the identity of the perpetrator.[19] Indeed, the right is an 'inherent' one and exists for states to protect themselves. Consequently, it would seem to undermine this principle if it was so restricted *ratione personae* purely to attacks by states.[20] However, as Oscar Schachter points out, 'this conclusion seems too simplistic in a world in which territorial sovereignty of states is a dominant principle'.[21] Indeed, the use of force against non-state entities in theory is one thing, in practice it is quite another.

In Practice

Whilst it may be feasible in theory to regard non-state entities as legitimate targets of actions in self-defence, the problems arise in establishing the practical elements

---

Platforms (Islamic Republic of Iran v United States of America) (Judgment) [2003] ICJ Rep. 161, paras. 51, 73 and 76–77.

16 J. Beard, 'America's New War on Terror: The Case for Self-Defence Under International Law' (2001–02) 25 *Harv.J.L.& Pub.Pol'y* 559, 559.

17 J.L. Kunz, 'Individual and Collective Self-Defence in Article 51 of the Charter of the United Nations' (1947) 41 *AJIL* 872, 879; T. Ruys and S. Verhoeven, 'Attacks by Private Actors and the Right of Self-Defence' (2005) 10 *JCSL* 289, 290; E.P.J. Myjer and N.D. White, 'The Twin Towers Attack: Unlimited Right to Self-Defence?' (2002) 7 *JCSL* 5, 7.

18 O. Schachter, 'The Lawful Use of Force by a State Against Terrorists in Another Country' (1989) Israel *Y.B.Hum.Rts.* 209, 216. Greenwood accepts that the notion is 'generally used with reference to the use of regular armed forces by states' although argues that 'there is no *a priori* reason why the term should be so confined'. See C. Greenwood, 'International Law and the "War Against Terrorism"' (2002) 78 *International Affairs* 301, 307.

19 S.D. Murphy, 'Terrorism and the Concept of "Armed Attack" in Article 51 of the UN Charter' (2002) 43 *Harv.Int'l L.J.* 41, 50; J. Paust, 'Use of Force Against Terrorists in Afghanistan, Iraq and Beyond' (2002) 35 *Cornell Int'l L.J.* 533, 534; Franck, supra n. 9, 840.

20 Thomas Franck has picked up on this point and argues that 'the right is expressly accorded in response to an "armed attack" and not to any particular kind of attacker'. Franck, Ibid., 840.

21 Schachter, supra n. 18, 216.

in carrying out such a response. Indeed, whilst measures in self-defence can be taken against entities on the high seas or in outer space,[22] this is not normally where they are located. Instead, the response in self-defence will normally need to occur on the territory of a state. In this case, 'if one would accept that private attacks can in themselves amount to "armed attacks" in the sense of article 51 of the Charter, this would lead to the absurd result that states would be exposed to military force, even if they have not committed an internationally wrongful act of their own'.[23] Consequently, forcible responses on the territory of a state have traditionally only been permissible if the actions of the non-state entities can be attributed to the territorial state.[24]

The traditional standard of attribution The traditional standard for attributing the actions of non-state entities to states for the purpose of self-defence emanates from the work of the ILC,[25] the *Definition of Aggression*,[26] and the jurisprudence of the ICJ.[27] This standard has been set relatively high so that under the traditional rules actions in self-defence will only be permitted if:

- the entity has been 'sent by or on behalf of a state';[28] or
- the entity is acting 'on the instruction of, or under the direction or control of a state';[29] or
- the territorial state 'acknowledges and adopts the conduct in question as its own'.[30]

In a similar vein, the ICJ, in drawing upon the *Definition of Aggression* in the *Nicaragua* case, set the standard as one of 'effective control'.[31] Whilst the ICTY has criticized this standard as being set too high and instead opted for one of

22 See A. Cassese, *International Law*, 2nd edn (Oxford: Oxford University Press, 2005), 476–79.

23 Ruys and Verhoeven, supra n. 17, 312.

24 As O'Connell notes, '[t]o take the attack to the territory of a state, the defending state must have evidence the territorial state is responsible for the acts'. See M.E. O'Connell, 'Evidence of Terror' (2002) 7 *JCSL* 19, 30.

25 ILC, 'Draft Articles on Responsibility of States for Internationally Wrongful Acts' (21 April–3 June 2001 and 2 July–10 August 2001) UN Doc. A/56/10 (hereafter DASR 2001).

26 UNGA Res. 3314 (XXIX) (14 December 1974) UN Doc. A/RES/29/3314 (XXIX).

27 *Nicaragua Case*, supra n. 2.

28 UN Doc. A/RES/29/3314 (XXIX), supra n. 26, Article 3(g) (as employed in the *Nicaragua Case*, supra n. 2, para. 195). See also DASR 2001, supra n. 25, Article 4.

29 DASR 2001, Ibid., Article 8.

30 DASR 2001, Ibid., Article 11. See also *United States Diplomatic and Consular Staff in Tehran (United States of America v Iran)* [1980] ICJ Rep. 3, para. 74.

31 *Nicaragua Case*, supra n. 2, para. 195.

'overall control',[32] the element of state control was still the key element. Problems arise, however, in other situations where 'the law is not entirely clear'.[33]

The first of these situations arises where a state, although not in direct control of the non-state entity, may be actively supporting it through the supply of weapons, financial aid, or logistical support. However, whilst the state may be in violation of its international obligation to refrain from such support,[34] whether this opens the state up to forcible measures has traditionally been a point of contention within both the primary and secondary interpretive communities. Indeed, whilst in the *Nicaragua* case the ICJ held that the supply of weapons or logistical or other support could only be considered an unlawful use of force or intervention in the internal affairs of states as opposed to an 'armed attack',[35] several judges sitting on the ICJ at the time and scholars within the secondary interpretive community disagreed with this restrictive view.[36] Nevertheless, when states have invoked the right of self-defence in response to this type of support it has proved controversial.[37]

Given that active support has not traditionally been viewed as sufficient to attribute the armed attacks of non-state actors to the state thus triggering a response in self-defence, it follows logically that neither will more passive support, such as acquiescence or toleration.[38] In this situation the state concerned will be in violation of the positive obligation to act with 'due diligence' to do all it can to eradicate

---

32 *Prosecutor v Tadic* (Appeals Chamber) IT-94-1-A (15 July 1999), para. 124.

33 A. Cassese, 'The International Community's "Legal" Response to Terrorism' (1989) 38 *ICLQ* 589, 599.

34 This duty flows from the *Declaration on Friendly Relations* which proclaimed that 'no state shall organize, assist, foment, finance, incite or tolerate subversive, terrorist or armed activities directed towards the violent overthrow of the regime of another state, or interfere in civil strife in another state'. See the *Declaration on Principles of International Law Concerning Friendly Relations and Co-operation Among States in Accordance with the Charter of the United Nations*, UNGA Res. 2625 (XXV) (24 October 1970) UN Doc. A/RES/25/2625 (XXV). See also *The Corfu Channel Case (United Kingdom v Albania)* [1949] ICJ Rep. 22.

35 *Nicaragua Case*, supra n. 2, para. 195.

36 Judges Jennings and Schwebel considered this to be an overly restrictive view. See their *Dissenting Opinions* at 543 and 346–47 respectively, *Nicaragua Case*, supra n. 2. See also R. Higgins, *Problems and Process: International Law and How We Use It* (Oxford: Clarendon Press, 1994), 250–51 and, generally, J.N. Moore, 'The Nicaragua Case and the Deterioration of World Order' (1987) 81 *AJIL* 151.

37 See, for example, France against Tunisia in 1958; Israeli against Jordan in 1968; South Africa and Southern Rhodesia against neighbouring states between 1976 and 1986; Senegal against Guinea-Bissau in 1992; Tajikistan against Afghanistan in 1993; Iran against Iraq in 1994; Sudan against Eritrea in 1996; Burundi against Tanzania in 1997; Burma against Thailand in 1995. See Ruys and Verhoeven, supra n. 17, 292–96.

38 Although this is only an inference from the *Nicaragua* case which did not expressly address the issue.

non-state entities from operating from its territory[39] but under the traditional rules this could only lead to countermeasures of a non-forcible kind.[40] Indeed, 'in the case the state has not acted due diligently, for example by merely tolerating the presence of armed private actors, then it still cannot be subjugated to actions of self-defence: it is only responsible for the breach of the customary duty to protect foreign states, governed by the due diligence rule, which cannot be qualified as an act of aggression'.[41] Again, the invocation of forcible measures by states in such circumstances has proved controversial[42] and only supported by the arguments of a few scholars.[43]

The last possibility arises where a state acts with due diligence, thus alleviating it of responsibility, but either lacks the capacity to prevent the non-state entity from operating from its territory, is not in control of a particular part of its territory, or simply fails in its efforts to prevent them from operating. In these circumstances, because the territorial state cannot be held responsible, the question is whether the victim state simply has to endure attacks against it without even the possibility of taking non-forcible countermeasures, there being no violation of international law, in an attempt to prevent the attacks? Whilst Israel[44] and Turkey[45] appear to have used force in these circumstances, at first sight the answer appears to be affirmative. However, it is perhaps arguable that if the territorial state finds itself in this position, as part of the due diligence principle it should invite other states, in particular the victim state, to operate on its territory with the aim of eradicating the non-state entity which is launching the attacks.[46]

Alternatively, it has been suggested by some within the secondary interpretive community that 'a doctrine of necessity'[47] or 'extra-territorial law enforcement'[48] becomes applicable as a circumstance precluding wrongfulness where the victim

39 See Ruys and Verhoeven, supra n. 17, 305–08; Gazzini, supra n. 8, 187. See, generally, R. Pisillo-Mazzeschi, 'The "Due Dilligence" Rule and the Nature of the International Responsibility of States' (1992) 35 *German Y.B.Int'l L.* 9.

40 Pissilo-Mazzeschi, Ibid., 36.

41 Ruys and Verhoeven, supra n. 17, 307.

42 See, for example, Portugal against Senegal in 1969; Israel against Lebanon in 1968; Israel against Tunisia in 1985; South Africa and Southern Rhodesia against Botswana, Zambia, and Angola in the 1970s and 80s; border tension between Liberia, Guinea, Burkina Faso and Sierra Leone in 2000. See Ruys and Verhoeven, Ibid., 292–96.

43 See, especially, Y. Dinstein, 'The International Legal Response to Terrorism' in P. Lamberti Zanardi *et al* (eds), *International Law at the Time of its Codification: Essays in Honour of R. Ago* (Milan: Giuffre, 1987), 139, 146.

44 At various times against Hezbollah in Southern Lebanon and in rescuing its nationals in Entebbe in 1976.

45 In Iraq throughout the 1990s and more recently in 2008 in its fight against the PKK.

46 Gazzini, supra n. 8, 187. See also Trapp, supra n. 14, 147 (n. 33).

47 D.W. Bowett, *Self-Defence in International Law* (Manchester: Manchester University Press, 1958), 10; Gazzini, supra n. 8, 205.

48 Dinstein, supra n. 8, at 244–47.

state acts forcibly to put an end to the terrorist activities in lieu of the territorial state. However, although Sir Derek Bowett, for example, believed that this doctrine could excuse the use of force, the ILC, which included 'necessity' as a circumstance precluding wrongfulness,[49] has maintained that its invocation must be 'in conformity with an obligation arising under a peremptory norm of general international law'[50] and thus arguably rules out the use of force. Furthermore, there is very little practice amongst the primary interpretive community in support of this doctrine and it has been relatively overlooked by the secondary interpretive community.[51]

As the above demonstrates, beyond an 'effective control' relationship between a state and a non-state entity, forcible self-defensive measures in response to attacks from a non-state entity are traditionally controversial at best. Whilst a handful of states have invoked self-defence (and occasionally the doctrine of necessity) to respond to the attacks of non-state entities, these have normally been controversial. Consequently, a restrictive approach on the issue can be identified. However, the US, in its practice in the post-Cold War era, has gradually attempted to expand this traditionally restrictive standard of attribution.

The United States and Self-Defence Against Terrorism: From Effective Control to Passive Support

Invoking the Effective Control Standard in Responding to Terrorism

On 26 June 1993, in response to an alleged plot to assassinate the former US President, George H.W. Bush whilst on a visit to Kuwait on 14–16 April 1993, US forces launched a missile attack on the Iraqi Military Intelligence Headquarters in Baghdad.[52] The strike consisted of 23 Tomahawk cruise missiles fired from US aircraft carriers in the Gulf and the Red Sea.[53] In justifying the strikes the US declared that it had acted 'in accordance with Article 51 of the United Nations Charter' in exercising 'its right of self-defence'.[54]

---

49 DASR 2001, supra n. 25, Article 25.

50 Ibid., Article 26.

51 Gazzini, a proponent of this doctrine, appears to recognize its unclear status by noting that when states are unable to curb the terrorist activities within its jurisdiction, they 'cannot invoke self-defence to counter the hostile military activities; they have to rely on other legal grounds, *presumably* the state of necessity'. Gazzini, supra n. 8, 190 (emphasis added).

52 *Keesing's* (1993) 39531. See also M. Walker, 'Clinton Hails Strike as Success' *The Guardian* (28 June 1993), 1.

53 *Keesing's*, Ibid.

54 US letter to the UNSC, UN Doc. S/26003 (26 June 1993). See also 'Challenges to UN Decisions Scrutinized: Baghdad Sites Attacked After Assassination Plot' *UN Chronicle* (September 1993), 20. This letter meant that the US had complied with the reporting requirement under Article 51. However, as Kritsiotis correctly notes, '[d]eference to this requirement is ... of evidential, rather than substantive, value: it is

Attributing responsibility There is no general standard of evidence in international law.[55] However, the US claimed to base Iraq's responsibility for the assassination attempt upon 'clear and compelling evidence'.[56] This evidence, which 'took time' to collect so that 'there was no rush to judgment', included 'forensic data, interviews with suspects and other intelligence'[57] and led the US Department of Justice and the CIA to conclude that 'Iraq planned, equipped and launched the terrorist operation'.[58] Furthermore, 'this assassination plot was directed and pursued by the Iraqi intelligence service'.[59] In particular, the two main suspects, of Iraqi origin, had informed the FBI how they had been 'recruited',[60] 'received orders',[61] 'instructed',[62] and provided 'with the car bomb and other explosive devices'[63] by the Iraqi intelligence service.

If the US's 'clear and compelling' evidence implicating the government of Iraq is to be believed, and many of those within the UNSC expressly accepted the assessment of it as 'clear and compelling' at face value[64] and those that did not also did not challenge this assessment, then the assassination attempt, which is a breach of an international obligation,[65] is attributable to Iraq under international law.[66] Indeed, given the evidence presented, it would appear that those individuals actually carrying out the attempt were acting under the 'effective control' of Iraq.

Reaction Whilst Iraq described the missile attacks as an 'act of aggression' and a violation of 'the norms of international law and the Charter'[67] and a few states

---

not a condition precedent for the lawful use of force in self-defence'. See D. Kritsiotis, 'The Legality of the 1993 US Missile Strike on Iraq and the Right of Self-Defence in International Law' (1996) 45 *ICLQ* 162, 174.

55 O'Connell, supra n. 24, 21.

56 UN Doc. S/26003, supra n. 54. In President Clinton's address to the nation it was claimed that 'compelling evidence' had been found. See R.F. Teplitz, 'Taking Assassination Attempts Seriously: Did the United States Violate International Law in Forcefully Responding to the Iraqi Plot to Kill George Bush?' (1995) 25 *Cornell Int'l L.J.* 569, 605.

57 UNSC Verbatim Record (27 June 1993) UN Doc. S/PV. 3245, US (4).

58 Ibid., 3.

59 Ibid., 4.

60 Ibid., 5.

61 Ibid.

62 Ibid., 6.

63 Ibid., 5.

64 Ibid., France (13), Japan (16), Brazil (18), UK (21), New Zealand (23) and Spain (24).

65 A.D. Surchin, 'Terror and the Law: The Unilateral Use of Force and the June 1993 Bombing of Baghdad' (1994–95) 5 *Duke J.Comp.& Int'l L.* 457, 470–71.

66 Indeed, '[t]he failure of the plotters to conduct the assassination is therefore immaterial in the determination of the actual international liability of Iraq'. See Kritsiotis, supra n. 54, 172.

67 UN Doc. S/PV. 3245, supra n. 57, 9 and 12. See also UN Doc. S/26004 (27 June 1993).

expressed mild rebuke towards the strikes[68] or urged restraint by all states,[69] general support was the consensus among those present in the UNSC on this occasion. Whilst caution must be taken in using the discussion and debate in this organ as representative of the view of the primary interpretive community concerned with interpreting and evaluating actions of self-defence, that is, the international community of states, it at least appeared that there was no significant negative reaction from those within this community. Furthermore, those from this broader community that were sitting in the UNSC claimed that the action was 'justified'[70] or expressed 'understanding'[71] for the strikes 'in the circumstances'[72] with some stating that any state would have taken the same action.[73] More specifically, whilst 'the traditional interpretation of article 51 leads to the conclusion that an unsuccessful assassination attempt on a former U.S. president which took place outside of the United States would not be an armed attack',[74] on this occasion 'the international community acquiesced in Ambassador Albright's characterization of the Iraqi plot as an "attack"'.[75]

Furthermore, the emphasis placed upon the action by the US was that it was a response to a 'continuing threat to United States nationals'[76] with the intention being 'to damage the terrorist infrastructure of the Iraqi regime',[77] 'frustrate future unlawful actions',[78] 'pre-empt such activities'[79] and to 'discourage'[80] and 'deter further acts of aggression against the United States'.[81] However, on this occasion none of those present within the UNSC required evidence of this threat whilst many asserted agreed with the preventative or deterrent nature of the

68 China said that it was 'deeply concerned' and stressed 'that disputes between or among countries should be settled through peaceful means of dialogue and consultation' and 'opposed … any action that can contravene the Charter of the United Nations and norms of international relations'. Ibid., China (21).

69 Ibid., Cape Verde, representing the NAM, (16). See also UN Doc. S/5657 (27 June 1993).

70 Ibid., Hungary (18), UK (21) and Russia (22).

71 Ibid., France (13) and Spain (24).

72 Ibid., France (13) and Japan (16).

73 Ibid., New Zealand (23).

74 Surchin, supra n. 65, 480. Kritsiotis also notes that 'it is unlikely that the foiled plot would come within the definition of an actual armed attack under Article 51 … it is doubtful whether the Clinton administration's perception of the Iraqi role in the assassination plan as an "armed attack" can be genuinely accommodated in law'. See Kritsiotis, supra n. 54, 172.

75 S.G. Baker, 'Comparing the 1993 US Airstrike on Iraq to the 1986 Bombing of Libya: The New Interpretation of Article 51' (1994) 24 *Ga.J.Int'l.& Comp.L.* 99, 112.

76 UN Doc. S/26003, supra n. 54.

77 UN Doc. S/PV. 3245, supra n. 57, 6.

78 UN Doc. S/26003, supra n. 54.

79 Ibid.

80 Ibid.

81 UN Doc. S/PV.3245, supra n.57.

strikes.[82] As Dino Kritsiotis correctly summarizes: 'By tying the missile strike to the prospect of similar, though unspecified, incidents, the Clinton administration struck a clear response in the international community. In the Security Council the missile strike was not perceived merely as a singular response to the assassination plot but was viewed as a general deterrence against possible future acts of state-sponsored terrorism by Iraq'.[83] Indeed, the general support, whether implicit or explicit, was that the action was both necessary[84] and proportionate.[85]

Qualifying the impact of the 1993 Iraq incident on the jus ad bellum In the aftermath of the missile strikes of June 1993 it at least appeared that there was intersubjective agreement that measures to suppress state-sponsored terrorism was an appropriate response. Indeed, given the condemnation of the US strikes against Libya in 1986 in response to an incident of state-sponsored terrorism in similar circumstances[86] it would seem at first glance that this turnaround suggested the setting of a new precedent. However, one should be cautious in overstating the precedential value of this incident for two reasons.

First, the apparent *opinio necessitatis* regarding the incident must be seen in the 'Iraq context'. As Sean Murphy notes, 'the extensive global intrusion into Iraqi sovereignty after its 1990 invasion of Kuwait, the establishment of the "no-fly zones" in northern and southern Iraq, and ultimately the launching of missile strikes against Iraq for the failure to comply with the U.N. weapons-inspection regime warrants caution in viewing the global reaction to the 1993 airstrike as reflecting a general shift in attitudes about the use of force norms'.[87]

Indeed, the fact that this incident involved action against the pariah state of choice at the time, Iraq, warrants caution as to claiming any impact upon the law. The necessity behind the strikes was set in the context of Iraq's general defiance of the will of the UNSC following the Gulf War two years earlier.[88] For example, because of 'the pattern of ... Iraq's behaviour, including its disregard for international law and Security Council resolutions'[89] the US 'concluded that there [was] no reasonable prospect that new diplomatic initiatives or economic measures [could] influence the current Government of Iraq to cease planning

82 Ibid., Brazil (17), Hungary (19–20) and UK (22).

83 Kritsiotis, supra n. 54, 168. Nevertheless, the action was branded as classic case of 'reprisal' action by many of those within the secondary interpretive community. See Kritsiotis, Ibid., 166; W.M. Reisman, 'The Raid on Baghdad: Some Reflections on its Lawfulness and Implications' (1994) 5 *EJIL* 120, 125; Baker, supra n. 75, 115; Surchin, supra n. 65, 492.

84 See, for example, UN Doc. S/PV. 3245, supra n. 57, Brazil (17) and Spain (24).

85 See, for example, Ibid., UK (21).

86 Greenwood, supra n. 7, 933.

87 Murphy, supra n. 19, 47 (n. 37).

88 UN Doc. S/PV. 3245, supra n. 57, 8–9.

89 UN Doc. S/26003, supra n. 54.

future attacks'.[90] Consequently, it was 'necessary to respond to the attempted attack and the threat of further attacks'.[91] Many other members within the UNSC also noted the general behaviour of Iraq.[92] Russia, one of those behind the establishment of the no-fly zones, whilst condemnatory of the US actions in Libya in 1986, and its actions in Afghanistan and Sudan in 1998,[93] expressed much support on this occasion. As noted in Chapters 4 and 5 there was a certain amount of support for actions taken against Iraq at this time, which seemed to come to an end in 1996 when the intersubjective agreement broke down due to the US beginning to unilaterally enforce what it perceived to be the will of the UNSC.[94]

Second, although the action was generally welcomed, there was a noticeable lack of *opinio juris* regarding the right of self-defence in these circumstances.[95] Indeed, only Russia referred to Article 51 of the UN Charter and the *legality*, as opposed to the *necessity*, of the action.[96] Even the US's closest ally, the UK, whilst offering unrestrained general support, preferred to describe it as 'legitimate' as opposed to lawful.[97] What appeared as subtle nuances in language amongst some was actually a significant indicator of negative intersubjective agreement as to any changes to the law as a result of this action. The presence of *opinio necessitatis* regarding the anti-terrorist military actions of the US on this occasion had the possibility of solidifying into *opinio juris* over time. Indeed, as Kritsiotis notes, '[g]iven the strength of the international support for the American action, and the discernible reluctance to depart from the accepted Charter rules on the use of force, it may well be the case that the legal basis of the missile strike, if any exists, is rooted in an extended notion of self-defence. However, a more coherent, legal endorsement from the strike's political advocates needs to be forthcoming if this indeed is the case'.[98] However, not only was this unlikely given the swing in the intersubjective agreement regarding the 'Iraq context',[99] but also it is not possible

90 Ibid. For support in the secondary interpretive community for this position see Teplitz, supra n. 56, 611; Kritsiotis, supra n. 54, 167; Surchin, supra n. 65, 474.

91 UN Doc. S/26003, supra n. 54.

92 Those who mentioned the violation of the disarmament obligations include Japan (16), Hungary (18), Spain (24), UK (22), UN Doc. S/PV. 3245, supra n. 57.

93 See infra *Pushing the Boundaries: Passive State Support Permitting the Use of Force Against Non-State Entities.*

94 See, generally, Chapters 4 and 5.

95 As Kritsiotis notes: 'Importantly, a respectable and diverse corps of states in the Security Council understood the need and the reasons for unilateral action and approved of the firm-handed use of force to combat state-sponsored terrorism. However, only a limited number of states endorsed the legal opinion provided by the Clinton administration'. See Kritsiotis, supra n. 54, 175.

96 UN Doc. S/PV. 3245, supra n. 57, Russia (22). France also mentioned it but only in connection with what the US had said. Ibid., France (3).

97 Ibid., UK (21).

98 Kritsiotis, supra n. 54, 175.

99 See Chapters 4 and 5.

to see a change in the law as a result of this incident as the future witnessed not the increase in state-sponsored terrorism under the 'effective control' standard but rather non-state entities acting on their own or with limited support from states.

Pushing the Boundaries: Passive State Support Permitting the Use of Force Against Non-State Entities

On 7 August 1998, the US embassies in Nairobi, Kenya, and Dar es Salaam, Tanzania, were bombed killing nearly 300 people, 12 of whom were US citizens.[100] Subsequently, it emerged that the wealthy Saudi-born Islamic militant, Osama bin Laden, leader of the al-Qaida terrorist network, had issued a fatwa justifying the attacks and US officials suspected his involvement.[101] The UNSC, on 13 August 1998, strongly condemned the terrorist bomb attacks.[102]

On 20 August 1998, the US responded by launching cruise missiles against what it claimed was a terrorist training base near Khost, Afghanistan and a pharmaceutical plant (Shifa Pharmaceutical Industries) said to make VX nerve gas ingredients in Khartoum, Sudan.[103] In reporting its actions to the UNSC,[104] the US stated that it had 'exercised its right of self-defence' in 'accordance with Article 51 of the Charter of the United Nations'.[105] This was the first time that the US had used force in response to a non-state terrorist attack.

Attributing responsibility In support of its action the US claimed to have 'obtained convincing information from a variety of reliable sources that the organization of Usama Bin Laden is responsible'[106] and, whilst not claiming that the training camp and factory were the source of the embassy attacks, the US in its letter did claim to have 'convincing evidence that further such attacks were in preparation from these ... terrorist facilities'.[107]

Furthermore, whilst the US claimed to have convincing evidence of the perpetrators, and convincing evidence that more attacks were forthcoming from the same sources and location, it did not say to have possession of 'convincing' evidence, or indeed any evidence at all, that Sudan and Afghanistan had 'effectively controlled' those individuals behind the embassy bombings or adopted them as

100 *Keesing's* (1998) 42434.

101 Ibid., 42434–35; S.D. Murphy, 'Contemporary Practice of the United States' (1999) 93 *AJIL* 161.

102 UNSC Res. 1189 (13 August 1998) UN Doc. S/RES/1189.

103 *Keesing's* (1998) 42435.

104 UN Doc. S/1998/780 (20 August 1998); *Keesing's* (1998) 42435. The US had thus once again satisfied the reporting requirement of Article 51. See supra n. 54.

105 Ibid.

106 Ibid. It is notable that the letter to the UNSC at no time named this organization as 'al-Qaida'.

107 Ibid.

their own under the traditional standard for the attribution of the acts of non-state entities to a state thus permitting measures in self-defence on their territory. Indeed, the US did not attribute the embassy attacks to Sudan and/or Afghanistan[108] and neither did it claim that they were 'actively' supporting al-Qaida. Rather, it appears that the US was claiming support of a more 'passive' nature from the states concerned by their failing to 'shut these terrorist facilities down and to cease their cooperation with the Bin Laden organization'.[109]

If one accepts this claim, then the states concerned were in violation of both their obligations to refrain from supporting terrorism and the due diligence principle to act to prevent the terrorist organization from operating from their territory.[110] However, under the traditional law outlined above, this passive support and violation of these obligations was not sufficient to permit the use of force upon the territory of those states in response. Instead, all that was permitted was proportional non-forcible countermeasures.[111]

Nevertheless, in an implicit argument that echoed that made by Israel in the aftermath of its strike against the PLO headquarters in Tunis in 1985,[112] the US claimed that the cooperation it had described permitted force to be used not against the states themselves, but against the bases and facilities of the terrorist organization operating from their territories. That is, the support did not make the armed attack attributable to the host state, but it rendered its territory open to forcible measures in response specifically against the non-state entities concerned. As Kimberley Trapp correctly asserts, '[t]he United States was charging the Taliban and Sudan with acquiescing in Bin Laden's terrorist activities, and basing its right to specifically target non-state actors in foreign territory on an inability to rely on the host states in counter-terror efforts'.[113]

Reaction In contrast to the aftermath of the missile strike in Iraq in 1993, no meeting of the UNSC was held to discuss the incident and the US did not present its evidence.[114] This proved a point of contention in connection with the pharmaceutical plant in Sudan. Indeed, the evidential basis for its claim that the pharmaceutical

108 At this time al-Qaida was depicted as acting on its own. See Trapp, supra n. 14, 149 (n. 47).

109 UN Doc. S/1998/780, supra n. 104.

110 See supra The Traditional Law Governing Responses to Self-Defence Against International Terrorism.

111 Ibid.

112 See infra n. 182.

113 Trapp, supra n. 14, 149.

114 This led Jules Lobel to claim that '[t]he attack demonstrates that the United States has the power to block any effort to question or challenge its factual assertions, and to, in effect, silence other international voices'. J. Lobel, 'The Use of Force to Respond to Terrorist Attacks: The Bombing of Sudan and Afghanistan' (1999) 24 *Yale J.Int'l L.* 537, 557.

plant was a chemical weapons facility received much condemnation from both the primary[115] and secondary interpretive communities.[116]

However, the attacks in Afghanistan received far less critical attention from the primary interpretive community with some of its western members such as Australia, France, Germany, Japan, Spain, and the UK offering support, or at least understanding, towards the actions taken by the US.[117] This led Trapp to offer the following tentative conclusion:

> To the extent that there has been any change in the *jus ad bellum* based on the 1998 military campaign in Afghanistan – it is not a shift in the rules on attribution, or the emergence of a right to violate a state's territorial integrity irrespective of that state's non-involvement in terrorist attacks launched from its territory. It is more likely a broader acceptance that non-state actors themselves (as distinct from the state from whose territory they operate) can be the target of defensive force under Article 51 when that use of force is necessary given an inability to rely on the host state's cooperation in counter-terrorism.[118]

However, what Trapp fails to realize is that the line of reasoning adopted by the US on this occasion *was* an attempted shift in the rules on attribution. Indeed, in stressing the necessity of its actions, the US clearly stated that '[t]hese attacks were carried out only after repeated efforts to convince the Government of the Sudan and the Taliban regime in Afghanistan to shut these terrorist activities down and to cease their cooperation with the Bin Ladin organization'.[119] Such acquiescence and non-cooperation can be labelled as 'passive' support which is one of the controversial bases of attribution noted above.[120] The fact that the US

115 UN Doc. S/1998/786 (21 August 1998) (Sudan); UN Doc. S/1998/789 (21 August 1998) (League of Arab States); UN Doc. S/1998/879 (21 August 1998) (Non-Aligned Movement).

116 See, for example, Lobel, supra n. 114. Although Wedgwood claimed that there was 'a relative lack of controversy over the El-Shifa'. R. Wedgwood, 'Responding to Terrorism: The Strikes against Bin Laden' (1999) 24 *Yale J.Int'l L.* 559, 574. Several chemical weapons experts, diplomats and journalists doubted the evidence advanced by the US indicating that the plant in Sudan was producing nerve gas. Sudan forwarded many articles to the UNSC and UNGA from newspapers and studies indicating that the factory was not involved in manufacturing chemical weapons, that the US had based its decision to attack on insufficient information and that it had no supporting evidence for its claims. See UN Docs. S/1998/793, 801, 880, 885, 888, 911, 937, 938, 1083, 1133, 1168; *Keesing's* (1998) 42436.

117 W. Drozdiak, 'European Allies Back US Strikes: Japan Says it Understands' *Washington Post* (21 August 1998), A20.

118 Trapp, supra n. 14, 150.

119 UN Doc. S/1998/780, supra n. 104.

120 See supra The Traditional Law Governing Responses in Self-Defence Against International Terrorism.

was making such a claim indicated a shift in the rules so as to open up the borders of states offering such support without having 'effective control' over the non-state entities. This then enabled forcible actions to be taken against the non-state entity located there and that carried out the attack.

However, as in the Iraq incident in 1993, one should be cautious in drawing too much from this reaction.[121] Whilst there was an increased awareness and recognition of the threat of non-state terrorism (indeed the UNSC condemned the terrorist attacks shortly afterwards)[122] no member of the primary interpretive communities expressly approved of the *legal* argument advanced. Those state members which appeared to approve rather expressed mere understanding.[123] However, both the arguments advanced by the US and the reaction of the primary interpretive community was to take a significant shift just a few years later in the aftermath of the events of 9/11.

The Harbouring Standard of Attribution: *Operation Enduring Freedom*

The facts of the 9/11 attacks are well known. Nevertheless, it is worth briefly recalling them to assist in setting out the US's proposed 'harbouring' standard of attribution. On 11 September 2001, four passenger aeroplanes were hijacked and flown into the Twin Towers of the World Trade Centre, the Pentagon, with the last one crashing in open space in Pennsylvania.[124] The attacks were widely condemned by the UN[125] and the final death toll for these attacks was 2,986.[126] Although no organization claimed responsibility and no evidence was publicly presented, it was speculated by intelligence experts that the attacks were perpetrated by the al-Qaida organization based in Afghanistan.[127] Subsequently, the US claimed to have 'clear

121 L. Campbell, 'Defending Against Terrorism: A Legal Analysis of the Decision to Strike Sudan and Afghanistan' (1999–2000) 74 *Tul.L.Rev.* 1067, 1096.

122 See supra n. 102.

123 Although it is true that without a meeting of the UNSC this reaction is somewhat hard to gauge. See Chapter 2.

124 *Keesing's* (2001) 44333; S. Schmemann, 'US Attacked, Hijacked Jets Destroy Twin Towers and Hit Pentagon in Day of Terror, President Vows to Exact Punishment for "Evil"' *New York Times* (12 September 2001), A2.

125 For condemnation by the UNGA see UNGA Res. 56/1 (12 September 2001) UN Doc. A/RES/56/1, para. 1 (adopted without vote); for condemnation by the UNSC see UNSC Res. 1368 (12 September 2001) UN Doc. S/RES/1368, para. 1 (unanimously adopted); for condemnation by the UNSG see UN Doc. SG/SM/7948 (11 September 2001). For condemnation by the President of the UNSC see UN Doc. SC/7141 (11 September 2001). See, generally, *Keesing's* (2001) 44335.

126 See http://www.worldhistory.com/wiki/S/September-11,-2001-attacks.htm [Accessed: 14 June 2007].

127 *Keesing's* (2001) 44333. It was suspected that al-Qaida had attacked US interests on previous occasions, for example in the attack on the World Trade Centre in 1993, the

and compelling information that the Al-Qaeda organization, which was supported by the Taliban regime in Afghanistan, had a central role in the attacks'.[128] Al-Qaida's involvement in the attacks was accepted by NATO and its links with the Taliban regime of Afghanistan were deemed 'clear and compelling'.[129]

Invoking the Harbouring Standard of Attribution

In responding to this attack, the US did not claim that the Taliban, the *de facto* Government of Afghanistan, had 'sent' the individuals that carried it out, had 'directed and controlled' them, or had 'acknowledged and adopted' the 9/11 attacks as its own thereby directly attributing the attacks to the Taliban and therefore the state of Afghanistan. Neither was it primarily claimed that the Taliban was 'actively' supporting al-Qaida by providing it with financial aid, weapons or logistical support. Instead, the claim was made that the support provided by the Taliban was of a 'passive' form by offering a base from which to operate: 'The attacks on 11 September 2001 … have been made possible by the decision of the Taliban regime to allow parts of Afghanistan that it controls to be used by this organization as a base of operation'.[130] Furthermore, the regime rejected US demands that it unconditionally close al-Qaida training camps in Afghanistan, surrender Osama bin Laden to the US, and open Afghanistan to inspections.[131] Consequently, the US claimed that '[d]espite every effort by the United States and the international community, the Taliban regime has refused to change its policy'.[132]

Whilst up to this point the claims appear similar to those made in 1998 when the US used force in self-defence against terrorist facilities in Sudan and terrorist training camps in Afghanistan,[133] the US now asserted a distinct shift in the permissible action in response to terrorist attacks. Indeed, in its newly launched 'war on terror', the US began to claim that it was necessary now to make 'no distinction between the terrorists who committed these acts and those who *harbour* them',[134]

1998 bombing of the US embassies in Kenya and Tanzania, and the attack on the USS *Cole* in Yemen in 2000. See S.D. Murphy, 'Contemporary Practice of the United States in Relation to International Law' (2002) 96 *AJIL* 237, 239.

128 US letter to the UNSC, UN Doc. S/2001/946 (7 October 2001).

129 See Statement by NATO Secretary-General, Lord Roberson (2 October 2001). Available at http://www.nato.int/docu/speech/2001/s011002a.htm [Accessed: 14 January 2010].

130 UN Doc. S/2001/946, supra n. 128.

131 *Keesing's* (2001) 44337.

132 UN Doc. S/2001/946, supra n. 128.

133 See supra *Pushing the Boundaries: Passive State Support Permitting the Use of Force Against Non-State Entities.*

134 President George W. Bush, 'Address to the Nation on the Terrorist Attacks' (2001) 37 *Weekly Compilation of Presidential Documents* 1301, 1301 (emphasis added). See S.R. Ratner, '*Jus ad Bellum* and *Jus in Bello* After September 11' (2002) 96 *AJIL* 905, 906; *Keesing's* (2001) 44334. On 14 September, the US Congress approved a joint

this assimilation thus permitting it to take measures not just against al-Qaida training camps but also against Taliban military installations. In this case both were viewed as legitimate targets of self-defence so that passive support in the form of harbouring entitled the use of force against non-state actors *and* the territorial state.

The Harbouring Standard in Practice: Operation Enduring Freedom

The US subsequently responded on 7 October 2001 by launching *Operation Enduring Freedom* and formally justified it as self-defence under Article 51 of the UN Charter.[135] Indeed, the US reported to the UNSC that '[i]n accordance with Article 51 of the Charter of the United Nations' and 'following the armed attacks that were carried out against the United States on 11 September 2001'[136] it had exercised 'its inherent right of individual and collective self-defence'.[137] Importantly, it was intended that this would 'include measures against al-Qaeda terrorist training camps *and military installations of the Taliban regime in Afghanistan*'.[138] Furthermore, most of the force employed on this occasion was directed against governmental infrastructure rather than against the terrorist organization which had perpetrated the attacks.[139] Fighting continued until 7 December 2001 when the remaining Taliban troops in the city of Kandahar were defeated by the Northern Alliance, an opposition group which the US (and UK) had been supporting in its fight against the Taliban.[140] However, *Operation Enduring Freedom* itself still officially continues today.

Reaction

The most notable point in this instance is not the US's assertion of new rights but rather the overwhelming support witnessed for the forcible response taken under the justification of self-defence. Indeed, not only did the primary interpretive community provide sympathy for the US and support for its actions in the months following the 9/11 attacks, but it also supported more specifically the right of self-defence in these circumstances and the classification of the attacks as 'armed attacks'.

---

resolution that authorized the President to 'use all necessary and appropriate force' against those behind the attacks and those who '*harboured* such organizations and persons … in order to prevent any future acts of international terrorism against the United States by such nations, organization or persons'. See (2001) 40 *ILM* 1282 (emphasis added).

135 UN Doc. S/2001/946, supra n. 128. See also letter to the UNSC from the UK, UN Doc. S/2001/947 (7 October 2001); *Keesing's* (2001) 44334.

136 UN Doc. S/2001/946, Ibid.

137 Ibid.

138 Ibid., (emphasis added). Indeed, both were viewed as legitimate targets of self-defence. See Trapp, supra n. 14, 151.

139 C. Gray, *International Law and the Use of Force*, 2nd edn (Oxford: Oxford University Press, 2004), 168.

140 *Keesing's* (2001) 44503.

This express support came from several other organizations. For example, NATO, for the first time in its history, invoked the collective self-defence provision of its constituent treaty.[141] Similarly, the OAS determined that the attacks on the US were an attack on 'all American states' and that member states shall provide 'effective reciprocal assistance'.[142] On 8 October 2001, the EU also declared its 'wholehearted support for the action that is being taken in self-defence'.[143]

Furthermore, Canada, France, Germany, the Netherlands and New Zealand offered ground troops to the US in building a coalition to respond to the attacks of 9/11.[144] Australia, on 23 November 2001, announced that it was invoking the 1951 ANZUS treaty in contributing land, air and naval units to the US.[145] Offers of support also came from many other states.[146] Only Iraq directly challenged the legality of the military action.[147] Significantly, from this reaction 'it would appear

141 The North Atlantic Treaty (1949), Article 5. For the text of The North Atlantic Treaty see http://www.nato.int/docu/basictxt/treaty.htm [Accessed: 28 November 2009]. The NATO Secretary-General stated that because it had been determined that the attack had been directed from abroad, it was 'regarded as an action covered by Article 5 of the Washington Treaty, which states that an armed attack on one or more of the Allies in Europe or North America shall be considered an attack against them all' so that any member state could take such action as they deemed necessary in the exercise of the collective right of self-defence. See Statement by NATO Secretary General, Lord Roberson (2 October 2001). Available at http://www.nato.int/docu/speech/2001/s011002a.htm [Accessed: 28 November 2009].

142 OEA/Ser.F/II.24RC.24/RES.1/01 (21 September 2001). Available at http://www.oas.org/oaspage/crisis/rc.24e.htm [Accessed: 2 July 2007]. Article 3(1) of the Rio Treaty provides that 'an armed attack by any state against an American state shall be considered as an attack against all the American states and, consequently, each one of the said Contracting Parties undertakes to assist in meeting the attack in the exercise of the inherent right of individual or collective self-defense recognized by Article 51 of the Charter of the United Nations'. Inter-American Treaty of Reciprocal Assistance (2 September 1947) T.I.A.S. No. 1838.

143 UN Doc. S/2001/967 (8 October 2001). In clear support of the harbouring standard of attribution opening up the way to self-defence, the letter also stated that 'despite repeated pressure, the Taliban regime has refused to take responsibility for handing over those suspected so that they could be brought to justice. The al-Qai'dah network and the regime that supports and harbours it are now facing the consequences of their action'.

144 See, respectively, UN Doc. S/2001/1005 (24 October 2001); UN Doc. S/2001/1103 (23 November 2001); UN Doc. S/2001/1127 (29 November 2001); UN Doc. S/2001/1171 (6 December 2001); UN Doc. S/2001/1193 (17 December 2001).

145 UN Doc. S/2001/1104 (23 November 2001).

146 Those states offering ground troops included the Czech Republic, Italy, Japan, Turkey and the UK. States such as Georgia, Oman, Pakistan, the Philippines, Qatar, Saudi Arabia, Tajikistan, Turkey, and Uzbekistan provided airspace and facilities. China, Egypt, Mexico and Russia publicly expressed approval of the strikes. See *Keesing's* (2001) 44335–36; S.D. Murphy, 'Contemporary Practice of the United States' (2002) 96 *AJIL* 237, 245 and 248–49.

147 B. Whitaker, 'Attack on Afghanistan: Iraqi Reaction' *The Guardian* (8 October 2001), 6.

that the relationship between Afghanistan and al-Qaeda – despite falling short of responsibility – was considered sufficient to render the former a legitimate target of self-defence. Extensive international support for the operation certainly supports this contention'.[148]

The Security Council Arguably the most significant of all of those who recognized this right was the UNSC which, immediately after the events of 9/11, 'recogniz[ed] the inherent right of individual and collective self-defence in accordance with the Charter' in Resolution 1368 (2001).[149] The recognition in these circumstances is remarkable for its unanimity, for the fact that there was no reference to possible state involvement (at the time it had not been established who was responsible for the attacks), and for the fact that this was the first time that the UNSC, an organ not prone to recognizing the right of self-defence, affirmed the right in response to terrorist attacks.

However, the resolution did not classify the attack as an 'armed attack' and instead, whilst recognizing the right of self-defence in the preamble, regarded the acts as a 'threat to international peace and security'.[150] This has led Antonio Cassese to claim that the resolution was 'ambiguous and contradictory' wavering between the right of self-defence and collective security.[151] Others within the secondary interpretive community, however, have claimed that by recognizing the right of self-defence this was an implicit recognition of the attacks as 'armed attacks'.[152] In any case, the intersubjective agreement at the time certainly seemed to suggest that the primary interpretive community generally believed that a right of self-defence existed in these circumstances.

Some Tentative Conclusions

The events of 9/11 and the overwhelming support from the primary interpretive community for the actions of the US might lead one to conclude that there has been

148 L. Moir, 'Reappraising the Resort to Force? *Jus ad Bellum* and the War on Terror' (2005) 8 *Y.B.N.Z.Juris.* 1, 13.

149 UNSC Res. 1368, supra n. 125, preamble. Later, the UNSC unanimously adopted Resolution 1373 which 'reaffirmed' this right and contained measures to be taken in order to combat terrorism. UNSC Res. 1373 (28 September 2001) UN Doc. S/RES/1373. It has been suggested that the language used in UNSC Resolution 1373 (2001) could be argued to be an authorization to use force to prevent terrorism. See M. Byers, 'Terrorism, the Use of Force and International Law after 11 September' (2002) 51 *ICLQ* 401, 401–02; Paust, supra n. 19, 544–55. However, given the absence of the commonly understood authorization to use 'all necessary means' and the lack of intersubjective agreement on this at the time and in the period since, this argument has proved to have had no legs.

150 UNSC Res. 1368, supra n. 125, para. 1.

151 A. Cassese, 'Terrorism is Also Disrupting Some Crucial Legal Categories of International Law' (2001) 12 *EJIL* 993, 996. For more on the collective security powers of the UNSC see Chapter 3.

152 Beard, supra n. 16, 568.

a significant shift in the law regarding actions in self-defence against terror attacks. Indeed, whilst not new, arguments that 'armed attacks' can clearly be carried out by non-state entities necessitating a forcible response in self-defence have been made with increased fervour by some within the secondary interpretive community.[153] Similarly, old arguments have been revived with increased enthusiasm after 9/11 that a delay in responding to a terrorist attack does not mean that it must be classified as an armed reprisal rather than an action of self-defence.[154] Furthermore, it has been claimed that forcible actions taken to prevent and deter future terrorist attacks may now be lawful.[155]

Yet perhaps the greatest perceived shift, and the one that has been the focus of this chapter, is in connection with the rules attributing the actions of non-state entities to certain states for the purposes of self-defence.[156] Whilst few have claimed that al-Qaida was actually under the 'effective control' of the Taliban,[157] some have suggested that they were under their 'overall control' thus attributing the 9/11 attacks to the state of Afghanistan under the *Tadic* standard and permitting the use of force in self-defence against it.[158] Others maintain that although the response against al-Qaida was lawful the response against the Taliban was 'impermissible' under the still relevant 'effective control' standard.[159]

However, this debate appears to miss the point. The states which undertook the action on this occasion based the right to take action against the Taliban on the basis that it provided passive support to al-Qaida, in particular providing it a 'harbour' from which to operate.[160] Furthermore, the primary interpretive community appeared to interpret this as acceptable on this occasion. Indeed,

---

153 See, for example, Franck, supra n. 9, 840.

154 Ibid.

155 M.E. O'Connell, 'Lawful Self-Defense Against Terrorism' (2001–02) 63 *U.Pitt. L.Rev.* 889, 899.

156 Derek Jinks has noted that '[s]ustained reflection reinforces the view that an important shift in the law of state responsibility – at least in the domain of antiterrorism – is indeed underway'. See D. Jinks, 'State Responsibility for the Acts of Private Armed Groups' (2003) 4 *Chicago.J.Int'l L.* 83, 88.

157 Although Moir claims that 'scholars have argued that the relationship between the Taliban and Al-Qaeda met the requirements of the *Definition of Aggression*' no evidence is provided of this and the current writer has come across no scholars who have expressly adopted this view. See Moir, supra n. 148, 12.

158 See O'Connell, supra n. 24, 32; C. Stahn, 'Terrorist Acts as "Armed Attack": The Right of Self-Defense, Article 51(1/2) of the UN Charter, and International Terrorism' (2003) 27 *Fletcher F. World Aff.* 35, 42–49. For more on this standard of attribution see supra The Traditional Law Governing Responses in Self-Defence Against International Terrorism.

159 Paust, supra n. 19, 540–44.

160 In this case O'Connell claims that 'the law clearly does not support a standard of responsibility in a case where a state merely harboured terrorists'. O'Connell, supra n. 155, 902. For support for the US's position see D. Brown, 'Use of Force Against Terrorism

'[u]nlike the military campaign in 1998, the international community viewed both Al-Qaeda and the Taliban as legitimate targets of defensive force'.[161] More significantly, regime change appeared to be accepted as a proportionate response to the provision of this level of support.[162] Indeed, overall it now appeared that 'harbouring' states were now legitimate targets of self-defence too.

However, one must take caution in drawing such conclusions. Given their unprecedented scale and magnitude those within the primary interpretive community were stunned at the audacity of these attacks on the territory of the US.[163] The fact that they occurred in such close proximity to the UN and the fact that the UNGA was in session at the time no doubt had an impact upon the response of both the UN as an organization and states individually. This combination of shock, sympathy for the US, and immediate fear for their own safety should not be translated as 'instant' custom.[164] Indeed, in order to show that a rule in general, and especially one of the importance of the prohibition of the use of force, has changed, something more is required.[165] In terms of precedential value, there are different ways in which the events and the response to them can be interpreted so that '[a]lthough there was considerable political support for the American action, from a legal point of view there was also considerable ambiguity'.[166] In this case, whilst there was undoubtedly *opinio necessitatis* generated in these arguably never to be repeated circumstances, it is only after the dust has well and truly settled that one is able to discern if this has solidified into *opinio juris* in connection with potential changes to the *jus ad bellum* regarding forcible responses to terrorism.

After September 11th: State Responsibility, Self-Defense and Other Responses' (2003–04) 11 *Cardozo J.Int'l & Comp.L.* 1, 15.

161 Trapp, supra n. 14, 151.

162 Although Myjer and White question this: 'Does an attack against a small part of the United States, albeit one with devastating consequences for the people in the area hit, justify an armed response against a whole country, with the aim not only to root out the terrorists but to destroy and remove the effective, though unrecognised, government?' See Myjer and White, supra n. 17, 8.

163 White notes that 'Afghanistan must be understood in the context of the emotions provoked by the horrific and profoundly symbolic destruction of the twin towers'. N.D. White, 'The Will and Authority of the Security Council after Iraq' (2004) 17 *LJIL* 645, 655.

164 Gray has written that the 'the massive state support for the legality of the US claim to self-defence could constitute instant customary international law and an authoritative reinterpretation of the UN Charter, however radical the alteration from many states' prior conception of the right of self-defence'. See C. Gray, 'The Use of Force and the International Legal Order' in M.D. Evans (ed.), *International Law*, 2nd edn (Oxford: Oxford University Press, 2006) 589, 602.

165 M.G. Kohen, 'The Use of Force by the United States after the End of the Cold War, and its Impact Upon International Law' in M. Byers and G. Nolte (eds), *United States Hegemony and the Foundations of International Law* (Cambridge: Cambridge University Press, 2003) 197, 224.

166 Ibid., 222.

The Harbouring Standard of Attribution: Life After *Operation Enduring Freedom*

After 9/11 the US persisted with the advocacy of its 'harbouring' standard. In particular, in its controversial *National Security Strategy* of 2002, the Bush administration formally advocated this standard of attribution by making clear that it made 'no distinction between terrorists and those who knowingly harbour or provide aid to them'.[167] This was subsequently reiterated in its 2006 *National Security Strategy* where it again, although perhaps in a less restrictive fashion,[168] claimed to make 'no distinction between those who commit acts of terror and those who support and harbour them'.[169] However, as Marcelo Kohen correctly points out:

> If the will of the international community is to review the existing rules regarding the use of force against terrorists, then one can expect the same attitude will be taken in other, similar situations. If it is not the case, then one has to conclude that what we are witnessing here is not a change in the rule or its interpretation, but rather a political attitude on the part of the majority of states supporting in one case only the political aims of one state.[170]

Indeed, if there is no repetition of the invocation of the harbouring standard 'in other, similar situations' then it is possible to argue that this represents a significant indicator of negative intersubjective agreement as to the harbouring standard of attribution. Furthermore, subsequent events in general will be determinative as to the impact that the US has wielded over changes to the *jus ad bellum* given its persistent advocacy of such changes since 9/11.

The Primary Interpretive Community

Being the primary makers and breakers of international law, the first port of call is to examine the practice of states within the interpretive communities.[171] What follows is a survey of some of the most relevant incidents to have occurred since the commencement of *Operation Enduring Freedom*.

---

167 The White House, 'The National Security Strategy of the United States of America' (20 September 2002), 5. Available at http://www.commondreams.org/headlines02/0920-05.htm [Accessed: 15 November 2009].

168 The requirement of 'knowingly' harbouring terrorist groups was removed.

169 The White House, 'The National Security Strategy of the United States of America' (16 March 2006), 12. Available at http://www.isn.ethz.ch/isn/Digital-Library/Publications/Detail/?ord516=OrgaGrp&ots591=0C54E3B3-1E9C-BE1E-2C24-A6A8C7060233&lng=en&id=15462 [Accessed: 15 November 2009].

170 Kohen, supra n. 165, 225.

171 Moir has noted that 'international law is based on what states say and what states do, and it is true that apparent abrogation from its rules can result in the evolution of new rules'. Moir, supra n. 148, 27.

Russia/Chechen rebels/Georgia (2002) In 2002, Russia, in invoking its right of self-defence against terrorist attacks by Chechen rebels,[172] accused Georgia of failing in its responsibility to prevent them from operating out of the Pankisi Gorge border area.[173] In particular, it claimed that '[i]f the Georgian leadership is unable to establish a security zone in the area of the border, continues to ignore Security Council Resolution 1373 and does not put an end to the bandit sorties and attacks on adjoining areas of Russia, we reserve our right to act in accordance with Article 51 of the UN Charter'.[174]

Whilst Russia did not directly claim that Georgia willingly harboured and cooperated with the Chechen rebels, it also did not merely claim that Georgia was unable to fulfil its responsibilities thereby negating it of any responsibility. Instead, it also claimed that Georgia had 'ignored' its obligations thereby claiming some form of acquiescence on the part of Georgia. As a result, 'the responsibility for the consequences of the armed incursion' into Russian territory 'lay fully with Georgia'.[175] However, Russia did not adopt the new 'harbouring' standard of attribution proposed by the US so as to take action against Georgia. Instead, it limited its response to Chechen positions within Georgian territory.

Surprisingly, even though the US accepted that Georgia had not established effective control over the eastern part of its territory and went as far as to accept a link between the Chechen rebels and al-Qaida, it failed to support Russia's claim.[176] Rather, it condemned the violations of Georgia's sovereignty and the actions taken by Russia 'under the guise of antiterrorist operations'.[177] This has led one notable commentator within the secondary interpretive community to correctly conclude that '[t]he reluctance by the USA to acknowledge the right of another state to invoke self-defence against terrorism, even in a neighbouring state, and even where it may legitimately claim to have a strong case, seems to make it more difficult to claim that the events of 9/11 and the response have established a new customary rule. Here, as elsewhere, we see the USA claiming rights for itself that it is unwilling to see exercised by others'.[178]

Israel/Islamic Jihad/Syria (2003) In October 2003, Islamic Jihad carried out a suicide bomb attack at a café in the Israeli town of Haifa.[179] After accusing Syria

172 See, for example, *Keesing's* (2002) 44630 and 44686.

173 See 'Putin Ups Georgia Strike Warnings' BBC News (12 September 2002). Available at http://www.bbc.co.uk/news [Accessed: 15 March 2007].

174 UN Doc. S/2002/1012 (12 September 2002). For Georgia's objection to Russia's interpretation of Article 51 see UN Doc. S/2002/1033 (16 September 2002).

175 UN Doc. S/2002/854 (31 July 2002).

176 Gray, supra n. 3, 230.

177 See *The Guardian* (24 and 26 August 2002).

178 Gray, supra n. 3, 231.

179 *Keesing's* (2003) 45673.

of providing a 'safe harbour' to Islamic Jihad,[180] Israel launched a missile strike in self-defence claiming to specifically target the Ein Saheb terrorist training camp in Syria.[181] This argument of Israel did not reflect the post-9/11 US 'harbouring' standard of attribution but was instead reminiscent of the argument Israel had adopted nearly 20 years previously when it specifically targeted the PLO headquarters in Tunisia.[182] It also reflected the arguments of the US in justifying its use of force against Sudan and Afghanistan in 1998.[183]

Whilst the US invoked its 'harbouring' standard of attribution in condemning Syria for 'harbouring and supporting the groups that perpetrate terrorist acts'[184] the response was widely condemned by those within the UNSC as either a violation of international law, a violation of Syrian sovereignty, as a disproportionate armed reprisal rather than self-defence, or as an attempt to destroy the peace process.[185]

However, it should be borne in mind that this example of state practice is associated with the long running Middle East situation. Indeed, it is difficult to draw too much from incidents involving Israel as there is a sense of 'business as usual' and because of the fact that it is an illegal occupier of land with predictable support and condemnation from different quarters. Regardless of this fact, there was no attempt at getting over this political hurdle by arguing that Israel may now have a right to carry out such strikes due to changes in the law as a result of the actions of the US in light of 9/11.

Israel/Hezbollah/Lebanon (2006) On 12 July 2006, Hezbollah[186] abducted two Israeli soldiers and launched a number of rockets from southern Lebanon into northern Israel.[187] In describing the 'Axis of Terror', Israel appeared to lay

180 Islamic Jihad is categorized as a terrorist organization by the EU. See Official Journal of the EU, Council Common Position 2005/847/CFSP (29 November 2005).

181 UNSC Verbatim Record (5 October 2003) UN Doc. S/PV. 4836, Israel (5). See Trapp, supra n. 14, 152; Cassese, supra n. 22, 475.

182 On this occasion, Israel, in justifying its actions, set out a different conception of the harbouring standard. Indeed, whilst claiming that Tunisia 'knowingly harboured the PLO and allowed it complete freedom of action in planning, training, organizing and launching murderous attacks from its soil …[i]t was against [the PLO] that our action was directed, not against their host country'. UNSC Verbatim Record (2 October 1985) UN Doc. S/PV. 2611, Israel (22–5).

183 See supra *Pushing the Boundaries: Passive State Support Permitting the Use of Force Against Non-State Entities*.

184 UN Doc. S/PV. 4836, supra n. 181, 10

185 Ibid. See, for example, Spain (9), UK (9), Germany (10) and France (11).

186 Hezbollah is categorized as a terrorist organization by the EU and the US. The US has asserted links between Hezbollah and al-Qaida. See *Keesing's* (2002) 44918.

187 See the UNSG's Reports on UNIFIL for the facts surrounding the outbreak of the conflict. See UN Doc. S/2006/560 (21 July 2006).

responsibility at the doors of Lebanon, Syria and Iran.[188] Whilst responsibility was attributed to Lebanon from 'whose territory these acts have been launched into Israel',[189] Syria and Iran were accused of 'support[ing] and embrace[ing] those who carried out this attack'.[190]

However, although Israel adopted the language of the US and its 'war on terror' in claiming that Lebanon provided 'a base for terrorism',[191] in contrast to the actions of the US in 2001, when Israel launched its action in self-defence it made clear that it was targeted at the non-state entity, Hezbollah, not the territorial state, Lebanon.[192] Indeed, '[a]s has been Israel's consistent practice, it claimed not to be acting against the territorial host state, but primarily against non-state terrorists'.[193] In doing so, there was some notable support for its position. Indeed, many within the primary interpretive communities recognized the right of self-defence.[194]

However, whilst Israel maintained this claim, in what turned out to be an extensive military campaign it eventually became clear that Lebanese infrastructure was being targeted and severely damaged with many civilian casualties.[195] This led to much condemnation by the international community, in particular, that the actions taken were disproportionate.[196]

What is significant is that whilst Israel in its rhetoric was prepared to invoke the 'harbouring' standard of attribution, it was not ultimately prepared to rely upon it to justify actions against Lebanon. This failure to rely upon this standard of attribution, and by one of the US's closest allies too, is a significant indicator of negative intersubjective agreement regarding the standard at this time. Furthermore, it was clearly not favoured by the interpretive communities. Indeed, 'the international community's reaction to Israel's 2006 military campaign in Lebanon, and its repeated calls for Israel to refrain from targeting Lebanese infrastructure, militate against' the emergence of a rule 'recognizing a state's acquiescence in, or failure to suppress, international terrorism as a basis of attribution'.[197]

---

188 UN Doc. S/2006/515 (12 July 2006). President Bush previously described Iran, Iraq and North Korea as an 'axis of evil'. See Chapter 4.

189 Ibid.

190 Ibid.

191 UN Doc. S/2003/96 (27 January 2003).

192 Israel said in the UNSC: 'Although Israel holds the Government of Lebanon responsible, it is concentrating its response carefully, mainly on Hizbollah strongholds, positions and infrastructure'. UNSC Verbatim Record (14 July 2006) UN Doc. S/PV. 5489, Israel (6). See also UNSC Verbatim Record (21 July 2006) UN Doc. S/PV. 5493, Israel (10–12).

193 Trapp, supra n. 14, 153–54.

194 UNSC Verbatim Record (14 July 2006) UN Doc. S/PV. 5489, Argentina (9), US (10), Japan (12), UK (13), Tanzania (14), Peru (14), Denmark (15), Greece (17) and France (17).

195 Gray, supra n. 3, 241.

196 See, generally, UN Doc. S/PV. 5493, supra n. 192.

197 Trapp, supra n. 14, 156.

Turkey/PKK/Iraq (2008) After threatening to do so in October 2007,[198] and with regular border scuffles occurring at this time,[199] Turkey finally launched a full-scale troop invasion into northern Iraq on 25 February 2008 in response to attacks by the PKK organization which was operating from there.[200]

There had been previous operations of such a scale in 1995, 1996, and 1997.[201] On these occasions Turkey did not offer self-defence as a justification and did not report its measures to the UNSC but instead made the general claim that it was 'resorting to legitimate measures which are imperative to its own security'.[202] These were taken in the belief that '[n]o country could be expected to stand idle when its own territorial integrity is incessantly threatened by blatant cross-border attacks of a terrorist organization based and operating from a neighbouring country, if that country is unable to put an end to such attacks'.[203] Whilst it was not condemned by the UNSC, condemnation was loudly pronounced by many within the primary interpretive communities including the Arab League, the Gulf Cooperation Council and the NAM.[204]

In 2008 very little changed. It did not offer a legal justification of self-defence and did not report its actions to the UNSC. The cross-border incursions were threatened unless Iraq and the US forces present there suppressed the activities of the PKK.[205] In September 2007 Iraq had pledged in a deal to deny the PKK a safe haven in northern Iraq.[206] Echoing the justification from previous incursions, the Turkish President, Abdullah Gul, stated: 'We have made it very clear that if the terrorist shelters there are not destroyed, then it is our legitimate right to destroy those shelters ourselves'.[207] Although condemnation came from some quarters, the raids received cautious support from others, including the US.[208]

---

198 The Turkish Parliament passed a resolution on 17 October 2007 which authorized a full-scale invasion against the PKK. See *Kessing's* (2007) 48219.

199 See, for example, 'Turkey bombards Kurdish rebel bases' *The Times* (17 December 2007), 19.

200 P. de Bendern, 'Turkish army advances on PKK' *The Guardian* (26 February 2008), 22. This organization is classified as a terrorist organization by both the EU and the US.

201 See Gray, supra n. 3, 141–42.

202 UN Doc. S/1995/605 (24 July 1995). This appears to be an invocation of the doctrine of necessity. See supra The Traditional Law Governing Responses in Self-Defence Against International Terrorism. Iran, for its incursions into Iraqi territory, expressly offered self-defence under Article 51. See UN Doc. S/25843 (26 May 1993).

203 Ibid.

204 See UN Doc. S/1997/461 (16 June 1997).

205 S. Erdem, 'Turkey Seeks Lost Troops as Pressure For Action Grows' *The Times* (23 October 2007).

206 *Keesing's* (2007) 48151.

207 M. Howard, 'Turkey Bombards Northern Iraq After Ambush' *The Guardian* (22 October 2007).

208 de Bendern, supra n. 200.

Whilst there were no claims made that Iraq was intentionally harbouring or providing support to the PKK, this incident is still significant as it could be expected that if the events of 11 September 2001 had created or confirmed a right for states to take forcible measures in self-defence against the attacks of non-state entities on the territories of other states, Turkey might have clarified and improved its general justifications from previous incursions. The fact that it did not is telling as to any impact that the claims and reaction after the events of 9/11 have had.

Colombia/Farc/Ecuador (2008) On 2 March 2008, Colombian troops crossed the border into Ecuador and killed members of Farc, a rebel group of Colombia, after claiming to have been targeted first.[209] Rather than depicting this group as a legitimate resistance movement, Colombia described it as an arm of international terrorism, and its actions as part of the 'war on terror'.[210] States in the region urged restraint, with Brazil demanding Colombia apologize to Ecuador and Chile offering condemnation.[211] The US, whilst backing Columbia's right to defend itself and stating that it would stand by Colombia in its fight against terrorism, urged dialogue.[212] However, whilst Colombia accused Ecuador of passive support for Farc and of providing a base from which to launch its operations, it did not go as far as to claim that this support was sufficient to attribute the acts to this state for the purposes of self-defence, thus serving as a further indicator of negative intersubjective agreement regarding the harbouring standard of attribution.[213]

Conclusions on state practice The practice from the primary interpretive communities briefly examined above regarding self-defence in the post-9/11 era does not exhibit any real differences from the pre-9/11 era, or indeed from the practice preceding the US's strikes against Sudan and Afghanistan in 1998. The actions have either been condemned, have been part of long running conflicts with no change in the actions taken, in the justificatory discourse engaged in or the reaction of other states, self-defence has not been argued, or the right in the particular case has been excluded by the US itself. Ultimately, the US 'harbouring' standard of attribution has made no discernible impact. Even Israel, who used language connected with this standard, failed to ultimately rely on it to carry out strikes against other states. All in all, the precedents do not bear witness to any shift in the rules on attribution.

---

209 P. Vallely, 'What's Behind The Crisis Gripping Colombia, Venezuela and Ecuador?' *The Independent* (5 March 2008), 32.

210 D. Howden, 'Colombia Demands Chavez Face Trial For Funding Farc Rebels' *The Independent* (5 March 2008), 29. It did not legally justify its actions as self-defence nor characterize the preceding actions of the group as armed attacks.

211 Vallely, supra n. 209.

212 Ibid.

213 Ibid.

However, whilst these actions may be significant, perhaps even more significant are the omissions to act by the primary interpretive communities. Indeed, many have not invoked the right of self-defence since 9/11 against al-Qaida even though there have been attacks during this period which have been attributed to it.[214] Further still, as the next section demonstrates, the UNSC has not shown the same resolve towards these incidents as it did in the immediate aftermath of the events of 9/11.

Actions and Decisions of the Security Council

As noted above, arguably the most significant recognition of the right of self-defence in the aftermath of 9/11 was that of the UNSC. However, of greater significance for the purposes of this work is the fact that the UNSC has not made a similar reference to self-defence regarding the activities of non-state entities since, even in the context of al-Qaida terrorist attacks.[215] The UNSC has condemned them as threats to international peace and security but has remained silent on either categorizing the attacks as 'armed attacks' or referring to the right of self-defence.

Even resolutions containing general declarations on the issue of terrorism do not contain any mention of the right of self-defence.[216] Instead, peaceful and multilateral means were stressed. Indeed, '[t]his failure to refer to self-defence in this context, or to take the opportunity to reaffirm the right to use force in self-defence mentioned in earlier resolutions, seems significant. It may be taken as an indication that the right to use force in self-defence against past terrorist acts may remain exceptional, perhaps available only in cases of attacks on territory rather than on nationals abroad'.[217] After being quick to recognize the right in the aftermath of 9/11, given the inconsistent approach by this organ since it may also represent a significant indicator of negative intersubjective agreement regarding any dramatic shifts in the *jus ad bellum* opening up new possibilities to use force in response to terrorist attacks.

Due to this paucity in recognition of the right by the UNSC, Gray has commented that the right of self-defence against terrorist attacks may be limited to situations where the UNSC has affirmed it in a prior resolution.[218] Indeed,

---

214 For example the attack on a Bali nightclub in Indonesia in 2002 (*Keesing's* (2002) 45034) and the bombings in Madrid in 2004 (*Keesing's* (2004) 45910).

215 See, for example, UNSC Res. 1450 (13 December 2002) UN Doc. S/RES/1450, which deplored the claims of responsibility by al-Qaida for the terrorist attacks in Kenya but made no reference to self-defence.

216 See UNSC Res. 1456 (20 January 2003) UN Doc. S/RES/1456. The UNGA also adopted the United Nations Global Counter-Terrorism Strategy in 2006 which focuses on peaceful measures. See UN Doc. A/60/825 (27 April 2006).

217 Gray, supra n. 3, 228.

218 Gray, supra n. 164, 603.

many within the primary interpretive communities regarded the UNSC backing provided in UNSC resolutions 1368 (2001) and 1373 (2001) as crucial to the US's claim of self-defence.[219] However, it also depicts that the *opinio necessitatis* of those within the primary interpretive communities for action in self-defence in the immediate aftermath of 9/11, with apparent acquiescence in the 'war of self-defence',[220] seems to have faded.

Jurisprudence of the International Court of Justice

Although this organ of the UN is not always regarded as being the last bastion of clarity, as a significant actor within the secondary interpretive community its pronouncements do make an authoritative contribution to the debate on the state of the law.[221] Indeed, 'much of the modern law regulating the use of force by states is a product of the Court's interpretation and application of the United Nations Charter and the rules of customary international law'.[222] Since 9/11, one advisory opinion and one decision has been handed down with relevance to the issues of self-defence against non-state entities.

The Wall *advisory opinion* In 2005, the ICJ gave an advisory opinion on the legality of Israel's security wall in the West Bank. In response to Israel's claim that the wall was a measure of self-defence against terrorist attacks, the Court, in a moment of great brevity, provided its position in a single paragraph:

> Article 51 of the Charter … recognizes the existence of an inherent right of self-defence in the case of armed attack by one state against another state. However, Israel does not claim that the attacks against it are imputable to a foreign state … [c]onsequently, the Court concludes that Article 51 of the Charter has no relevance in this case.[223]

Attention has been given in the secondary interpretive community to the Court's apparent characterization of the right only being able to be invoked 'by one state against another state'. In particular, this would appear to unnecessarily read too much into the text of Article 51[224] and reject the occasionally observed trend in state practice that acts of non-state entities could be armed attacks justifying the right

219 Ibid.

220 W.M. Reisman, 'In Defense of World Public Order' (2001) 95 *AJIL* 833, 835.

221 See Chapter 2.

222 C.J. Tams, 'Light Treatment of a Complex Problem: The Law of Self-Defence in the *Wall* Case' (2005) 16 *EJIL* 963, 964.

223 Legal Consequences of the Construction of a Wall in the Occupied Palestinian Territories (Advisory Opinion), [2004] ICJ Rep. 136, para. 139.

224 Tams says that this 'is very curious indeed' as Article 51 'contains no reference to state involvement in the armed attack, but speaks of an "armed attack" without any

of self-defence.[225] This was noted and criticized even by some of the judges in the Court.[226] Whilst it has been noted that the Court's methodology and the criticism which this part of the advisory opinion received 'arguably limits the authoritative nature of the decision as regards self-defence against non-state actors',[227] the remarkably conservative opinion does stand in stark contrast to the changes that some argue have occurred in the *jus ad bellum* as a result of the events of 9/11. However one interprets the Court's jurisprudence on this occasion, it does indicate that the right of self-defence against non-state actors is still of a controversial nature in the UN's 'principal judicial organ'[228] and the actions and assertions of the US have had a limited impact in this respect.

Because the attacks Israel was claiming to defend itself against were not of an 'international phenomena',[229] that is, they did not emanate from foreign territory, the Court did not examine either the issue of the legality of the use of force on a third state's territory in response to terrorist armed attacks or the issue of attribution. These issues were of more relevance in the *DRC v Uganda* case.

The DRC v Uganda *case* The 'harbouring' standard of attribution was confronted head on in this particularly complex case[230] in which Uganda claimed that the DRC was responsible for the attacks it was suffering at the hands of armed bandits operating from its territory. This responsibility arose out of the active military and logistic support that the DRC had provided to the rebels and because of its passive toleration and acquiescence in their presence on its territory. Consequently, although it had not been attacked directly by the forces of the DRC, Uganda argued that its use of force in self-defence was directed not just at rebel military operations on the border region, but also took the form of whole scale military assaults on the DRC (thousands of miles away from the border).[231]

Whilst the Court rejected this argument on the evidence provided by Uganda as to the DRC's involvement in the attacks, in a clear rejection of the US's post-9/11 'harbouring' standard the Court also stuck with the traditional 'effective control'

---

additional qualification'. Tams, supra n. 222, 973. See supra The Traditional Law Governing Responses in Self-Defence Against International Terrorism.

225 Ibid., 972–73.

226 Separate Opinion of Judge Higgins, para. 33; Separate Opinion of Judge Kooijmans, para. 35; Declaration of Judge Buerganthal, para. 6.

227 Trapp, supra n. 14, 144. See also Tams, supra n. 222, 978.

228 UN Charter (1945), Article 92.

229 The words of Judge Kooijmans. See Separate Opinion of Judge Kooijmans, para. 36.

230 *Armed Activities on the Territory of the Congo (Democratic Republic of Congo v Uganda)* (Merits), Judgment of 19 December 2005. Available at www.icj-cij.org [Accessed: 20 July 2009]. An in-depth overview of the facts is beyond the scope of this work. For such an account see J. Kammerhofer, 'The Armed Activities Case and Non-State Actors in Self-Defence Law' (2007) 20 *LJIL* 89.

231 *DRC v Uganda*, Ibid., para. 147.

standard of attribution.[232] Consequently, because Uganda did not claim to have been subjected to an armed attack by the armed forces of the DRC and the attacks could not be attributed to the DRC, the conditions for the exercise of a right of self-defence by Uganda *against* the DRC were not present.[233]

If the response to 9/11 really had caused a dramatic shift in the *jus ad bellum*, and in particular the rules attributing the actions of non-state entities to states for the purposes of self-defence, it is arguable that the ICJ would not have been so coy in touching upon the issue. Whilst it may be argued that it did not rule out the possibility of the use of force solely against terrorist groups, because on the facts Uganda had taken widespread action against the DRC, it did expressly reject the US's 'harbouring' standard of attribution as propounded after 9/11.

Events at the United Nations

Events at the UN in the post-9/11 era have also not demonstrated any significant changes. Indeed, the organization has failed to address the issue on occasions when it was opportune to do so. The Report of the High-Level Panel on Threats, Challenges and Change recognized that '[t]he maintenance of world peace and security depends importantly on there being a common global understanding, and acceptance, of when the application of force is both legal and legitimate'.[234] However, no mention was made of the right of self-defence against terrorist activities. Whilst it touched briefly upon the issue of the 'harbour[ing] or support[ing]' of 'non-state actors', this was in the context of Chapter VII action.[235] The UNSG's report, *In Larger Freedom*, which gave scant consideration to the right of self-defence, did not mention anything at all about the events of 9/11 and the aftermath.[236] Lastly, at a time when states themselves had the opportunity to put forward their views on the issue at the UN World Summit in September 2005, whilst reiterating the obligation 'to ensure that their territories are not used for [terrorist] activities',[237] the Outcome document simply reaffirmed 'that the relevant provisions of the Charter are sufficient to address the full range of threats to international peace and security'.[238]

Although these documents did not rule out the use of force against terrorist non-state actors alone, or the terrorists *and* those that harbour them, given the emphasis

232 Ibid., paras. 131–35 and 146.

233 Ibid., para. 147.

234 Report of the High-Level Panel on Threats, Challenges and Change, 'A More Secure World: Our Shared Responsibility' (2004) UN Doc. A/59/565, para. 184.

235 Ibid., at 193.

236 Report of the UN Secretary-General, 'In Larger Freedom: Towards Security, Development and Human Rights for All' (2005) UN Doc. A/59/205.

237 2005 World Summit Outcome Document (2005) UN Doc. A/60/L.1, para. 86 (this is a reference to the due diligence principle).

238 Ibid., para. 79.

on terrorism at the time it would have been the perfect opportunity to have offered some clarification on the law. The fact that they did not do so is no doubt a sign of the controversy and division surrounding the issue since *Operation Enduring Freedom*.

Conclusion

Whilst the US has taken actions in self-defence against terrorism in the post-Cold War era it appeared to base its earlier actions on either the accepted standards of attribution or on standards which had been used by other states previously. However, in the aftermath of the attacks of 9/11 and in *Operation Enduring Freedom* there appeared to be a change in standards or, even more fundamentally, a change in world view, by many states.

The adoption of the 'harbouring' standard of attribution by the US presented the possibility of a radical shift in the permissible responses to terrorist attacks. The threat to international peace and security posed by widespread acceptance of this standard was clear with many states becoming possible targets of force in the 'war on terror'. Indeed, this opened up the possibility of far greater numbers of civilian deaths. To calm fears, the US did not refine its proposed standard any further into a more coherent regime for attribution. Indeed, it is still not clear the exact level of state support that was necessary before this standard of attribution became applicable.[239]

However, subsequent events militate against a reading of a change in the *jus ad bellum* to incorporate such a standard. Indeed, although the collective security system has arguably taken a knock by the US opting for self-defence when UNSC authorization would undoubtedly have been granted,[240] 'it is open to question how far any change on the law on the use of force has resulted from the terrorist attacks and their aftermath'.[241] For example, whilst such a standard may have been workable against a governmental structure such as the Taliban, its utility should perhaps be doubted against those of a more established, legitimate, and powerful nature. Practice since by relevant actors within the international community perhaps bears witness to this realization and *Operation Enduring Freedom* remains the only incident where the international community accepted the use of force against non-state actors *and* the harbouring state.[242]

239 Although, as described in the first part of the chapter, the traditional rules are also 'far from unambiguous'. See Cassese, supra n. 22, 472.

240 As Kohen has remarked, '[h]arbouring terrorist groups acting abroad clearly constitutes a threat to international peace and security, which in turn can justify forcible action as decided upon by the Security Council under Chapter VII of the Charter'. See Kohen, supra n. 165, 207.

241 Gray, supra n. 3, 193.

242 Trapp, supra n. 14, 152. The reaction to the attacks of 11 September 2001 can be viewed as *sui generis* in connection to that particular set of events. As Gray notes, 'it is not yet

It is quite possible that the lack of enthusiasm for this particular tool for fighting the 'war on terror', witnessed also in the UNSC, the UN more generally, and the jurisprudence of the ICJ, is a by-product of the divisions created over *Operation Iraqi Freedom*.[243] Whilst the US generated a large amount of support in connection with the immediate action taken after 9/11, the controversy surrounding the invasion of Iraq just a few years later appeared to have damaged this. In particular, the US can be viewed as having acted outside of the intersubjective agreement as to the boundaries of any 'war on terror' inhibiting the development of *opinio juris* as to the mechanisms proposed to fight it.[244] In short, whilst on the basis of the reaction to the 9/11 attacks and *Operation Enduring Freedom* it may have appeared as though the international community had accepted this standard, the enormous sympathy shown towards the US on this occasion has not subsequently translated into a radical shake-up of the rules on attributing the acts of non-state entities to states for the purposes of forcible self-defensive measures.

---

clear whether these events have brought about a radical and lasting transformation of the law of self-defence or whether their significance should be narrowly construed in that *Operation Enduring Freedom* was essentially a one-off response to a particular incident based on Security Council affirmation and (almost) universal acceptance by states'. See Gray, Ibid., 194.

243 See Chapter 4.

244 As Gray notes, '[t]he temporary agreement between those few states which argued that the legal right to use force against terrorist attacks was already established and those far more numerous states who after 9/11 were apparently for the first time willing to accept it as a new development in the interpretation of Article 51 has since dissipated in the disagreement as to whether to use military force against Iraq'. See Gray, supra n. 3, 194.

Chapter 7
The Doctrine of Pre-Emptive Self-Defence

> We must adapt the concept of imminent threat to the capabilities and objectives of today's adversaries.[1]

Introduction

Whilst the preceding chapters of this book have generally focused on both actions and justifications by the US, this chapter focuses simply on a doctrine advanced by the US for consideration by the interpretive communities but which is yet to be used in justification for action.[2] Whilst the advocacy of a doctrine of unilateral pre-emptive self-defence[3] is not novel for the US,[4] its inclusion in the 2002 *National Security Strategy* (hereafter '*NSS*'), accompanied by a legal argument, was a significant move in light of the 9/11 terrorist attacks and the discussion and debate as to how to deal with global terrorism.[5] However, the US went further. It also advocated such a doctrine in the realms of dealing with other states which possessed weapons of mass destruction (hereafter 'WMD').

Given that the adoption of a right of unilateral pre-emptive self-defence would appear to bend beyond breaking the point the text of Article 51 of the UN

---

1 The White House, 'The National Security Strategy of the United States of America' (20 September 2002), 15. Available at http://www.commondreams.org/headlines02/0920-05.htm [Accessed: 15 November 2009].

2 That is, unless one takes *Operation Iraqi Freedom* as an example of this doctrine in operation. The problem with this is that whilst pre-emption formed a background to the invasion, the US primarily justified it as authorized by the UNSC. See Chapter 4.

3 'Pre-emptive' self-defence is that used to destroy a threat that a state perceives as possibly coming to fruition at some point in the future. This should be contrasted with that which is 'anticipatory', that is self-defence in situations where there is the imminent prospect of an attack. The main difference between these types of action is the temporal nature of the threat which they are responding to. Although this is the terminology adopted in this book, there is a lack of any universally agreed terminology regarding the different modes of self-defence.

4 Previous administrations of the US have made similar, if not as explicit, claims to pre-emption. See W.M. Reisman and A. Armstrong, 'The Past and Future of the Claim of Preemptive Self-Defense' (2006) 100 *AJIL* 525, 527–32.

5 The other major aspect regarding forcible measures against terrorism has been discussed in the previous chapter of this Part of the book. Whilst incidents were included in that chapter which had as their aim the prevention of further terrorist attacks, this chapter focuses on 'pure' pre-emptive self-defence prior to any attack from the target source.

Charter and its requirement for the occurrence of an 'armed attack', the debate has traditionally focused on whether a right of 'anticipatory' self-defence exists within this rubric.[6] Consequently, and to set the US's more recent extensive claims in context, the debate in the secondary interpretive community surrounding this right will first be discussed. Following this, the claims themselves will be set out with a brief discussion of whether the Iraq crisis in 2003 was a test case for the doctrine. The chapter then addresses, through the primary and secondary interpretive communities, the discernible impact that these claims have had upon the *jus ad bellum* in light of the 2002 claims. Lastly, the Bush administration's persistence in advocating the doctrine is addressed followed by some conclusions.

The Traditional View of Anticipatory Self-Defence

In 1837, an anti-British insurrection was taking place in Canada. Although the US and Britain were in a state of peace, the *Caroline*, a ship owned by US nationals, was allegedly providing assistance to the rebels in Canada. On the night of 29 December 1837, British troops boarded the ship, killed several US nationals, set the ship on fire, and sent it over the Niagara Falls.[7]

In the aftermath of this incident, the British claimed that they were acting in self-defence but, after an exchange of diplomatic correspondence with the US, it was agreed that such action could be justified only if there was a 'necessity of self-defence, instant, overwhelming, leaving no choice of means, and no moment of deliberation' and if nothing 'unreasonable or excessive' was done.[8] Although the use of force was not prohibited at the time, it nonetheless established agreement as to when force could be used to avert an attack from occurring.

However, '[w]ith the inception of the UN Charter in 1945 the legality of anticipatory self-defence became less clear'[9] so that the question was now whether Article 51 of the Charter, agreed to over a hundred years later and now by all but a few states, modified the principle established in the *Caroline* case. The main doctrinal division surrounds the inclusion in Article 51 of the phrase '*inherent*

6 For a definition of this notion see supra n. 3.

7 See *The Caroline Case* (1837) 30 BFSP 195–96. For an extensive account of the *Caroline* case see, generally, R. Jennings, 'The Caroline and McLeod Cases' (1938) 32 *AJIL* 82; A.C. Arend, 'International Law and the Preemptive Use of Military Force' (Spring 2003) *Washington Quarterly* 89, 90.

8 Letter from Daniel Webster, Secretary of State of the United States, to Henry S. Fox, Esq., Envoy Extraordinary and Minister Plenipotentiary of Her Britannic Majesty (24 April 1841), reprinted in (1857) 29 BFSP 1129, 1138. This standard gave rise to the principles of 'necessity', 'proportionality' and 'immediacy' that have become a part of modern customary international law and which inform the UN Charter in gauging whether action taken in self-defence is lawful. See Chapter 6 (nn. 7, 8 and 9).

9 A. Garwood-Gowers, 'Pre-emptive Self-Defence: A Necessary Development or the Road to International Anarchy' (2004) 23 *Aust YBIL* 51, 54.

right of … self-defence'.[10] To set the discussion of the practice of the primary interpretive communities in context, and given the doctrinal nature of the right, a discussion of how the issue has been addressed by some of those within the secondary interpretive community in light of the introduction of Article 51 shall be addressed first.

The Secondary Interpretive Community

Scholarly debate A review of the scholarly literature on this provision indicates a clear division between two sets of scholars. The 'restrictionists'[11] claim that the intent of Article 51 was to specifically limit the right of self-defence to those circumstances where an 'armed attack' has actually occurred or is actually occurring. It is submitted that under this view the inclusion of the word 'inherent' simply refers to the obvious right of states to engage in self-defence if attacked. Some argue that the limits imposed on self-defence in Article 51 would be meaningless if a wider customary law right to self-defence survived unfettered by these restrictions.[12] Furthermore, although there is no hierarchy between custom and treaties as sources of law, applying the principle of *lex posterior derogate priori* would mean that a later law repeals an earlier one.[13] The consequence of this for the right of anticipatory self-defence is that the 'restrictive' Article 51 with its requirement of an 'armed attack' takes precedence over the customary practice that had developed before that.[14]

On the other hand, the 'expansionists'[15] claim that the intent of the Charter was not to restrict the customary law right of anticipatory self-defence and the mention of the occurrence of an 'armed attack' was just one circumstance in which a state may act in self-defence. However, under the expansionist approach, the question

---

10 See Chapter 6 for Article 51 of the UN Charter.

11 See, for example, I. Brownlie, *International Law and the Use of Force by States* (Oxford: Clarendon Press, 1963), 275–78; Y. Dinstein, *War, Aggression and Self-Defence*, 4th edn (Cambridge: Cambridge University Press, 2005), 187–92; L. Henkin, *How Nations Behave*, 2nd edn (Columbia: Columbia University Press, 1979), 143–44; I. Detter, *The Law of War*, 2nd edn (Cambridge: Cambridge University Press, 2000), 86; C. Gray, *International Law and the Use of Force*, 3rd edn (Oxford: Oxford University Press, 2008), 160–65.

12 Gray, Ibid., 118.

13 A. Cassese, *International Law*, 2nd edn (Oxford: Oxford University Press, 2005), 154.

14 M. Byers, *War Law: International Law and Armed Conflict* (London: Atlantic Books, 2005), 73.

15 See, for example, D. Bowett, *Self-Defence in International Law* (Manchester: Manchester University Press, 1958), 184–93; M. McDougal and F. Feliciano, *Law and Minimum World Public Order* (New Haven: Yale University Press, 1961), 232–44; A.C. Arend and R.J. Beck, *International Law and the Use of Force: Beyond the UN Charter Paradigm* (New York: Routledge, 1993), 71–79; T.M. Franck, *Recourse to Force: State Action Against Threats and Armed Attacks* (Cambridge: Cambridge University Press, 2002), 98.

remains as to why the drafters of the Charter only included 'armed attack' as a situation when self-defence would be legitimate and did not include other, less obvious circumstances? In response to this, Belatchew Asrat submits that 'in the immediate atmosphere of the Second World War, armed attack was obviously a principal preoccupation of the drafters of the Charter'.[16]

Although Yoram Dinstein has long disagreed with this proposition and maintains that action taken in self-defence before an 'armed attack' is not permitted under Article 51, he does talk of 'interceptive' self-defence as being a legitimate use of force.[17] It is submitted that Dinstein's use of the term 'interceptive' is the same as the use of the term 'anticipatory' in this work, that is, self-defence in the face of an 'imminent' armed attack.[18] Although it is clearly stated by Dinstein that a strike which pre-empts an attack that is 'merely "foreseeable" (or even just "conceivable")' is unlawful, interceptive (or anticipatory) self-defence 'is lawful, even under Article 51 of the Charter'.[19] Essentially, the question of whether a strike in self-defence is lawful comes down to when one determines that an armed attack has begun. Dinstein submits that this occurs when the 'other side has committed itself to an armed attack in an ostensibly irrevocable way'.[20] In other words, although an armed attack may not have actually taken place, there must be a high level of certainty that one will occur imminently if nothing is immediately done to prevent it from occurring. To interpret Article 51 more restrictively would mean that the UN Charter is a 'suicide club'; the right of self-preservation in such circumstances only being available to non-members.[21]

Jurisprudence of the International Court of Justice Given this scholarly division it is unfortunate that the ICJ has not authoritatively determined the precise meaning of Article 51 in regards to the right of anticipatory self-defence. In the *Nicaragua* case in 1986, the Court merely stated that 'the issue of the lawfulness of a response to the imminent threat of an armed attack has not been raised' and therefore 'the Court expresses no view on this issue'.[22] However, the Court did construe the existence of the word 'inherent' in Article 51 to be a reference to customary international law although it did not specify the contents of the customary rules referred to.[23] Therefore, this important decision of the Court cannot support any

16 B. Asrat, Prohibition of Force Under the UN Charter: A Study of Article 2(4) (Uppsala: IUSTUS Forlag, 1991), 210.

17 Dinstein, supra n. 11, 191.

18 See supra n. 3 for the definitions of the different terms used in this work.

19 Dinstein, supra n. 11, 191.

20 Ibid.

21 Franck has claimed that to place states in such a position would be a '*reductio ad absurdum*'. However, permitting 'unilateral recourse to force whenever a state feels potentially threatened could lead to another *reduction ad absurdum*'. Franck, supra n. 15, 98.

22 *Case Concerning Military and Paramilitary Activities in and Against Nicaragua (Nicaragua v United States of America)* (Merits) [1986] ICJ Rep. 14, para. 194.

23 Ibid., para. 176.

interpretation narrowing or broadening Article 51 with regard to anticipatory self-defence and the issue in the aftermath of this case remained relatively undecided.

The continuing nature of the doctrinal debates as to the existence of the right of anticipatory self-defence in the Charter and the fact that the ICJ has never given any assistance on the matter is perhaps indicative of the matter being unresolved amongst the primary interpretive communities of the UN Charter and customary international law. However, the next section will explore the practice of these primary interpretive communities in the period after the Charter was adopted to determine if this practice has either helped supply meaning to the ambiguous language of Article 51 or given rise to a new rule of customary international law in its own right that would allow for anticipatory action in self-defence.[24]

The Primary Interpretive Communities

Perhaps one of the leading examples of state practice in this area is that of the Cuban missile crisis.[25] On 22 October 1962, the US indicated that it had sufficient evidence that Russian nuclear missiles were being brought to Cuba by Russian ships. Accordingly, the US announced a naval 'quarantine' so that all ships going to Cuba were to be examined and any found to be carrying such weapons would not be permitted to pass.[26] When the US brought the issue before the UNSC it did not attempt to justify this action by invoking the doctrine of anticipatory self-defence but instead relied on regional peacekeeping under Chapter VIII.[27] However, the issue was raised as to whether the action taken by the US was lawful under Article 51 and even several states that condemned the action seemed not so much to reject a doctrine of anticipatory self-defence as to question whether the criteria established in the *Caroline* case were met in this instance.[28]

On 5 June 1967, Israel launched a military campaign against Egypt, Jordan and Syria and won the 'Six-Day War'.[29] In the UNSC, Israel did not expressly rely on the doctrine of anticipatory self-defence to justify its actions but instead argued that it was acting in self-defence under Article 51. Although, evaluated alone, no steps taken before the launch of this campaign qualified as an 'armed attack', this was the way

---

24 This later customary international law may repeal the earlier Article 51 if the *usus* and *opinio juris* elements are present.

25 Franck, supra n. 15, 99. For a comprehensive analysis of the crisis see, generally, M. McDougal, 'The Soviet-Cuban Quarantine and Self-Defense' (1963) 57 *AJIL* 597; Q. Wright, 'The Cuban Quarantine' (1963) 57 *AJIL* 546.

26 S.A. Alexandrov, *Self-Defense Against the Use of Force in International Law* (The Hague: Kluwer, 1996), 154–55.

27 UN Doc. S/5181 (22 October 1962).

28 See, for example, UNSC Verbatim Record (24 October 1962) UN Doc. S/PV. 1024, Ghana (51).

29 1967 *UNYB* 166.

Israel viewed all of the measures taken together.[30] Furthermore, states that supported the Israeli action refrained from a discussion of the permissibility of anticipatory self-defence whilst others simply saw Israel's first strike as aggression.[31] However, although there was no clear consensus opposed to the doctrine of anticipatory self-defence in the UNSC on this occasion, due to the adoption of a UNSC resolution that required the withdrawal of the Israeli forces from the occupied territories,[32] it was clear that Israel's claim of self-defence found little support, albeit from within the primary interpretive community of the UNSC.[33]

After the US had mistakenly shot down a civilian Iran Airbus in July 1988 during the Iran–Iraq war,[34] it argued that it had acted in self-defence in response to the prior shooting down of a US helicopter by Iran and as part of being engaged in an ongoing battle.[35] It is striking that the US did not expressly rely on anticipatory self-defence even though its rules of engagement had been altered to allow its forces to take action against enemy ships and aircraft displaying 'hostile intent'.[36] In a debate that took place within the UNSC, many members argued that Article 51 does not allow anticipatory self-defence and that the US action amounted to aggression.[37] Whilst the UK offered support for the US action in general terms, it did not expressly support anticipatory self-defence.[38]

Whilst in the above cases the justification of anticipatory self-defence was not expressly invoked, this was not the case after Israel attacked the Osiraq nuclear reactor in Iraq on 8 June 1981.[39] Israel argued that the scope of the right of self-defence had broadened to include the right of anticipatory self-defence because of the potential use of nuclear weapons which had not been foreseen by Article 51.[40] This was countered by Iraq which claimed that self-defence was permissible only against an 'armed attack'.[41] Significantly, Israel could only call on support for its

30 These included the ejection of the UN Emergency Force, the closure of the Straits of Tiran and the buildup of Egyptian forces along the borders of Israel. See Franck, supra n. 15, 101–02.

31 See the statements of Morocco (UNSC Verbatim Record (6 June 1967) UN Doc. S/PV. 1348, 122) and the Soviet Union (UNSC Verbatim Record (8 June 1967) UN Doc. S/PV. 1351, 61).

32 UNSC Res. 242 (XXII) (22 November 1967) UN Doc. S/RES/242 (XXII).

33 Alexandrov, supra n. 26, 154.

34 It was claimed by the US that it thought that the Airbus was a hostile Iranian military aircraft.

35 UN Doc. S/19989 (6 July 1988); Gray, supra n. 12, 162.

36 Ibid.

37 UNSC Verbatim Record (14 July 1988) UN Doc. S/PV. 2818.

38 Gray, supra n. 11, 162.

39 UNSC Verbatim Record (12 June 1981) UN Doc. S/PV. 2280, Israel (16); See, generally, A. D'Amato, 'Israel's Air Strike Upon the Iraqi Nuclear Reactor' (1983) 77 *AJIL* 584.

40 UN Doc. S/14510 (8 June 1981).

41 UN Doc. S/PV. 2280, supra n. 39, Iraq (16).

position from writers and was not able to rely on any clear state practice.[42] Whilst many within the UNSC believed that the Charter clearly defined self-defence as an inherent right only if an 'armed attack' occurs and that the notion of anticipatory strikes was unacceptable,[43] others argued that the anticipatory use of force could be permissible under the Charter provided that it could be demonstrated that there was an imminent threat and that other means of addressing the threat had been exhausted.[44] Whilst the UNGA and UNSC condemned Israel for these attacks[45] and condemned the justification of anticipatory self-defence in circumstances in which the conditions of imminent danger were not present, it was not completely clear that it rejected the notion of anticipatory self-defence *per se*.[46]

The above has shown that traditionally even the doctrine of anticipatory self-defence has proved to be at best controversial. Furthermore, the 'reluctance of states to explicitly invoke anticipatory self-defence as a legal justification undermines the credibility of claims that such a right exists'.[47] However, on the basis of the above practice, even if 'one accepts the existence of a right of anticipatory self-defence' this appeared to be 'strictly limited by the criteria laid down in the *Caroline* incident'.[48] Indeed, the *Caroline* formula 'is as far as pre-emptive self-defence possibly goes under current international law'.[49] Set in this context, the sharp break from traditional interpretations proposed by the US, under the administration of President George W. Bush, becomes particularly notable.

The Enunciation of a Doctrine of Pre-Emptive Self-Defence in 2002

Within a year of the 9/11 terrorist attacks, the US had begun to build a case for widening the conventional right of self-defence so as to include taking traditionally unlawful unilateral pre-emptive military action against the 'new' threats of global terrorism and WMD.

The first indications of the doctrine came in the justification for *Operation Enduring Freedom* on 7 October 2001. John Negroponte, the US Permanent Representative to the UN, wrote to the President of the UNSC declaring that the action was taken in self-defence in accordance with Article 51 of the UN

42 Ibid., paras. 98, 99 and 100.

43 Those who took this view included Egypt, Mexico, Syria, Guyana, Pakistan, Spain and Yugoslavia.

44 Those who took this view included Sierra Leone, the UK, Malaysia, Niger and Uganda.

45 UNGA Res. 36/27 (13 November 1981) UN Doc. A/RES/36/27; UNSC Res. 487 (19 June 1981) UN Doc. S/RES/487.

46 Because of the clear lack of 'imminency' the Osiraq incident is an example of pre-emptive self-defence as opposed to anticipatory self-defence.

47 Garwood-Gowers, supra n. 9, 55.

48 Ibid., 56.

49 M. Bothe, 'Terrorism and the Legality of Pre-emptive Force' (2003) 14 *EJIL* 227, 231.

Charter and stressed the 'ongoing' terrorist threat to the US posed by al-Qaida and the Taliban.[50] However, in his letter Ambassador Negroponte went beyond simply invoking the right of self-defence solely in regards to the perpetrator of the attacks, al-Qaida, and its harbour state, Afghanistan.[51] Indeed, as he later wrote: 'We may find that our self-defence requires further actions with respect to *other organizations and other states'*.[52] It is now clear that the letter was an early attempt to secure advanced support for an extension of the right of self-defence to encompass the unlawful sphere of unilateral pre-emption.[53]

Further evidence of the US expounding a broader doctrine of self-defence came in the January 2002 State of the Union address where President Bush declared that the greatest danger to America lay where terrorism, rogue states, and WMD intersected and that there was an 'axis of evil' consisting of Iran, North Korea and Iraq.[54] Another important piece fell into place in the development of this new doctrine when, at the beginning of June 2002, the President claimed for the first time the right to launch pre-emptive strikes on states deemed a threat, before the US itself had been attacked.[55] President Bush stated that the US must 'confront the worst threats before they emerge'[56] and that it must 'be ready for pre-emptive action when necessary'.[57]

However, what came to be known as the 'Bush doctrine' finally took formal shape in the Bush administration's first *NSS*, unveiled in September 2002.[58] Recognizing the change in adversaries, it appeared that the doctrines of containment and deterrence, used to great effect during the Cold War had been abandoned in light of the twenty-first century threat of international terrorism and WMD.[59] In other words, because the concern was now the threat of 'shadowy terrorist networks with no nation or citizens to defend'[60] and 'unbalanced dictators with weapons of mass destruction',[61] a corresponding strategic shift was necessary.[62] Indeed, the

50 UN Doc. S/2001/946 (7 October 2001).

51 For more on the US's proposed 'harbouring' standard of attribution see Chapter 6.

52 UN Doc. S/2001/946, supra n. 50 (emphasis added).

53 C. Henderson, 'The Bush Doctrine: From Theory to Practice' (2004) 9 *JCSL* 3, 6.

54 President George W. Bush, 'State of the Union Address' (29 January 2002). Available at http://archives.cnn.com/2002/ALLPOLITICS/01/29/bush.speech.txt/ [Accessed: 19 June 2009].

55 'Remarks by the President at 2002 Graduation Exercise of the United States Military Academy at West Point' (1 June 2002). Available at http://www.mtholyoke.edu/acad/intrel/bush/westpoint.htm [Accessed: 19 June 2009].

56 Ibid.

57 Ibid.

58 2002 *NSS*, supra n. 1.

59 R. Wedgwood, 'The Fall of Saddam Hussein: Security Council Mandates and Preemptive Self-Defense' (2003) 97 *AJIL* 576, 583.

60 West Point speech, supra n. 55.

61 Ibid.

62 M.N. Schmitt, 'Preemptive Strategies in International Law' (2003) 24 *Mich.J.Int'l L.* 513, 517.

NSS made it clear that the US would exercise its 'right of self-defence by acting pre-emptively against such terrorists'.[63]

In legally justifying the Bush doctrine, the *NSS* made an implicit reference to the *Caroline* case and its requirement of 'imminency' as outlined above:

> For centuries, international law recognized that nations need not suffer an attack before they can lawfully take action to defend themselves against forces that present an imminent danger of attack. Legal scholars and international jurists often conditioned the legitimacy of pre-emption on the existence of an imminent threat – most often a visible mobilization of armies, navies, and air forces preparing to attack ... We must adapt the concept of imminent threat to the capabilities and objectives of today's adversaries.[64]

Essentially, the Bush administration's view was that the legitimacy of any forcible measures in self-defence taken before an armed attack had actually occurred hinged on the existence of an 'imminent' threat, although it sought to expand the definition of imminence in the light of the new threats of global terrorism and WMD.[65]

The Rationale Behind a Wider Interpretation of 'Imminence'

International law relating to the recourse to force was founded so as to address states, traditionally the main actors in international relations, and did not generally consider terrorist groups. Along with this, the law also only addressed traditional threats that existed at the time and did not anticipate real threats of WMD. The fact that terrorism and WMD can strike at states in ways that international law did not anticipate[66] was the main impetus for the development of the doctrine of pre-emptive self-defence, particularly in the post-11 September period. Indeed, as the *NSS* made clear:

> Rogue states and terrorists do not seek to attack us using conventional means. They know such attacks would fail. Instead, they rely on acts of terror and, potentially, the use of weapons of mass destruction – weapons that can be easily concealed, delivered covertly, and used without warning.[67]

---

63 2002 *NSS*, supra n. 1, 6.

64 Ibid., 15.

65 Ronzitti has stated that 'President Bush's doctrine on "preventive war", as spelled out in the 2002 National Security Strategy of the United States, is in reality a new and expanded interpretation of the notion of imminence of armed attack, which affords new possibilities to react in self-defence'. See N. Ronzitti, 'The Expanding Law of Self-Defence' (2006) 11 *JCSL* 343, 347.

66 Arend, supra n. 7, 98.

67 2002 *NSS*, supra n. 1, 15.

Consequently, the threats had changed so that 'if we wait for threats to fully materialize, we will have waited too long'.[68]

Previously, if a state was attacked in the conventional way using conventional means, the *Caroline* criteria meant that it could defend itself and survive the attack. The soon-to-be aggressor would be taking enough overt actions and the attack itself would require mobilization that would give the victim enough lead time.[69] Now it was argued that the *Caroline* requirements 'cannot rationally be claimed to apply *in havec verba* to the possibility of an attack with modern technology and advanced WMD, launched by terrorists acting secretly with state support'.[70] In addition, Rein Müllerson argued that terrorists 'intentionally target defenceless civilians and civilian objects' and therefore, 'in many cases preventative … self-defence is the only effective method of stopping terrorists from achieving their goals'.[71] In other words, by the time the use of a nuclear weapon or a terrorist attack had become 'imminent' under the traditional standard, it would be extremely difficult, if not impossible, for a state to mount an effective defence.

Under the proposed interpretation, in attacking terrorist groups such as al-Qaida, and those that harbour and support them, pre-emption would not really be an issue as the state could simply argue that it was engaged in self-defence against an ongoing armed attack,[72] but if it was a terrorist group that had not yet committed an armed attack, when would such an attack be 'imminent'? The *NSS* clearly saw the case for taking unilateral pre-emptive action as 'compelling … even if uncertainty remain[ed] as to the time and place of the enemy's attack'.[73] It would appear from this that the Bush administration was propounding a rule that accepted that whenever and wherever a terrorist group or possible threat from a state is located, it should be destroyed without necessarily acting within the intersubjective agreement of the interpretive communities. The potential difficulties in accepting the Bush doctrine in this raw unilateral form are obvious.[74] In particular, if a threat is recognized as serious enough recourse should be had to

68 West Point speech, supra n. 55.

69 Arend, supra n. 7, 98.

70 A.D. Sofaer, 'On the Necessity of Pre-emption' (2003) 14 *EJIL* 209, 214.

71 R. Müllerson, '*Jus Ad Bellum*: Plus Ça Change (Le Monde) Plus C'Est La Même Chose (Le Droit)? (2002) 7 *JCSL* 149, 180.

72 Arend, supra n. 7, 99.

73 2002 *NSS*, supra n. 1, 15.

74 Franck is of the opinion that the doctrine of pre-emptive self-defence found in the 2002 *NSS* 'aims at ending all collective control over the U.S. recourse to force'. See T.M. Franck, 'What Happens Now? The United Nations after Iraq' (2003) 97 *AJIL* 607, 620. See also, for example, R. Falk, 'What Future for the UN Charter System of War Prevention' (2003) 97 *AJIL* 590; R.N. Gardner, 'Neither Bush Nor the "Jurisprudes"' (2003) 97 *AJIL* 585; J. Brunnée and S. Toope, 'The Use of Force: International Law and Iraq' (2004) 53 *ICLQ* 785; Henderson, supra n. 53; Garwood-Gowers, supra n. 9; M. Sapiro, 'Iraq: Shifting Sands of Preemptive Self-Defense' (2003) 97 *AJIL* 599; C. Gray,

the UNSC which has within its jurisdiction the powers to use force to pre-empt 'threats to international peace and security'.[75]

Ultimately, the asserted break in interpretation was significant for two reasons. First, the Bush administration made a conscious effort to offer an argument to shift traditional notions of what the law was rather than to simply assert a sharp break to traditional interpretations. This at least showed some influence of the law upon the US and that it intended for it to be a right available to all states under international law.[76] Second, by talking of 'adapting' the traditional law on the subject, the US recognized that it was operating within the *lex ferenda* which militated against any finding of *opinio juris* even on behalf of the doctrine's proponent state.[77] Instead, by having asserted that the primary interpretive community 'must' adapt the concept of imminence to the nature of today's adversaries, the US was expressing *opinio necessitatis* as to the right of unilateral pre-emptive self-defence.[78] Whilst it expressly reserved the right for itself to take such action, any impact upon the law depended upon positive intersubjective agreement of the primary interpretive communities associated with both the UN Charter and customary international law emerging as to the perceived need to take action in these circumstances and the reinterpretation of the *jus ad bellum*. Before this issue is addressed, an example of the dangers of such a doctrine in practice will first be briefly discussed.

Operation Iraqi Freedom: A Test Case?

Upon the launching of *Operation Iraqi Freedom* in March 2003 the US wrote to the UNSC basing its case for taking action almost entirely on the 'revival' of authority to use force under UNSC Resolution 678 (1990).[79] However, in the last paragraph of this letter it also briefly stated that the action taken was necessary 'to defend the United States and the international community from the threat posed by Iraq and to restore international peace and security in the area'.[80] Some commentators

---

'The US *National Security Strategy* and the New "Bush Doctrine" on Preemptive Self-Defense' (2002) 1 *Chinese J.Int'l L.* 437.

75 See Chapter 3.

76 There is nothing in the *NSS* to suggest that the doctrine of pre-emption is restricted to use by the US. For the proposition that 'pre-emptive self-defense is only an American doctrine' see W.M. Reisman, 'Assessing Claims to Revise the Laws of War' (2003) 97 *AJIL* 82, 90.

77 As Paulus noted, '[e]ven the National Security Strategy does not consider "preemption" as part of international law on force'. See A. Paulus, 'The War Against Iraq and the Future of International Law: Hegemony or Pluralism?' (2003–04) 25 *Mich.J.Int'l L.* 691, 702.

78 For more on this element in the process of normative change, see Chapter 2 (n. 70).

79 See Chapter 4.

80 UN Doc. S/2003/351 (21 March 2003).

viewed the Bush administration's comments regarding pre-emption in Iraq as no more than 'rhetorical flourish'[81] and the final paragraph of the letter as a 'causal afterthought'.[82] Indeed, '[i]t is difficult to distinguish official legal justifications from the accompanying political rhetoric ... but once this is achieved it is clear that the right of self-defence against Iraq was not formally asserted'.[83]

Nevertheless, given the temporal proximity between the advocacy of the doctrine and the launching of *Operation Iraqi Freedom* it may not have been that straightforward. Indeed, even if *Iraqi Freedom* was not a *legal* precedent for a right of pre-emptive force, by the time it had commenced 'public opinion ... had [already] come to view Iraq as the first application of the new "preventive war" doctrine'.[84] Furthermore, some commentators assessed the events in Iraq against the backdrop of the doctrine of pre-emptive self-defence as it 'appeared to be the perfect test case for this standard of imminency'.[85]

In this respect, and viewed in light of the events that have occurred, concerns regarding the doctrine of pre-emptive self-defence as enunciated in the 2002 *NSS* look to have been realized. As Chapter 4 described, whilst there was agreement within the primary interpretive community of the UNSC that Iraq should be disarmed, there were differences as to how to achieve this aim. The US and UK on the one side urged the use of immediate force to eradicate the threat, others wanted to first exhaust the inspection process.[86] The views of the latter group on how to proceed were ultimately vindicated as, after spending 16 months searching, the Iraq Survey Group stated in its final report on 30 September 2004 that it had failed to discover any WMD, or serious programmes of.[87] Indeed, the invasion led to disaster rather than disarmament and proved that Iraq at the time had no WMD. If the inspection process had have been continued this reality would have been discovered with far less tragic consequences.

A central part of any possible right of unilateral pre-emptive self-defence is the ability to rely on the intelligence services in providing accuracy in regards to the nature of any threat. *Operation Iraqi Freedom* highlighted the serious inadequacy of the services' ability in this respect. Embarrassingly for the US, the aftermath of the invasion witnessed a frenzy of publicity on the failure of the pre-war intelligence estimates.[88]

---

81 D. Kritsiotis, 'Arguments of Mass Confusion' (2004) 15 *EJIL* 233, 249.

82 Ibid., 251.

83 L. Moir, 'Reappraising the Resort to Force? *Jus ad Bellum* and the War on Terror' (2005) 8 *Y.B.N.Z.Juris.* 1, 19.

84 Gardner, supra n. 74, 589.

85 Henderson, supra n. 53, 16.

86 See Chapter 4.

87 See the 'Comprehensive Report of the Special Advisor to the DCI [Director of Central Intelligence] on Iraq's WMD' (30 September 2004). Available at https://www.cia.gov/library/reports/general-reports-1/iraq_wmd_2004/index.html [Accessed: 20 October 2009]. See also *Keesing's* (2004) 46280.

88 Indeed, in the pursuit of improving intelligence, the United States established an investigation to examine the failures of the intelligence which was relied upon in the run

As early as 2003, Miriam Sapiro perceptively predicted the result of adopting *Operation Iraqi Freedom* as a test case for the doctrine of unilateral pre-emptive self-defence:

> Perhaps Iraq will be the case that highlights the risks of adopting a new doctrine of pre-emptive war, whilst persuading the sceptics that the restraints governing the more traditional justifications of anticipatory self-defense make sense. Although the war in Iraq would not have fit the criteria of anticipatory self-defense, it helps demonstrate why these constraints represent the right balance between addressing new threats to security and avoiding the pitfalls of an expansive new doctrine.[89]

Indeed, this assessment was arguably reflected in the subsequent years in the way in which the interpretive communities addressed the issue.

Reaction to the 2002 Assertions of the Doctrine

The above section demonstrated that whilst the theory behind the Bush doctrine had its supporters within the scholarly community, it also caused 'considerable consternation' amongst others.[90] This consternation has also been visible within the primary interpretive community where even the US's closest allies have shown restraint in opting for such a doctrine in combating contemporary threats, thus providing evidence of a significant indicator of negative intersubjective agreement regarding the doctrine. Furthermore, the various reports emanating from the UN and the decisions handed down by the ICJ have also reflected this restraint. Indeed, the proposed shift in the interpretation of 'imminence' by the US has, in general, not been well received.

The Primary Interpretive Communities

North Korea Whilst some within the primary interpretive communities, for example Israel,[91] France,[92] and Russia,[93] have expressed some support for the doctrine in

---

up to the invasion. See 'Commission on the Intelligence Capabilities of the United States Regarding Weapons of Mass Destruction' (31 March 2005). Available at http://www.wmd.gov/report/wmd_report.pdf [Accessed: 3 January 2007].

89 Sapiro, supra n. 74, 607.

90 Kritsiotis, supra n. 81, 246.

91 'Disengagement Plan of Prime Minister Ariel Sharon – Revised (28 May 2004), paras. 3(One)(3) and 3(Two)(2). Available at http://www.knesset.gov.il/process/docs/DisengageSharon_eng_revised.htm [Accessed: 25 May 2009].

92 Ministry of Defence, '2003-2008 Military Programme, Bill of Law'. Available at http://www.info-france-usa.org/atoz/mindefa.pdf [Accessed: 17 February 2007].

93 'Putin: Russia Preparing Action Against Terrorists' *foxnews.com* (17 September 2004). Available at http://www.foxnews.com/story/0,2933,132687,00.html [Accessed: 4 September 2008]; *Keesing's* (2006) 47119.

connection with their individual security concerns regarding non-sate actors, these same members have not elicited any discernible support for its use against other states, including those posing a threat of WMD. Indeed, the only member of the primary interpretive communities other than the US to have claimed a right of pre-emption against a state adversary has been North Korea and this was, ironically, in response to the US's classification of it as part of the 'axis of evil' in 2002 and its subsequent advocacy of the Bush doctrine.[94] As Christine Gray points out, this evidences '[t]he destabilizing impact of the "Bush" doctrine and the perverse incentive it offers to states to hasten to acquire weapons of mass destruction'.[95]

Australia However, since the enunciation of the Bush doctrine in 2002, undoubtedly its greatest supporter has been Australia. Nevertheless, even this state has been somewhat ambivalent in its support. In light of the terrorist bombings in Bali on 12 October 2002, when Australian citizens were killed and injured,[96] the Prime Minister at the time, John Howard, claimed that Australia was ready to take pre-emptive action against terrorists in neighbouring Asian countries.[97] However, Mr Howard's open advocacy of the Bush doctrine received much criticism, particularly from Asian countries that felt that such statements posed a threat.[98] Significantly, and echoing the rationale adopted by the US, it was also claimed that international law could no longer cope with the changed circumstances confronting the world where the most likely threat to any nation's security was from non-state terrorism.[99] However, this was recognition that any claim of pre-emptive self-defence was *lex ferenda*. This expressed belief that such use of force was not lawful under the *lex lata* may be reflected in the fact that no mention was made of the doctrine in Australia's *National Security Strategy* in either 2003 or 2005.[100] Whilst there was rhetoric by

94 UN Doc. S/2003/681 (1 July 2003); *Keesing's* (2003) 45238.

95 C. Gray, 'A Crisis of Legitimacy for the UN Collective Security System?' (2007) 56 *ICLQ* 157, 162 (n. 24).

96 A. Spillius and B. Dutter, '182 Dead in Club Bombing' *The Daily Telegraph* (14 October 2002), 17.

97 R. Beeston, 'Australians Ready to Hit First Against Terrorists' *The Times* (1 November 2002), 14; N. Frankland, 'Australia Supports Pre-Emptive Strikes' *The Guardian* (2 December 2002), 19.

98 'Howard Outrages South East Asian Nations' *The People's Daily* (3 December 2002) Available at http://english.peopledaily.com.cn/200212/03/eng20021203_107860.shtml [Accessed: 17 May 2007].

99 See 'Interview by Neil Mitchell with Prime Minister John Howard' (29 November 2002). Available at http://www.pm.gov.au/news/interviews/2002/interview2013.htm [Accessed: 19 June 2007].

100 See 'Australia's National Security Strategy: A Defence Update' (26 February 2003). Available at http://www.defence.gov.au/ans2003/Report.pdf [Accessed: 26 September 2008]; 'Australia's National Security Strategy: A Defence Update' (15 December 2005). Available at http://www.defence.gov.au/update2005/defence_update_2005.pdf [Accessed: 26 September 2008].

Australia, ultimately it has not set out to support the Bush administration's claim that it was necessary to incorporate this as a right under the *jus ad bellum*.

The United Kingdom Arguably the US's closest ally and friend, the UK, has noticeably distanced itself from supporting the doctrine. Whilst an adherent to the notion of anticipatory self-defence, the UK has rejected any form of self-defence which is not in reaction to an 'imminent' attack. Indeed, in February 2003, the Foreign Secretary at the time, Jack Straw, stated in response to a Foreign Affairs Committee report, that the Government was of the opinion that it was legitimate to take action in self-defence in the face of an 'imminent' threat, not only from states but also from terrorist groups and that it did not find it necessary to review this policy in light of the publication of the US's 2002 *NSS*.[101] Furthermore, in light of a recommendation that the Government should try and 'work to establish a clear international consensus on the circumstances in which military action may be taken by states on a pre-emptive basis', the Foreign Secretary stated:

> There is already scope under international law to take into account all the circumstances, including the likelihood, nature and seriousness of any attack, in determining whether any threat is imminent. The Government will not speculate on the precise circumstances in which the UK would take military action, not least because of the advantage this would present to potential adversaries. We would therefore not wish to attempt to reach consensus internationally on the precise circumstances in which military action in anticipatory self-defence may be taken by states.[102]

It is submitted that by not giving a definition or example of the word 'imminent', Mr. Straw was purposely leaving the door open as to the circumstances required before force may be used in anticipation of an armed attack. However, any arguments that this could somehow be aligned with the widened interpretation of imminence advanced by the US were soon extinguished by the UK Attorney-General in his legal advice on the war in Iraq. Whilst he maintained the Foreign Secretary's line in stating that '[f]orce may be used in self-defence if there is an actual or imminent threat of an armed attack' and '[t]he concept of what is imminent may depend on the circumstances'[103] he then explicitly set this in the context of the Bush doctrine:

---

101 Response of the Secretary of State for Foreign and Commonwealth Affairs to the Second Report of the Foreign Affairs Committee, 'Foreign Policy Aspects of the War Against Terrorism' (Session 2002–2003) Cm 5793. Available at http://www.fco.gov.uk/Files/kfile/CM5739.pdf [Accessed: 20 January 2008].

102 Ibid., 8.

103 See 'Attorney General's Advice on the Iraq War: Resolution 1441' (2005) 54 *ICLQ* 767, para. 3.

> I am aware that the USA has been arguing for recognition of a broad doctrine of a right to use force to pre-empt danger in the future. If this means more than a right to respond proportionately to an imminent attack (and I understand that the doctrine is intended to carry that connotation) this is not a doctrine which, in my opinion, exists or is recognized in international law.[104]

Indeed, it is telling that whilst the US made some reference to self-defence in its justification of *Operation Iraqi Freedom*, neither the UK nor Australia followed suit.[105]

The European Union The EU has shown some support for the theory behind pre-emptive action, even if not for the unilateral format in which it was presented by the US.[106] Indeed, in June 2003 the EU endorsed a strategy to combat the spread of nuclear, biological and chemical weapons that for the first time included a reference to possible military action against states or terrorist groups that acquired such arms.[107] However, while accepting the possible use of force as a last resort if diplomatic preventative measures and international relations failed, the EU insisted that 'the UN Security Council should play a central role',[108] indicating that it fundamentally disagreed with the unilateralist approach to pre-emption taken by the US and instead preferred the security of multilateralism. Six months later, in its own *European Security Strategy*, it was again open in its support for the theory behind pre-emption although again stressed the need for multilateralism and the UNSC's primary responsibility for the maintenance of international peace and security.[109]

Events at the United Nations

In the wake of the advocacy of the right of pre-emptive self-defence in the 2002 *NSS*, the UN High-Level Panel on Threats, Challenges and Change issued its report, the UNSG issued his response to this, and the 2005 UN World Summit took place. These were all opportunities for actors within both the primary and secondary interpretive communities to have their say and, in light of the US's

---

104 Ibid.

105 See UN Doc. S/2003/351 (20 March 2003) and UN Doc. S/2003/352 (20 March 2003) respectively.

106 Reuters, 'EU Moves Towards US "Pre-Emption" Doctrine' (17 June 2003). Available at http://www.reuters.co.uk/news.jhtml [Accessed: 15 May 2007].

107 'Basic Principles for an EU Strategy against Proliferation of Weapons of Mass Destruction' (10 June 2003). Available at http://ue.eu.int/pressdata/EN/reports/76328.pdf [Accessed: 26 March 2004].

108 Ibid., para. 4.

109 'A Secure Europe in a Better World: European Security Strategy' (12 December 2003), 7. Available at http://ue.eu.int/uedocs/cmsUpload/78367.pdf [Accessed: 26 August 2007].

advocacy, provided an opportunity for the right of pre-emptive self-defence to crystallize or positive intersubjective agreement regarding it to become discernible. This did not occur. Instead, the particular interpretation proposed by the US failed to be reconciled with the *lex lata* by those within the interpretive communities. However, this did not mean that there were no innovations in these reports. Indeed, Article 51 was interpreted 'in a way that UN bodies have been loath to do until now' by supporting the interpretation embodied in the theory of 'anticipatory self-defence'.[110]

The Report of the High-Level Panel on Threats, Challenges and Change (2004) After noting the 'restrictive' nature of Article 51, the High-Level Panel report went on to recognize that 'a threatened state, according to long established international law, can take military action as long as the threatened attack is *imminent*, no other means would deflect it and the action is proportionate'.[111] 'The problem arises', the report acknowledged, 'where the threat in question is not imminent but still claimed to be real: for example the acquisition, with allegedly hostile intent, of nuclear weapons-making capability'.[112]

In response, and acknowledging the concerns of the proponents of such a doctrine, the report adopted the position that 'if there are good arguments for preventive military action, with good evidence to support them, they should be put to the Security Council, which can authorize such action if it chooses to. If it does not so choose, there will be, by definition, time to pursue other strategies, including persuasion, negotiation, deterrence and containment – and to visit again the military option'.[113]

Although it is conceded that this does not completely rule out unilateral action,[114] the report was clearly opposed to the doctrine of pre-emptive self-defence:

> For those impatient with such a response, the answer must be that, in a world full of perceived potential threats, the risk to the global order and the norm of non-intervention on which it continues to be based is simply too great for the legality of unilateral preventive action, as distinct from collectively endorsed action, to be accepted.[115]

---

110 Ronzitti, supra n. 65, 346

111 Report of the High-Level Panel on Threats, Challenges and Change, 'A More Secure World: Our Shared Responsibility' (2004) UN Doc. A/59/565, para. 188 (emphasis added).

112 Ibid.

113 Ibid., para. 190.

114 A. Ghafur Hamid, 'The Legality of Anticipatory Self-Defence in the 21st Century World Order: A Re-appraisal' (2007) 54 *NILR* 441, 483.

115 Report of the High-Level Panel, supra n. 111, para. 191. However, in the debate over this Report, the NAM, representing 118 states, explicitly rejected the doctrine representing a significant indicator of negative intersubjective agreement. See 'Comments on the High-Level Panel Report' (2 December 2004) UN Doc. A/59/565, paras. 26–28.

Furthermore, in expressly rejecting any notions of US exceptionalism the report clearly based its conclusions on the fact that '[a]llowing one to so act is to allow all'.[116] In short, 'the Report rejects the doctrine of pre-emption theorized by the US President George W. Bush in the 2002 National Security Strategy document'.[117]

The Report of the United Nations Secretary-General: In Larger Freedom (2005) The position of the High-Level Panel appeared to be entirely endorsed by the UNSG in his subsequent report in March 2005, 'though less directly and in less dramatic language'.[118] Indeed, the UNSG noted that '[i]mminent threats are fully covered by Article 51, which safeguards the inherent right of sovereign states to defend themselves against armed attack'.[119] Echoing the 2002 *NSS*, he also claimed that '[l]awyers have long recognized that this covers an imminent threat as well as one that has already happened'.[120] However, this is where the similarities ended as the UNSG expressed full support for the UNSC in its ability to deal with threats under the US's proposed conception of imminence: 'Where threats are not imminent but latent, the Charter gives full authority to the Security Council to use military force, including preventatively, to preserve international peace and security'.[121]

The United Nations World Summit Outcome Document (2005) Perhaps in recognition of some disagreement on the right of self-defence, the World Summit did not pronounce on the issue of self-defence, let alone pre-emptive self-defence. Indeed, '[g]iven the controversial nature of the positions taken by the High-Level Panel and *In Larger Freedom*, it is not surprising that the *Summit Outcome Document* avoids the issue of self-defence'.[122] This follows the line taken in many of the UNGA resolutions adopted since 1945 which have addressed issues of the use of force.[123]

However, to dismiss the Outcome document as having nothing to say on the matter is perhaps an oversight. Indeed, a reading of the document does elicit an implied rejection of the Bush doctrine as found in the 2002 *NSS*. For example

116 Ibid., para. 191.

117 Ronzitti, supra n. 65, 345. Gray also notes that '[t]his amounts to an implicit rejection of the USA in the National Security Strategy (September 2002) where the USA had called for the concept of imminent threat to be adapted to the capabilities of today's adversaries'. See Gray, supra n. 95, 161.

118 Gray, Ibid.

119 Report of the UN Secretary-General, 'In Larger Freedom: Towards Security, Development and Human Rights for All' (21 March 2005) UN Doc. A/59/205 (2005), para. 124.

120 Ibid.

121 Ibid., para. 125.

122 Gray, supra n. 95, 163.

123 See, for example, the *Declaration on Principles of International Law Concerning Friendly Relations and Co-operation Among States in Accordance with the Charter of the United Nations*, UNGA Res. 2625 (XXV) (24 October 1970) UN Doc. A/RES/25/2625 (XXV).

it recognized that 'many of *today's* threats … must be tackled … in accordance with the Charter and international law'.[124] In particular, 'the obligation of states to settle their disputes by peaceful means' was emphasized[125] and 'the obligation of all Member states to refrain in their international relations from the threat or use of force in any manner inconsistent with the Charter' was reiterated.[126] In specific recognition of the concern of global terrorism the Outcome document recognized 'that international cooperation to fight terrorism must be conducted in conformity with international law, including the Charter and relevant international conventions and protocols. States must ensure that any measures taken to combat terrorism comply with their obligations under international law'.[127]

Furthermore, the Outcome document stressed the 'commitment to multilateralism'.[128] In particular, 'the importance of promoting and strengthening the multilateral process and of addressing international challenges and problems by strictly abiding by the Charter and the principles of international law' was reiterated[129] and the document expressed determination 'to take effective collective measures for the prevention and removal of threats to the peace and for the suppression of acts of aggression or other breaches of the peace'.[130] In this respect it was reaffirmed 'that the Security Council has primary responsibility in the maintenance of international peace and security'.[131] In short, the Outcome document reaffirmed 'that the relevant provisions of the Charter are sufficient to address the full range of threats to international peace and security'.[132] When viewed in light of these provisions, there is little room left for the US's doctrine of unilateral pre-emptive self-defence.

Jurisprudence of the International Court of Justice

Since the advocacy of the doctrine by the US in 2002 there have been two cases and one advisory opinion of the ICJ involving self-defence: the *Oil Platforms* case, the *Wall* advisory opinion, and the *DRC v Uganda* case. However, in none of these cases did 'the ICJ … clarify whether a right of anticipatory self-defence was available to states'.[133]

Nevertheless, in the *DRC v Uganda* case the Court did make reference to the issue. Indeed, whilst it noted that the security needs specified by Uganda were 'essentially preventative', Uganda itself had 'insisted in this case that [its operation] was not a

124 2005 World Summit Outcome Document (2005) UN Doc. A/60/L.1, para. 71 (emphasis added).
125 Ibid., 73.
126 Ibid., 77.
127 Ibid., 85.
128 Ibid., 78.
129 Ibid., 78.
130 Ibid., 77.
131 Ibid., 80.
132 Ibid., 79.
133 Ronzitti, supra n. 65, 345.

use of force against an anticipated attack'.[134] Consequently, the Court likened the circumstances with that in the *Nicaragua* case where because the issue had not been raised the Court expressed no view on it.[135] The Court did state, however, in an implicit rejection of the Bush doctrine, that 'Article 51 of the Charter may justify a use of force in self-defence only within the strict confines there laid down. It does not allow the use of force by a state to protect perceived security interests beyond these parameters. Other means are available to a concerned state, including, in particular, recourse to the Security Council'.[136] As Gray notes, '[t]he Court therefore implicitly indicated that it would not accept pre-emptive action as self-defence'.[137] However, regardless of this rejection, and the negative intersubjective agreement witnessed elsewhere, the Bush administration continued to persist with its claims.

The 2006 *National Security Strategy*: Pre-Emptive Use of Force and the Persistent Advocate

Despite the failures in Iraq, the equivocal at best reception of the doctrine by its allies, and the rejection of the doctrine by many within the primary and secondary interpretive communities, on 16 March 2006, the Bush administration persisted with its advocacy of the doctrine in the release of its second *NSS*.[138] Although the publication was a more low-key affair than its 2002 predecessor, the 2006 *NSS* was not without some notable content.

Released nearly four and a half years after the terrorist attacks of 9/11, the impact of the tragic events of that day continued to reverberate poignantly through the core of the document. 'America is at war'[139] are the first words of the letter by President Bush which preceded its substantive sections. Even the 2002 *NSS*, released less than a year after these attacks, was less striking in this assertion.[140] Nevertheless, the promotion of democracy in preventing terrorism and the importance of international diplomacy in persuading states to refrain from

134 *Armed Activities on the Territory of the Congo (Democratic Republic of Congo v Uganda)* (Merits), judgment of 19 December 2005, para. 143. Available at http://www.icj-cij.org [Accessed: 20 July 2009].

135 Ibid., para. 143.

136 Ibid., para. 148.

137 Gray, supra n. 11, 216.

138 The White House, 'The National Security Strategy of the United States of America' (16 March 2006). Available at http://www.isn.ethz.ch/isn/Digital-Library/Publications/Detail/?ord516=OrgaGrp&ots591=0C54E3B3-1E9C-BE1E-2C24-A6A8C7060233&lng=en&id=15462 [Accessed: 15 November 2009]. See C. Gray, 'The Bush Doctrine Revisited: The 2006 National Security Strategy of the USA' (2006) 5 *Chinese J.Int'l L.* 555; C. Henderson, 'The 2006 National Security Strategy of the United States: The Pre-emptive Use of Force and the Persistent Advocate' (2007) 15 *Tulsa J.Int'l & Comp.L.* 1.

139 2006 *NSS*, Ibid., i.

140 See 2002 *NSS*, supra n. 1.

WMD development were underlying themes throughout the document and were given greater emphasis than in the 2002 *NSS*.[141] Indeed, the 2006 document was a slightly moderated version of its predecessor, with more reliance on alternatives to military measures.[142] Nevertheless, the claim to a right of unilateral pre-emptive use of force against threats of terrorism and WMD was firmly re-advocated. Indeed, the 2006 *NSS* clearly stated that:

> [i]f necessary … under long-standing principles of self defense, we do not rule out the use of force before attacks occur, even if uncertainty remains as to the time and place of the enemy's attack. When the consequences of an attack with WMD are potentially so devastating, we cannot afford to stand idly by as grave dangers materialize. This is the principle and logic of preemption. *The place of preemption in our national security strategy remains the same.* We will always proceed deliberately, weighing the consequences of our actions. The reasons for our actions will be clear, the force measured, and the cause just.[143]

It is notable that any reference to the requirement of 'imminence' was omitted from its claim to pre-emptive self-defence on this occasion. Indeed, '[t]he claim of a right to take pre-emptive action in self-defence is not expressed in terms of a call for change in the law, nor is it expressly based on the existing law'.[144] This is perhaps an indication that the Bush administration desisted in its attempt to argue that the meaning of this requirement in customary international law should be reinterpreted so as to expand its temporal nature in light of the contemporary threats of terrorism and WMD, as it had done in the 2002 *NSS*. The document made no mention of the controversy that assertions of the right had caused. Nevertheless, the *opinio necessitatis* as to the right were still very much present.

However, other members of the primary interpretive community did not similarly come round to the US's way of thinking and adopt this view. Indeed, since the reiterated advocacy of the right in the 2006 document the position of these members as outlined above does not appear to have changed[145] and its

141 The 2006 *NSS* is 18 pages longer than its 2002 predecessor essentially due to the increased volume of Section II: Champion Aspirations for Human Dignity.

142 Reisman and Armstrong, supra n. 4, 531–32. The 2006 *NSS* does not advocate the use of force in promoting democracy and freedom.

143 2006 *NSS*, supra n. 138, 23 (emphasis added).

144 Gray, supra n. 139, 563.

145 Indeed, the NAM has reiterated its objection to the doctrine of pre-emption since the release of the 2006 *NSS*: 'Article 51 of the UN Charter is restrictive and … it should not be re-written or re-interpreted' and it '[o]ppose[d] and condemn[ed] … the adoption of the doctrine of pre-emptive attack'. 'Final document of the 14th Summit Conference Of Heads Of State Or Government Of The Non-Aligned Movement' (16 September 2006), paras. 20(2) and 22(5). Available at http://www.cubanoal.cu/ingles/index.html [Accessed: 25 September 2007]. This is an example of persistent objection and is significant due to the number of states which NAM represents. Indeed, this was a significant indicator of negative

contribution to the US's case for building a wide right of pre-emptive self-defence under international law appeared somewhat limited.

Conclusion

The advocacy of a doctrine of pre-emption by the Bush administration and its calls for the necessity of widening the concept of 'imminence' in light of the contemporary threats has led to a reassessment of the law in this area. Indeed, the publication of the reports by the UN, the UNSG and then the World Summit has meant that members of the interpretive communities have had the opportunity to clarify their positions on this point. Whilst there was still some discontent at the prospect of anticipatory self-defence, it also apparently found much support both in the reports and elsewhere.[146] However, the doctrine of pre-emption was a different matter. Whilst the US did not claim exceptional rights for itself, indeed it cleverly invoked the *lex lata* in proposing *lex ferenda*, it is clear that this was perceived as a sharp break by those within the interpretive communities. Significantly, the intersubjective agreement surrounding this issue included the US's closest allies and friends who, whilst not condemning the US for its claim, generally steered clear of adopting it.

Whilst the US exhibited clear *opinio necessitatis* for a right of pre-emptive self-defence, the persistent advocacy of the claim in 2006 did not lead to this becoming more widespread. The current crisis concerning Iran's nuclear ambitions has also not evinced any greater perceived need for the use of pre-emptive force in dealing with this threat. Perhaps as a cautious reminder of the errors concerning the intelligence regarding Iraq's WMD in 2003, a US joint intelligence report was issued in 2007 claiming that Iran had halted its nuclear weapons programme as early as 2003.[147] Nevertheless, even in the face of the opinion of its own intelligence agencies, the US, under President George W. Bush, maintained a hostile approach towards Iran with the threat of force firmly on the table.[148] However, any strike against Iran under the present circumstances and contemporary *lex lata* would be unlawful.[149] Perhaps in recognition of this fact, no justification was presented by Israel after it had carried

intersubjective agreement as to the Bush administration's persistent advocacy of a right of pre-emptive self-defence. For the NAM's previous objection see 'Comment on the High-Level Panel Report', supra n. 115.

146 See, for example, E. Wilmshurst, 'The Chatham House Principles of International Law on the Use of Force in Self-Defence' (2006) 55 *ICLQ* 963.

147 National Intelligence Estimate, 'Iran: Nuclear Intentions and Capabilities (November 2007). Available at http://www.dni.gov/press_releases/20071203_release.pdf [Accessed: 25 November 2007].

148 T. Baldwin and S.C. Frenkel, 'The Report Changes Nothing: Iran is Still a Threat, Says Defiant Bush' *The Times* (5 December 2007), 13.

149 M.E. O'Connell. 'The Ban on the Bomb – and Bombing: Iran, the U.S., and the International Law of Self-Defense', (2007) 57 *Syracuse L.Rev.* 497; Henderson, supra n. 138.

out a strike on Syria in 2007.[150] Indeed, whilst such a strike demonstrated *usus* for a right of unilateral pre-emptive self-defence, the fact that again one of the US's closest allies has not demonstrated any *opinio necessitatis*, let alone *opinio juris*, is telling as to the impact of the US's claim upon the *jus ad bellum*.

150 See 'Syria Air Strike Target "Removed"', BBC News (26 October 2007). Available at http://www.bbc.co.uk [Accessed: 26 January 2008].

Chapter 8
Conclusion

Since the end of the Cold War the US has been the sole superpower with connected military might far greater than any other state. As demonstrated throughout this book, the US has used force in some controversial situations, and perhaps due to its status of sole remaining superpower, has had less to fear in terms of repercussions. Nevertheless, when it has acted it has normally offered a justification of a legal nature for its actions, thereby recognizing the reality of international law and providing some support for the proposition that the law is not simply epiphenomenal, even for a superpower. Indeed, with a few exceptions, the US has recognized the importance of offering a justification under international law. Whilst this has often been in connection with actual uses of force, as Chapter 7 demonstrated, there have also been attempts to modify the law in the abstract.

These two factors mean that the US can be seen as an important actor from which to take a lead in carrying out a study of the impact of state practice on the *jus ad bellum*. However, the central theme of this work was to highlight that simply because such a state *can* act and either implicitly or expressly propose changes to the law in doing so, with perhaps less to fear in terms of direct repercussions, this does not simply translate into modifications to the law. This has been demonstrated by reference to the reaction not only of the relevant primary interpretive community associated with interpreting the sources of the *jus ad bellum* but also by reference to the interpretation of other interested and knowledgeable actors within the global interpretive community. Indeed, in addressing subsequent practice this study has widened its focus so as to include actors other than simply states, or those within the primary interpretive community, to include others which, although not possessing as decisive authority in interpreting and judging actions and discourse, make a contribution to the debate as to impact.

In reference to the practice of the global interpretive community, it has been discerned that the sources of the *jus ad bellum* have remained relatively robust to the influence and pressure of the US. Indeed, whilst the prohibition of the use of force is now held in many quarters to be *jus cogens*, very often the changes proffered by the US have not even been unequivocally accepted by the US's closest allies, let alone by the 'international community of states as a whole'.

This book has demonstrated that the sole area where solid changes have taken place in the *jus ad bellum* is where the US has acted in the multilateral context to incrementally shift the collective security system so as to incorporate the authorization technique. Whilst the collective security system as envisaged in the UN Charter did not incorporate such a practice within its strictures, the 'authorization' of states to use 'all necessary means' is now an accepted common understanding in UNSC resolutions and a settled interpretation of the competence of the UNSC. Not only has this led to a reinterpretation of the Charter but, it has been argued here, this informal modification of the Charter has also led to an evolution in customary international law. Indeed, there is nothing to suggest that the two main sources have diverged to any extent as a result of the generation of this practice.

The authorization technique emerged as a response to Iraq's invasion of Kuwait in 1990. This invasion established what has been termed here as the 'Iraq context', that is, given the negative way that Iraq was viewed by the international community the boundaries of intersubjective agreement incorporated limited forcible measures in the initial years after its invasion of Kuwait despite a lack of contemporary authorization to do so. However, the boundaries of this agreement soon changed when the US was perceived to be acting without the consultation of others within the primary interpretive community and going beyond the agreement as to appropriate measures. Consequently, the US took to making controversial arguments which can be expressly and implicitly linked back to the authorization technique. Firstly, the US claimed that the authorization bestowed upon it in UNSC Resolution 678 (1990) could be revived so as to enforce the disarmament obligations imposed upon Iraq at the end of the Gulf War. Secondly, the US began to imply that it had the right to unilaterally enforce the collective will contained in UNSC resolutions which, whilst not providing express authorization, stressed concern about a situation and imposed obligations upon certain states.

Although the revival doctrine had a complex legal argument attached to it, this was lacking in the collective will doctrine. Nevertheless, whilst the authorization technique was recognized by the primary interpretive community of the UNSC as a necessary incremental shift in the *jus ad bellum*, the revival and collective will doctrines ended as failed attempts at creating sharp breaks. It is argued here that this was based upon the fact that at the heart of the attempts by the US to insert further unilateral elements into the collective security system was the notion that it could determine if and when force was necessary to deal with a situation despite the UNSC's involvement. The intersubjective agreement amongst the primary interpretive community was that consultation and true collectiveness regarding any decision to use force under the auspices of the UNSC was too important to sacrifice. Furthermore, although *Operation Allied Force* in 1999 had the potential to set a precedent for a dramatic shift in the *jus ad bellum* so as to permit a collective group of states, many of whom were members of the UNSC, to take action despite the objections of some of the permanent members, given that similar action has not occurred since, its exceptional, if unlawful, nature has to be acknowledged.

Furthermore, the negative intersubjective agreement regarding any proposed sharp breaks from traditional interpretations of the law has been confirmed by the subsequent practice of the interpretive communities. Indeed, the ambiguous language used, such as 'material breach' and 'serious consequences' has been notably absent from UNSC resolutions since. Additionally, UNSC resolutions have been drafted more tightly as a result of these actions by the assertion that it is the UNSC which will make the decisions regarding the resolution's enforcement and by the fact that they have been adopted under Article 41 of the UN Charter, the provision entitling the UNSC to take non-forcible measures only.

However, the unilateral enforcement of the collective will was not simply about the unilateral enforcement of UNSC resolutions. Additionally, some states in the enforcement of the no-fly zones in Iraq and the NATO *Operation Allied Force* in 1999 in the FRY, including the US, evidenced *opinio necessitatis* as to a right of unilateral humanitarian intervention. Indeed, one of the themes that emerges from this book is that actions, even if not fulfilling the formal requirements to make them lawful, may be found to be acceptable by the interpretive communities if they are perceived necessary. This *opinio necessitatis* has the potential for normative change. However, whilst this was present in the justificatory discourse of some of the acting states, it was also rejected by many of the non-acting states, including Russia, China, and the NAM. Consequently, no solid changes to the *jus ad bellum* have been discerned from these incidences.

Nevertheless, whilst the *jus ad bellum* remained intact, since *Operation Allied Force* the terms of the debate regarding the use of force for humanitarian purposes have discernibly widened. Indeed, the UNSG, the International Commission on Intervention and State Sovereignty, the High-Level Panel on Threats, Challenges and Change, and states themselves at the 2005 World Summit have pledged their allegiance to the notion of a 'responsibility to protect'. However, whilst such a principle can be found in the discourse of these actors, as the Darfur crisis has also demonstrated, an actual meaningful capability to protect in practice is something quite different.

Part II of the book addressed US practice in the realms of self-defence. Following the 11 September 2001 terrorist attacks, the efforts of the US to test the boundaries of international law have increased, arguably with a sense of righteousness given the horrendous attacks that it had suffered and near universal sympathy which it received. Indeed, it was claimed by some in the secondary interpretive community that the declaration of a 'war on terror' by the US was the death knell for the prohibition of the use of force. This perception was arguably fuelled by the fact that the US made no attempt to act thorough the collective security system to fight this particular 'war', but rather attempted to expand unilateral rights, in particular the right of self-defence. This perception also appeared to be supported by the overwhelming support in the immediate aftermath of the attacks for *Operation Enduring Freedom*. This was an action in self-defence not just against the perpetrators of the attacks, al-Qaida, but *also* against the 'harbouring' state, Afghanistan.

The US's attempt at impacting upon not only the *jus ad bellum* but also the rules on state responsibility, whilst apparently initially supported, has virtually been ignored since. Whilst it has crept into the discourse of some states, it has not ultimately been relied upon by any. Furthermore, the right of self-defence recognized in 2001 has not been seen in the subsequent practice of the UNSC, reinforcing the view that this was a *sui generis* set of circumstances. Lastly, the UN has taken a cautious line, and the ICJ has maintained its restrictive view, or at least has certainly not welcomed the wide right. Indeed, it is argued here that this is an example of the interpretive communities recognizing an exceptional right to take action in one particular incident, thus widening the terms of the debate in connection with forcible responses to terrorism, without ultimately having any discernible impact upon the law itself.

Other than the harbouring standard of attribution, the US has also attempted to reinterpret the *jus ad bellum* so as to incorporate a right of pre-emptive self-defence. Whilst the US attempted to present the doctrine as an incremental shift in the *lex lata* governing self-defence, that is, a widening of the requirement of imminence to match the nature and capabilities of the contemporary adversaries of rogue states possessing WMD and global terrorism, this was instead perceived as a sharp break by others within the interpretive communities. Indeed, despite the concerted efforts of the US, under the Bush administration, to establish it as a legal right, it has received very little support, significantly even from some of the US's closest allies providing a clear and significant indicator of negative intersubjective agreement over the issue. It has also been rejected explicitly or implicitly by the UN, the UNSG, and the ICJ. The fact that it has continued to persist with its advocacy of such a right in 2006 does not seem to have changed things. In any case, the NAM, representing 118 States, has persistently objected providing another significant indicator of negative intersubjective agreement. Only Israel appears to have accepted it, even showing a willingness to put it into practice, but in this respect nothing can be said to have changed here from 1981 when it attacked the Osiraq nuclear reactor in Iraq, thus militating against a reading of Israel's strike against Syria in 2007 as subsequent practice following the claims of the US. In any case, it was not explicit about this strike and certainly did not offer any justification of pre-emptive self-defence, thus not exhibiting any *opino juris* as to its place in international law.

Ultimately, this monograph has demonstrated that whilst the *jus ad bellum* cannot always prevent the most powerful of states from acting, this does not mean that it ignores international law or that its actions have a direct impact upon the law. Furthermore, it could in fact be argued that these actions and associated discourse have had a positive effect in that by testing the boundaries of the intersubjective agreement of the primary interpretive communities and international law, the law has been clarified through provoking discussion and debate and, as this book has demonstrated, the rejection of a wide view of permissible unilateral action under the *jus ad bellum*. Ultimately, it has demonstrated that the most fundamental aspect of the international legal system can survive breaches by powerful states, which it is hoped provides some reassurance for its future.

Postscript

Whilst this book has included events up to the end of the reign of President George W. Bush, something should be said about President Barack Obama who, at the time of writing this postscript, has been in office for one year nearly to the day. When President Obama took control in the Oval Office there was little doubt that he was going to offer some stark contrasts to his predecessor. These have been visible both in style and in substance and have included a widely recognized shift towards multilateralism by virtue of many diplomatic initiatives[1] and the identification of different priorities and policies.[2] In response, although perhaps prematurely, President Obama has been honoured with the Nobel Peace Prize for 'his extraordinary efforts to strengthen international diplomacy and co-operation between peoples'.[3] However, a troubling aspect of the President's first year in the Oval Office has been his failure to outline clearly his policy on the use of force and the confusion over his position on the permissible limits imposed by international law.

Given that President Obama has failed to meet the deadline of 15 June 2009 for the publication of his administration's *National Security Strategy*, as imposed by the 1986 Goldwater-Nichols Act,[4] we are left to analyse other sources in an attempt to garner the position of the President on this issue, whether it can be distinguished from that of his predecessor, and whether it can be reconciled with the limits imposed by contemporary international law. Whilst some within the media have questioned whether there is an 'Obama doctrine',[5] on the basis of the evidence obtained so far it appears that there is one emerging.

---

1 These have included a widely hailed speech in Egypt; a willingness to negotiate with Iran (despite the criticisms of many Republicans); a willingness to be tough with Israel; the nuclear arms reduction treaty with Russia; and the opening of certain barriers with Cuba.

2 These can be seen in the closure of Guantanamo Bay; its critical position on the use of torture; concerns regarding climate change; the reversal of the missile defence programme; and negotiations on nuclear disarmament. Perhaps one can add to this the fact that Obama has refrained from using the phrase 'war on terror'.

3 Obama acknowledged the controversy surrounding him receiving the Prize at this stage of his presidency and agreed that his 'achievements were still slight'. See The White House, 'Remarks by the President at the Acceptance of the Nobel Peace Prize' (10 December 2009). Available at http://www.whitehouse.gov/the-press-office/remarks-president-acceptance-nobel-peace-prize [Accessed: 10 January 2010].

4 The Goldwater-Nichols Department of Defense Reorganization Act of 1986 Pub. L. No. 99–433. However, he is not alone here; no administration has ever met this deadline.

5 See, for example, 'America's Foreign Policy: Is There an Obama Doctrine?' *The Economist* (19 December 2009), 78.

The earliest, and to this day most direct, indication we have of Obama's position regarding the use of force and the legal limits imposed upon it is his response to a survey conducted by the American Society of International Law in which several questions were posed to the Presidential candidates in the run-up to the elections in 2008.[6] Rather on point, one of the questions posed was '[w]hat views do you have regarding any legal constraints on US use of force?'[7] In answering this question much of what Barack Obama said may equally as well have come from the mouth of George W. Bush:

> The U.S. has today and has always had the right to take unilateral military action, including the pre-emptive use of force, to eliminate imminent threats to our country and security. No nation or organization has a veto over our right of self-defense – and none ever will. In fact, Article 51 of the U.N. Charter recognizes this right of self-defense for every nation.[8]

Furthermore, whilst President Obama went on to recall 'the so-called Bush doctrine' and noted that '[t]he preventive use of force – in anticipation of potential threats that may not be imminent – is a different matter',[9] he also, and rather confusingly, was clear that '[s]ometimes, the preventive use of force may be necessary'.[10] This was hardly a resounding rejection of the Bush doctrine and President Obama gave no indications of what conditions might make it 'necessary' or indeed what *his* interpretation of 'imminence' was. Given a somewhat veiled criticism of preventive force and the national security policy of his predecessor whilst at the same time making it clear that it would be resorted to when 'necessary', it could be questioned whether this was the beginning of an Obama doctrine of 'necessary force'? To date there is nothing to suggest that Obama has shifted from this position since taking up residence in the White House and the use of force in other contexts has also been described as 'necessary'. Whilst in none of his major speeches since becoming President has Obama expressly accepted the preventive use of force under international law as he did in the American Society of International Law survey neither has he ruled it out. However, his position does give cause for concern.

In contrast to his predecessor, President Obama did not choose to use his speech at West Point on 1 December 2009 to set out his position on the use of force.[11] Instead, in his speech, which was given over almost entirely to the war in

---

6 'International Law 2008 – Barack Obama', *American Society of International Law*. Available at http://www.asil.org/obamasurvey.cfm [Accessed: 10 January 2010].

7 Ibid.

8 Ibid.

9 Ibid.

10 Ibid. It is submitted here that President Obama is using the term 'pre-emptive' as this book has used 'anticipatory' and uses 'preventive' as this book has used 'pre-emptive'. See Chapter 7 (n. 3).

11 The White House, 'Remarks by the President in Address to the Nation on the Way Forward in Afghanistan and Pakistan' (1 December 2009). Available at http://

Afghanistan, there were no direct references to when the use of force would be justified or 'necessary'. More significant in this respect was his speech in Oslo upon accepting his Nobel Peace Prize on 10 December 2009 where he took the opportunity to speak 'at some length to the question that must weigh on our minds and our hearts as we choose to wage war'.[12] On this occasion, Obama was assertive in his belief 'that all nations – strong and weak alike – must adhere to standards that govern the use of force'[13] and 'that adhering to standards, international standards, strengthens those who do, and isolates and weakens those who don't'.[14] However, again, he was similarly assertive that he 'reserve[ed] the right to act unilaterally if *necessary* to defend [his] nation'.[15] Whilst on the face of it this statement, taken as a whole, was uncontroversial, and in many respects commendable, it is when one reads more into it that points of contention become apparent.

The first of these was his failure to elaborate on what the 'standards' were that he was referring to. For example, were they of a political or legal nature? If we are to assume that they were of a legal nature, talking about 'standards' is meaningless unless one elaborates upon what one is referring to. Given the auto-interpretive nature of international law, clarity in the choice of terminology to convey meaning is required. Although references to international law were in short supply during the Bush era, given the attempt in the 2002 *NSS* to offer a reinterpretation of 'imminence' in light of the perceived new threats of terrorism, and particularly terrorists in the possession of weapons of mass destruction,[16] Bush would no doubt have argued that he was similarly adhering to standards that govern the use of force, albeit that a shift was necessary to cope with these new threats. In this light, Obama's reference to the 'standards' governing the use of force needs clarifying, especially after claiming himself that the 'new threats' of terrorism and nuclear proliferation to terrorist groups have caused the 'architecture to keep the peace', including the 'United Nations' and 'mechanisms to govern the waging of war', to 'buckle'.[17] Whilst similar sentiments were expressed in many documents published since the attacks of 11 September 2001 and the emergence of the Bush doctrine, the consensus remained both amongst the authors of these reports and states themselves that the current architecture and mechanisms, whilst not perfect, are capable of dealing with these threats.[18] Obama needs to be clearer whether he agrees with this conclusion and, if not, what exactly it is that he is proposing.

www.whitehouse.gov/the-press-office/remarks-president-address-nation-way-forward-afghanistan-and-pakistan [Accessed: 17 December 2009].

12 Oslo speech, supra n. 3.

13 Ibid.

14 Ibid.

15 Ibid. (emphasis added).

16 See Chapter 7.

17 Oslo speech, supra n. 3.

18 Report of the High-Level Panel on Threats, Challenges and Change, 'A More Secure World: Our Shared Responsibility' (2004) UN Doc. A/59/565 (2004), paras 190–91;

The second point of contention was his use again of the concept of 'necessity' in asserting the right of unilateral defence. As Chapters 6 and 7 highlighted, in the context of the customary international legal regulation of the right of self-defence this term has a particular meaning. Furthermore, whilst the boundaries of this term, and the others of 'proportionality', 'immediacy', 'imminence' and 'armed attack' in judging forcible actions have been placed differently by different actors and some have today been open in their acceptance today of a right of anticipatory self-defence,[19] the response to the Bush doctrine[20] and the invasion of Iraq in 2003[21] provides strong evidence of the fact that they do not stretch as far as to incorporate a right of pre-emptive self-defence. Consequently, Obama must be clearer in his use of the term 'necessity', particularly in his discourse on the doctrine of self-defence.

Furthermore, whilst 'necessity' is generally considered to be reference to a situation where 'there is no choice of means', a last resort, or to the exhaustion of peaceful measures, Obama appears to be proposing that this is not the case when confronting 'evil' actors in the world:

> Evil does exist in the world. A non-violent movement could not have halted Hitler's armies. Negotiations cannot convince al-Qaeda's leaders to lay down their arms. To say that force may sometimes be *necessary* is not a call to cynicism – it is a recognition of history; the imperfections of man and the limits of reason.[22]

Since coming to power, President Obama's efforts in strengthening international diplomacy have been noted.[23] Indeed, in his Oslo speech he also spoke of the need for 'engagement with repressive regimes',[24] rhetoric that is to be welcomed. However, given President Bush's use of the phrase 'axis of evil',[25] the fact that Obama chose to characterize any as 'evil' is surprising. Of more significance is that it appears that in the face of adversaries which could be categorized as such, a dilution of the standard of 'necessity' in international law is required so that in dealing with such actors not only is there no longer any requirement for a prior 'armed attack' but also that in this context the exhaustion of means other than the

---

Report of the UN Secretary-General, 'In Larger Freedom: Towards Security, Development and Human Rights for All' (2005) UN Doc. A/59/205, para. 125; 2005 World Summit Outcome Document (2005) UN Doc. A/60/L.1, paras 79–80.

19 For arguably the most notable acceptance see Report of the UN Secretary-General, Ibid., para. 124.

20 See Chapter 7.

21 See Chapter 4.

22 Oslo speech, supra n. 3.

23 See supra nn. 1 and 2.

24 He expanded: 'I know that engagement with repressive regimes lacks the satisfying purity of indignation. But I also know that sanctions without outreach – condemnation without discussion – can carry forward only a crippling status quo. No repressive regime can move down a new path unless it has the choice of an open door'. Oslo speech, above n. 3.

25 See Chapter 7.

use of force is no longer required, thus opening the door to the use of pre-emptive force. If indeed this is being proposed, elaboration on such a shift is required from the President so that the interpretive communities are fully aware of his interpretation of the standards governing the use of force.

However, the emerging Obama doctrine, as described in this postscript as one of 'necessary force', has also apparently endorsed the other key element of the Bush doctrine, that of the 'harbouring' standard of attribution for actions in self-defence against non-state actors and those states that 'harbour' them. Indeed, President Obama has chosen not to associate this standard with the 'war on terror' era of the Bush administration and reject it or distinguish himself from it. On the contrary, if anything, he has endorsed it. As he noted in his West Point speech, 'Al-Qaeda's base of operations was in Afghanistan, where they were *harbored* by the Taliban – a ruthless, repressive and radical movement that seized control of that country'.[26] The President went on to indicate that whilst the Taliban and the state of Afghanistan did not carry out the attacks, or send or control those that did, this did not prevent the use of force against it. Indeed, not only did Obama recall the fact that 'Congress authorize[d] the use of force against al-Qaeda and those who *harbored* them – an authorization that continues to this day',[27] but also that '[t]he world rallied around America after the 9/11 attacks, and continues to support our efforts in Afghanistan, because of the horror of those senseless attacks and *the recognized principle of self-defense*'.[28] The increased efforts by Obama in *Operation Enduring Freedom*, an operation based upon self-defence, and the fight to destroy the Taliban are further indications of his adoption of the harbouring standard of attribution.

In the immediate aftermath of 9/11 there appeared at first glance to be a significant shift in the law governing the attribution of the actions of non-state actors to states for the purposes of self-defence.[29] Indeed, some questioned whether this was 'instant' customary international law. However, as Chapter 6 demonstrated, the practice of the primary interpretive communities, events at the UN, and the jurisprudence of the ICJ are indicative of the fact that at this stage it cannot be considered to form, as yet, a part of the *jus ad bellum*. However, in linking the pieces together it appears that Obama has incorporated the harbouring standard under his emerging doctrine of 'necessary force' by his categorization of this conflict as a 'war of necessity'.[30] Given that it does not have a place within the *jus ad bellum* if Obama is claiming, whether wittingly or not, that this standard is, or should be, a part of the *jus ad bellum* he needs to be clear about it.

---

26 West Point speech, supra n. 11.

27 Ibid.

28 Oslo speech, supra n. 3 (emphasis added).

29 See Chapter 6.

30 See 'The Making of the President's Foreign Policy: The Decider' *The Economist* (28 November 2009), 51.

Breaking away from self-defence, there appears to be another piece to the emerging Obama doctrine of 'necessary force', that is, the use of force that is 'not only *necessary* but *morally justified*'.[31]

The concept of 'just war' dates back centuries and long before the current legal regulation of the use of force was realized.[32] The historical basis of this concept did not elude Obama. Indeed, in his Nobel speech he noted the just war concept as 'suggesting that war is justified only when certain conditions were met: if it is waged as a last resort or in self-defense; if the force used is proportional; and if, whenever possible, civilians are spared from violence'.[33] Whilst noting that 'for most of history, this concept of "just war" was rarely observed',[34] in claiming that 'wars within nations' had also caused the original architecture to 'buckle',[35] Obama made the argument that this state of affairs required the interpretive communities to think '*in new ways* about the notions of just war and the imperatives of a just peace'.[36] Indeed, '*[m]ore and more*, we all confront difficult questions about how to prevent the slaughter of civilians by their own government, or to stop a civil war whose violence and suffering can engulf an entire region'.[37]

As Chapter 5 of this book demonstrated, a right of humanitarian intervention is not one that currently exists within the *jus ad bellum*. Nevertheless, Obama was open in his belief not that he would like to see a principle *emerge* permitting the unilateral use of force on humanitarian grounds, but:

> that force *can* be justified on humanitarian grounds, as it was in the Balkans, or in other places that have been scarred by war. Inaction tears at our conscience and can lead to more costly intervention later. That's why all responsible nations must embrace the role that militaries with a clear mandate can play to keep the peace.[38]

After claiming that the international community would have to 'think in *new* ways' and 'more and more' about how to prevent humanitarian catastrophes through just wars, the President seems here to have put the cart before the horse in claiming that such a right of humanitarian intervention already existed. Proposing that a right should emerge is one thing, and indeed can form a constructive contribution to the development of international law, but claims that one already exists is another with implications for the international legal order of a quite different nature.

---

31 Oslo speech, supra n. 3 (emphasis added).

32 See I. Brownlie, *International Law and the Use of Force by States* (Oxford: Clarendon Press, 1963), 1–18 for more on this concept.

33 Oslo speech, supra n. 3.

34 Ibid.

35 Ibid.

36 Ibid. (emphasis added).

37 Ibid. (emphasis added).

38 Oslo speech, supra n 3.

Furthermore, whilst Obama has made overtures to multilateralism and the standards governing the use of force, not only did he not mention the collective security system in his speeches but appeared to intentionally avoid mentioning it in the context of humanitarian interventions by stating that these actions would take place either 'individually or *in concert*'.[39] As noted in Chapter 5, at present actions taken 'in concert' but not under the auspices of the Security Council possess no more legality than those taken individually. Without the Security Council's authorization or agreement this is still a unilateral use of force prohibited under the *jus ad bellum* as it currently stands.

Obama has never claimed to be a pacifist and his belief that the use of force will sometimes by 'necessary' has been made clear. Indeed, this postscript has argued that under the rhetoric so far there is an evolving doctrine of 'necessary force' becoming increasingly discernible. However, of concern here is the President's refusal so far to expand upon what was meant by his use of the term 'necessary'. Was this to be taken to be understood as it is in traditional legal parlance of the *jus ad bellum*? If not, what conditions have to pertain to make the use of force 'necessary'?

What is worrying about this doctrine is not the assertion of wide rights but the complete lack of clarity as to what is permissible under it. One could of course argue that it is politically wise not to provide too much information to your adversaries on when you are prepared to use force. However, if Obama is serious about respecting the 'standards' of international law and the need for reciprocity here he needs to be clearer as to what he believes these standards to be before he can begin judging others. If Obama leaves the door so wide open as to what these are, as he has done so far under the doctrine of 'necessary force', this encourages others, including potential adversaries, to do the same so that ultimately no one is clear as to what the 'standards' are that they are supposed to be respecting.

Many of President Obama's initial decisions whilst in the White House are commendable and witness America trying, if not always successfully,[40] to move more in line with its international legal obligations. However, whilst it is too soon at this stage to make any assessment of the impact that the Obama administration has had, or may come to have, on the *jus ad bellum*, if what has been set out above are the early signs of an Obama doctrine emerging, more needs to be provided to set out the boundaries of this as, as it stands, it is more open to unilateral possibilities than his predecessor's controversial doctrine and ultimately cannot be reconciled with the contemporary limits imposed by the *jus ad bellum*. However, although under the Obama administration it appears that the perception of the US as a 'persistent advocate' lives on, as this book has demonstrated, its success is far from guaranteed.

39 Oslo speech, supra n 3.

40 For example, the closure of Guantanamo Bay has yet to become a reality.

Index

www.ingramcontent.com/pod-product-compliance
Ingram Content Group UK Ltd.
Pitfield, Milton Keynes, MK11 3LW, UK
UKHW021721240926
475702UK00029BA/1731
9781138272170